Communication Policy
in Developed Countries

edited by

Patricia Edgar
Syed A. Rahim

Kegan Paul International
London, Boston and Melbourne
in association with
The East-West Center
Honolulu

First published in 1983
by Kegan Paul International
39 Store Street, London WC1E 7DD, England
9 Park Street, Boston, Mass. 02108, USA
296 Beaconsfield Parade, Middle Park,
Melbourne, 3206, Australia
Printed in Great Britain by
Redwood Burn Ltd, Trowbridge, Wilts

ISBN 0-7103-0060-3

TABLE OF CONTENTS

ACKNOWLEDGMENTS

This project originated from a discussion between the editors at the Communication Institute, East-West Center, Honolulu, Hawaii in July 1977. Over the next twelve months, Dr. Patricia Edgar contacted the contributors and explored possibilities for organizing workshops to discuss the draft contributions. A workshop organized by Dr. Patricia Edgar and attended by Dr. Syed A. Rahim was held in May 1979 at La Trobe University, Melbourne with a group of Australian participants to discuss Geoff Evans's paper on communication policy in Australia. Those Australian participants are acknowledged in a footnote on the first page of Evans's paper. In January 1980, another workshop was organized by Dr. Syed A. Rahim at the Communication Institute, East-West Center, Honolulu where the editors and contributors reviewed and discussed the draft chapters of the volume.

We wish to acknowledge the financial support for this project provided by the Communication Institute, East-West Center, Honolulu, Hawaii; the Centre for the Study of Educational Communication and Media, La Trobe University, Melbourne, Australia; and the Associated Broadcasting Services Limited and the Southern Cross Communications Limited—both regional broadcasting services in Australia.

The editors and contributors also acknowledge the support and cooperation of the program and secretarial staffs of the Communication Institute and the Centre for the Study of Educational Communication and Media.

Patricia Edgar
Centre for the Study of Educational
  Communication and Media
La Trobe University
Melbourne

Syed A. Rahim
Communication Institute
East-West Center
Honolulu, Hawaii

1

Introduction

Patricia Edgar
Syed A. Rahim

As the world has advanced, the task of communication has become ever more complex and subtle—to contribute to the liberation of mankind from want, oppression and fear and to unite it in community and communion, solidarity and understanding. However, unless some basic structural changes are introduced, the potential benefits of technological and communication development will hardly be put at the disposal of the majority of mankind.—International Commission for the Study of Communication Problems, UNESCO, 1979

Communication policy issues are now being debated intensely in various international fora, particularly in the United Nations Educational, Scientific and Cultural Organization (UNESCO) and the International Telecommunication Union (ITU). UNESCO's intergovernmental general conferences and the UN General Assembly sessions have made several attempts over past years at formulating international norms and standards for communication in promoting peace and understanding. In 1948 the United Nations adopted a resolution upholding the concept of free flow of information and the fundamental human right to freedom of expression. But with the growth of many newly independent nations and an upsurge in nationalism, a growing concern about existing imbalances in the international flow of information has been expressed strongly. Uncertainty about the impact of new communication technology has further aggravated that concern.

The Third World nations have initiated a call for "a new world communication and information order" that would remedy the unsatisfactory situation in world communication. The umbrella concept of "a new order" has become a controversial matter for debates and decisions on international communication. The concept encompasses a wide

1

variety of issues and problems: a free and balanced flow of information; equitable access to communication resources; prior consent of states for direct satellite broadcasting and remote sensing by communication satellites; protection of privacy in transborder data flows; transfer of communications technology; the cultural impact of communications development; communication planning for efficient and equitable resource allocation across nations; international cooperation for communication development in the developing countries; and institutional reform in the established order of communications systems dominated by a few developed countries.

In 1978 the UNESCO general conference in Paris adopted by acclamation a declaration on the fundamental principles governing the use of mass media for international peace and understanding. This declaration and a follow-up UN resolution endorsed the need for a more just and effective world communication order based on the free and better-balanced flow of information, and urged nations to cooperate in developing communication systems in less developed countries. In 1979 the World Administrative Radio Conference (WARC) sponsored by the ITU took far-reaching decisions relating to the allocation and use of radio spectrum and geostationary satellite orbits. Here again the main principle adopted was that of an equitable and effective allocation of limited natural communication resources for all countries of the world. With that, the ITU abandoned its older tradition of the "first come, first served" principle of resource allocation. The 1979 WARC could not settle all the issues concerning access to and equitable and effective allocation of resources, but decided to hold special conferences in the 1980s to formulate specific policies and plans for better utilization of the shortwave radio frequency for broadcasting, and the orbital space for communication satellites.

The participants in the international debates over communication policy have lacked access to well-organized information on communication problems in a world context. To help alleviate the situation, UNESCO constituted an international commission to study the totality of communication problems and make recommendations for practical action. Under the chairmanship of Sean MacBride from Ireland, the commission, with members from Belgium, Canada, Chile, Colombia, Egypt, France, India, Indonesia, Japan, Netherlands, Nigeria, Soviet Union, Tunisia, United States, Yugoslavia, and Zaire, completed its study in late 1979 (MacBride 1980). The commission made a strong case for communication policy and planning. In its view, the role and function of communication in modern society has become a matter of central importance, hence communication policymaking and planning should be incorporated into overall national policy and planning for development and progress, and a better mechanism should be developed for international coordination and cooperation. The commission identified a number of specific areas where the challenge for concerted action is very serious. Among these are the problems of imbalance in international communication flows, distortion of content in communication, undesirable effects of external communication on national cultures, barriers to the democratic flow of communication, rights and responsibilities of journalists, international cooperation for the development and better use of communication, and special problems of improving the communications infrastructure in developing countries.

The international debates about communication policy analysis and long-range planning raise difficult questions and problems for the developed industrial countries as well as the developing countries. While the nature of the problems in the developed and the developing countries is different, finding solutions requires collaboration and concerted efforts by all countries. An understanding of the differences, the similarities, and the common issues is essential for collaboration and effective solution of the problems. The problems stemming from the communications revolution in developed countries relate more to employment issues, life-style changes, philosophical issues relating to freedom of information and privacy, and concerns about the way communication resources are being developed and distributed. The Third World countries face the same problems as they attempt to develop and modernize their communication systems. They also face (or at least perceive) an additional problem of the threat to their national sovereignty and cultural integrity posed by the new technology combined with the commercial push from the transnational communication enterprises.

At one end of the development spectrum is the United States, a country that since the end of the Second World War has been a massive supplier of media products—books, news, film, television—to the rest of the world, yet its communication system is not dependent on foreign products. The United States' dominant position in communication technology and in world communication markets is one example of its economic power. The communication sector of the United States, which ranks higher in terms of growth and profitability than many other sectors of industry, today is a very important sector indeed. A 1980 survey of U.S. industries shows that 100 out of 1,000 large public companies with annual sales of $3,000 million or more are communication-information enterprises. The enormous size and growth of the communication industry in the United States can be seen from Table 1-1.

Other communication industries in the United States are also very large and growing operations. The 1979 figures showing sales of products and services of some of these industries include: photographic equipment and supplies $13,300 million, consumer electronics $6,700 million, motion picture box office receipts $3,000 million, and advertising agency billings $23,300 million. The U.S. commitment to private ownership and to the profit motive is unique in its application to the formulation of communication policies compared with other developed countries. Other Western countries have evolved a range of models that

Table 1-1
Financial Growth of the U.S. Communication Industry

Industry	1979 Revenue ($ millions)	1980 Expected Growth (percent)	Export Value (US$ millions)		Employment (millions of workers)
			1979	1980	
Printing and publishing	62,500	10.0	1,000	N.A.	1.0
Telephone and telegraph services	56,800	9.8	1,900	2,300	1.1
Telephone and telegraph equipment	9,100	10.0	N.A.	N.A.	N.A.
Computer products and services	21,100	10.0	5,300	N.A.	N.A.
Broadcasting radio, TV, and cable TV	12,200	14.0	N.A.	N.A.	1.6
Advertising	13,400	N.A.	N.A.	N.A.	N.A.

Source: U.S. Department of Commerce, 1980.
Note: N.A. = not available.

incorporate both public and commercial control of the media within a context of free speech and democratic ideals. Often government intervention and public control of the media have been a direct result of the influence of the free flow of American information and technology around the world.

In response to this enormous growth in the communication industries and the social and political problems that have emerged, there has been significant development in the academic field of communication. Academic research on the political economy of communication and on the information economy is striving to find new rationales, concepts, and methods for the policy analysis and planning of communication systems. The concept of the "information society" proposed in the works of American writers such as Machlup (1962), Bell (1973), Drucker (1968), and Porat (1976) is providing one foundation for a new paradigm for policy research and analysis. The approach is based on the notion that advanced industrial society is moving toward a new stage where the production, processing, and distribution of information will be the central societal activity. This is reflected in the trends of the economy, industrial growth, work organization, the leisure activities of people, and various social and economic transactions based on the exchange of information. A similar intellectual movement in Japan compares the evolution of industrial society to biological evolution. As the brain and nervous system in human biology are at the most advanced stage of evolution, so is the information industry in the industrial society. The rise of the information industry is a step forward on the path of evolution, its dominance indicating the coming of the information society (Ito 1979). (Ito reviewed the work of Japanese scholars and the Japanese concept of information society [Johoka].)

In a recent study of the U.S. economy, Marc Porat claims that the United States is now "an information economy." He shows that the production, processing, and distribution of information account for about half of the gross national product and more than half of the wages in the U.S. economy. He argues that since communication capability is closely linked to the power and wealth of society it is essential that public policy deal effectively with the emerging problems of communication, and he places high priority on these issues. The technological revolution is creating great potential for expansion and change of the communication infrastructure, and therefore the focus of attention of communication policymaking should be at the level of the infrastructure. Porat believes that the crucial communication factors do not belong to the cultural superstructure of society, but rather are concerned with the basic technological and economic foundations of the information society (Porat 1976, 1978).

The technology-centered framework for communication policy analysis is proposed by scholars from the two countries most advanced in communication technology and industry: the United States and Japan.

5

This shows that an integral relationship exists between the development of material conditions in a society, the intellectual pursuit of knowledge, and the practical concern for the application of knowledge. The research approach that examines the information economy is still emerging, and its application is limited to a few projects, including studies initiated by Lamberton in Australia and by an Organization for Economic Cooperation and Development (OECD) group working on information, computer, and communication policy.

Scholars who analyze communication problems from a cultural-theoretical framework are also reacting to the trend of expanding communication industries in advanced capitalist economies. In some recent academic works, a call for a major revision within cultural theory demonstrates the effects of that reaction. British academics—Raymond Williams, Nicholas Garnham, Stuart Hall, Graham Murdock, and Peter Golding—argue that in the increasingly complex structure of the advanced industrial society it is impossible to separate the process of production and distribution of communication from other economic processes (Curran, Gurevitch, and Woollacot 1979; Garnham 1979). Moreover, as the communication industry becomes dominant, its relationship to culture grows stronger and more complex. The theoretical formulations of earlier years—including the classical Marxian metaphor of the economic base and the cultural superstructure in which communication and culture belong to the superstructure; the associated view that the mass media operate as ideological apparatuses of the ruling class, providing ideological support for the economic base; the cultural-theoretical elaboration of the concept of relative autonomy of the superstructure from the economic base, with the mass media playing a distinctive and independent role in shaping that economic base—do not seem to provide adequate theoretical formulations and tools for a proper analysis of the objective conditions of communication in advanced industrial societies. Hence, a theoretical refinement of the conceptual categories and the place of communication in them has become necessary.

The case for elaboration of a political economy of mass communication presented by Garnham (1979) and Murdock and Golding (1977) stresses the importance of examining the economic structure of the growing communication industry and its relationship to the state. In their view the production and distribution of information or the "culture industry" is an essential element of the economic base in the Marxian sense, and the ideological and legal aspects of communication are in the category of a superstructure. It follows logically that an analysis of communication problems should begin with a study of the ownership, management, and economic structure of the communication industry, and then move into a critical cultural study of content, effects, and audiences. Only then can the problems be understood properly in their appropriate contexts. Such an approach, they argue, will be "intensely practical," and will bring to light the real nature of the communication policy problems in advanced capitalist societies.

To understand the impact of the technological, economic, and political forces on the process of communication development in industrial countries, the necessary first step is to look at the totality of the communication system at the national level. The various components of national communication systems—the press and publications, cinema, broadcasting, telemetric and informatics, and telecommunications—need to be examined from both an economic and a cultural perspective. In every country the government plays a major role in influencing the communication sector through direct policy intervention, indirect regulatory control, or, as in the United States, a policy of relative nonintervention. Therefore the relationship between the government and the autonomous or private communication enterprises is an important aspect of the communication system to be examined for policy analysis.

Government initiative in studying the changing environment of communication and assessing its long-range implications for policymaking and planning is evident in a number of reports published recently. In Australia the national Telecommunications Commission conducted extensive studies on long-range policy and effective planning approaches. There were seven inquiries into aspects of communication occurring in Australia in 1981. A commission for the development of telecommunications systems constituted by the West German government has examined the problem of integrating the new communication technology and services into the existing communication establishments. In Britain, three different study commissions reviewed the press, broadcasting, and the telecommunications policy problems. The Canadian government initiated a series of studies focusing on the problems of external dependency and internal coordination in developing a communication system that it could use effectively to realize national goals. Similar national studies have been conducted in Finland, France, Japan, Sweden, and other countries. These recent moves on the part of developed countries to examine and recommend on their communication policies appear to have been triggered by growing international concern, along with uncertainties about the rapid changes in technology that have occurred in the 1970s. Ironically, while there is a call for an international approach to communication issues, when one looks at the systems that have developed within different Western countries, there is little evidence to show that communication policies have emerged as a result of rational planning, or to show that the various sectors of the communication industry are considered as a whole within any one nation. Despite the rhetoric at international fora, local politics seems to be the overwhelming determinant in the formulation of communication policies.

This book contains studies of the communication systems of seven developed countries: the United States, the United Kingdom, Canada,

Sweden, the Federal Republic of Germany (FRG), Australia, and New Zealand. Each chapter combines a description of present-day policies with critical discussion of those policies and methods of policy formation. Each chapter reflects the background of the author(s) and thus approaches taken differ. The variety of approaches illustrates the scope for policy analysis from different perspectives. The seven chapter overviews, while they reveal similar trends within industrial countries, demonstrate how unique communication systems have emerged as a result of cultural differences.

Throughout the chapters there is a recurrent theme that relates to the two distinct sources from which a nation's communication policy can be studied. One consists of official statements about goals and means embodied in legislation, regulations, reports of commissions and committees, parliamentary speeches, and the like. The other consists of the observable results of communications decisions and practices. The difference is often between rhetoric and intention, and as in the international arena, no apparent fit between explicit and implicit communication policies can be assumed.

In Australia and the FRG, for example, explicit policies have often been expressed and then watered down or undermined in practice. The United Kingdom, on the other hand, has been hesitant to develop explicit communication policy statements and, as Anthony Smith states in his chapter, "the repertoire of governmental roles and guises is so multitudinous and varied as virtually to preclude the notion of overall national policy." For reasons quite unlike those that prevail in the United States, there is also a political stand-off from government intervention in media systems and institutions that is basic to Britain's media culture and respected by both major political parties. Despite this, as Smith's paper demonstrates, British communications systems have developed under the direction of clear and powerful policies implicit in the society— British society has a communication policy as undoubtedly as it possesses a foreign policy. But while a foreign policy is deliberately made explicit, in communications, implicit policies exist and are just now beginning to go through the process of being made explicit.

Sweden by contrast has an explicit basis for its communication policy—that of the maintenance of strong libertarian values including the right of people to participate in decision making in society and to be well informed for that purpose. These rights are protected by direct state intervention in media systems. The state is aiming "to maintain a diversified and pluralistic media arrangement in a market that would otherwise be dominated by strong capital interests, creating oligopolistic conditions." Most mass media systems in Sweden enjoy some form of state support, but that support is given in order to guarantee a diversified flow of information and the state has limited its role to this function.

The FRG inherited from the years of Allied occupation both a quasi-imposed set of constitutional ideals and a determination to achieve them and bury the recent past. But Ed Wittich describes how party political interests and business interests within a country can operate to undermine the democratic ideals expressed in communication policies. The FRG provides a case study in conflicts and contradictions. The dominance of strong private interests over communication media is regarded as undesirable, yet attempts to control press monopolies have met with failure. Broadcasting, on the other hand, is funded basically through the levy of licensing fees, and advertising is stringently limited by law to preserve the independence of broadcasting from sponsors. These advertising regulations set German broadcasting apart from the other countries represented in this volume. Furthermore, attempts by newspaper interests to enter the broadcasting field have met federal government resistance. Thus Germany has been protected from the growth of multimedia monopolies and media cross-ownership—a situation that exists in most of the countries discussed in this volume.

Both Australia and New Zealand present a less ideal political picture than Sweden or the FRG. Decisions on communication policies in both countries have, particularly in recent years, been subject to the different political values of the two major parties and a determination to use the media, particularly broadcasting, for political purpose and favor. Therefore the overriding picture that emerges is one of ad hoc decision making, with decisions being taken as a result of lobbying from industry interests and other strong pressure groups.

Geoff Evans describes the Australian system as conservative and characterized by a low respect for planning and comprehensive social philosophy. There has often been a lack of theoretical analysis and information and this has been financially marked in communications. In practice an informal college of policymakers is composed of members of political parties, the bureaucracy, commercial interests, activist groups and individuals, the media, and academics. Evans argues that there have been policy statements by various elements within the elite but that these statements serve multiple functions, ranging from fair statements of belief and intent to propaganda. But generally they contain political tactical content, designed to advance the interest concerned, and tend to be almost worthless as guides to intention. He believes it is highly unlikely that any government in Australia will ever issue an official policy statement that is detailed enough to be very useful.

Another common strand runs through the chapters on Canada, Australia, New Zealand, and to a lesser extent Sweden and the FRG—that is, the influence of the U.S. and British communications systems upon these countries. While the United States has difficulty coming to terms with, or even acknowledging the international implications of its free marketplace ideology, even the non-English-speaking countries of Sweden and Germany are not free from the impact of U.S. cultural products and technology. The problems this domination causes are indicative of the growing concerns of developing countries about the threat to national sovereignty implied by U.S. preeminence in computers, remote sensing, and communication technology; the cultural imperialism reflected in U.S. exports of publications, films, and television; and the bias of American news agency coverage of foreign affairs.

While Americans may see these issues as separate, Third World interests argue that together they represent a unified information order that operates systematically against the interests of developing countries. But as the chapters in this book reveal, the problem is not unique to Third World countries. The Canadian chapter describes the influence of both U.S. and British values on Canadian policy. Canadians do not have the American distaste for government involvement in broadcasting. However, the attitudes of many Canadians are shaped by proximity to the United States and its communications media, and the Canadian broadcasting interests invoke the American ideals of freedom of the press and the free marketplace of ideas in their protests against Canadian regulatory practice. Nearly everywhere along the Canadian border, where most of the population lives, it has been possible to receive U.S. radio and television broadcasts, and this proximity to the United States has been a major factor influencing the development of Canadian communication policy on radio, television, satellites, and computer networks. In the publishing, feature film, and television industries, Canada is an importer rather than an exporter of product; therefore in virtually every field in the discussion of Canadian communication policy, the geographical proximity to the United States has been the most significant influence. In this respect, Canada has been decades ahead of other countries in the world that are today experiencing similar problems of cultural and economic sovereignty because of the instantaneous transmission capabilities of international satellites.

This same technical-cultural influence has been felt in Australia and New Zealand, where the television, film, and music industries, although located on the other side of the globe, have been dominated by American product; even the United Kingdom has not escaped this influence. Britain's technology and content are both received and indigenous; it is a victim of American invasion of its cinema, but a major exporter of systems and content in its own right. This conflict underlies policy development in the United Kingdom, for while attempting to Europeanize its culture, Britain cannot find a way to permit a flow of foreign-language material while trying to staunch the inward flow of American material. In the telecommunications field also, Britain leans toward a European consortium even though the American link is always more convenient, cheaper, and less politically problematic in the medium term.

While subject to the pressures of American "flow," Britain has also exerted a major influence on the communication systems of other countries including the Commonwealth countries of Canada, Australia, New Zealand (as well as Sweden and the FRG)—particularly through commitment to the model of the BBC. The result has been the establishment of the Canadian Broadcasting Corporation (CBC), the Australian Broadcasting Commission (ABC), the New Zealand Broadcasting Commission (NZBC), and Sveriges Radio (the Swedish Broadcasting Corporation). During the years of Allied occupation, the British bequeathed to the FRG a significant broadcasting legacy that left a highly centralized structure controlled by public representatives, not the government or any one interest.

But the standards and traditions of the BBC were not always implanted with the structure. Don Stewart and Logan Moss describe the party political controversy surrounding the decision on a television structure to be adopted in New Zealand and express the view that it was cause for regret that the opportunity to shape the television medium "in accordance with a specifically New Zealand culture was lost" at that time. In Australia, the ABC was not granted the independence of the BBC, its budget is subject to political whim and pressure, its goals are unclear, and it has three competing commercial networks against it in well over half the Australian market. The British idea for broadcasting did not receive a fair trial in either country, but the examples illustrate how ideas from another culture can be borrowed and implanted in a communication system with little planning or rationale to support them.

As Anthony Smith remarks, a future-oriented communication policy is "impossible where connections have clearly not been made between the disparate elements of a national communications system." The lack of coherent and all-embracing policy or philosophy is apparent in every country, with the possible one exception of Sweden. The confusion that exists is most apparent when the authors are examining each country's attempts to cope with the new technology. It is within this area that opportunities still exist to determine policies appropriate to each country and its people. But the general trend toward deregulation and competition in industry, which has been adopted in the United States and followed in other countries including Australia, makes it almost inevitable that the United States will be the major influence on the systems adopted by other Western countries. The concerns expressed in international fora do not appear to be having much impact on U.S. policies.

The chapters in this book together illustrate that the questions relating to future communication policy are not simply those of the interests of developed versus developing countries, but relate in a very basic way to political and cultural values. Communication issues have not been given sufficient attention in the past and systems have often been allowed to develop in an ad hoc way. The revolution in communications technology, along with the energy and inflation crises, is forcing nations to reexamine their values, goals, and structures and to pay more attention to the potential role of communication in shaping alternative futures. This book identifies trends and major issues in seven developed countries concerned with the communication policy debate. The problems of new communication technologies and systems must first be understood at the national level if policy is to devise ways for communication systems to resolve the present international controversies and serve to better the human condition.

References

Bell, Daniel
1973   *The Coming of Post Industrial Society*. New York: Basic Books.

Curran, James; Gurevitch, Michael; and Woollacot, Janet, eds.
1977   *Mass Communication and Society*. Beverly Hills: Sage Publications.

Drucker, Peter
1968   *The Age of Discontinuity*. New York: Harper & Row.

Garnham, Nicholas
1979   "Contributions to a Political Economy of Mass Communication." *Media, Culture, and Society* 1 (2):123–46.

Ito, Youichi
1979   "Johoka Policies: Japan's Communication Policies in the 1970s." Mimeographed. Honolulu: East-West Communication Institute.

MacBride, Sean
1980   *Many Voices, One World*. London: Kogan Page; New York: Unipub; Paris: UNESCO.

Machlup, Fritz
1962   *The Production and Distribution of Knowledge in the United States*. Princeton: Princeton University Press.

Murdock, Graham, and Golding, Peter
1977   "Capitalism, Communication and Class Relations." In *Mass Communication and Society*, edited by James Curran, Michael Gurevitch, and Janet Woollacot, pp.12–43, Beverly Hills: Sage Publications.

Porat, Marc U.
1976   *The Information Economy*, vol. 1. Ann Arbor, MI: University Microfilms International.

1978   "Communication Policy in an Information Society." In *Communications for Tomorrow*, edited by Glen O. Robinson, pp. 3–60. New York: Praeger.

U.S. Department of Commerce
1980   *U.S. Industrial Outlook*. Washington, D.C.

2

Communication Policy in the United States: Diversity and Pluralism in a Competitive Marketplace

Anne W. Branscomb

Anne Branscomb describes what she calls the "balkanization" of policy-making in the United States that derives from a philosophy of equality, decentralization, local ownership and control, freedom of speech and information, and an unregulated marketplace. Communication policy and decisions are described as driven by competition, controversy, and confrontation. There is neither a planning process nor a centralized forum for decisions. It is assumed that there is no right and proper way of doing things: the strongest and most persuasive voice prevails. While a nationalized postal service, a system of local, publicly supported libraries, and a commitment to teach all citizens to read and write to give them access to print media were commitments undertaken by U.S. governments in the nineteenth century, no such public commitment has been made with respect to telegraphy, telephones, broadcasting, or computers. The future, Branscomb suggests, is more likely to lead to investment in communicative skills and nationwide availability of facilities than centralized planning; the United States is unequivocally dedicated to a potpourri of policy options.

Although the various modes of communication media in the United States are fast converging into a blended service of voice, video, and data transmission, regulation of the different types of communication facilities and services is treated very differently by the substantive law, as though each were completely separate and independent. Furthermore, because policy development occurs in different forms and in different

---

While the author takes full responsibility for the content of the chapter, appreciation must go to the following who provided useful review and criticism: Henry Geller, National Telecommunications and Information Administration; Jack Valenti, Motion Picture Association of America; Max Frankel, the *New York Times*; Erwin Krasnow, National Association of Broadcasters; Tony Oettinger, Harvard University; Lee Mitchell, Sidley & Austin; Kas Kalba, Kalba Bowen Associates.

arenas, it is difficult to achieve an integrated view of communication policy within the United States. The process is further complicated by the many policy initiatives that come not from the federal government or even state or local governments, but from private initiatives or nonprofit foundations whose major activity is policy analysis and development. In order to understand this balkanization of policymaking, I will briefly review the current status of different communication technologies under United States law and public policy. I include for this purpose:

- the print media—including newspapers, magazines, books, and special purpose newsletters;
- motion pictures—including audiovisual documentaries and made-for-television movies;
- broadcasting—including radio, television, and cable television;
- common carrier—including telephone, telegraphy, microwave, satellites, and digital transmissions.

In order to better understand the complexities and peculiarities of U.S. communication policy, it is useful to keep in mind the basic philosophy that underlies the overall system.

1. The cornerstone of U.S. policy is the Declaration of Independence, which establishes that all men are created equal. From this basic principle comes a strong bias toward equitable access to communication facilities and nationwide coverage for all services.

2. The United States is a country of some 228 million people who, except for a tiny fraction of native American Indians, have come from other lands. Over half are of European origin, about one-fifth Anglo-Saxon, about one-eighth African, about one-twelfth Latin American, and only one-twentieth Asian. In keeping with the "melting pot" concept, United States communication policy has been motivated by both a respect for religious, ethnic, and racial differences and a desire for national unity. These are reflected in a long history of support for free public libraries and a strong concern for fair treatment of minority interests in the broadcast media.

3. The United States has a constitutional system that establishes a formal government of free and independent states and sets up a government of checks and balances among three equally powerful institutions—the executive, the legislative, and the judicial branches. This constitutional system also explains the penchant for balkanization of power in the communication system, so that no centralized control over the media would ever be possible.

4. A three-tiered system of federal, state, and local government means that regulation is shared at all levels.

5. Historically, there has been a strong bias in favor of local ownership and control of the media. The actuality has come to be far different as the economic realities of both news gathering and program

production and distribution tilt heavily in the direction of centralized institutional management, and both newspaper and broadcasting chain ownership have become more the rule than the exception. However, the commitment to local ownership is deeply rooted in U.S. historical development as well as philosophical faith.

6. The Bill of Rights to the Constitution clearly establishes not only the freedom of the press (enlarged to include all mass media) from government control, but also the right of freedom of speech for every individual. The First Amendment states, "Congress shall make no law ... *abridging* the freedom of speech, or of the press." Wrestling with what the First Amendment actually means with respect to the various technologies of communication has been a major preoccupation of U.S. policy development, largely through judicial determination. The courts have never quite agreed on whether the amendment merely prohibits Congress from curtailing free speech or whether there is a positive thrust mandating action to protect and enlarge freedom of expression (Branscomb 1975). However, the basic philosophy favors a free marketplace in which ideas are distributed by their progenitors without censorship and with the faith that such free and unfettered competition will somehow produce truth. As Judge Learned Hand once commented, "To many this is, and always will be, folly; but we have staked upon it our all" (*U.S.* v. *Associated Press* 1943).

7. Accompanying the concept of a free marketplace of ideas is the economic commitment to an unregulated commercial marketplace in which it is assumed that both products and services will be generated at the lowest cost by the pull of consumer demand. Thus, there is an underlying strong commitment to a competitive marketplace unless realities dictate otherwise, as the scarcity of spectrum justified licensing of broadcast facilities and local telephone service was deemed to be a natural monopoly to be regulated with respect to rates and service areas.

8. U.S. communication policy is in a state of dynamic flux in which new rights and obligations are being forged, many of which have few historical roots, including proprietary rights in information about oneself, rights of reply to derogatory or controversial messages over the mass media, and the right not merely to speak but to hear or be heard. Conversely, there are, in the pandemonium that such complete democratization of the mass media produces, evolving rights to be left alone, such as the right to privacy, the right to be removed from mailing lists, and the right to have an unlisted telephone number so as not to be deluged with unwanted publicity or unsolicited mail and telephone calls. These issues are being addressed in litigation, administrative hearings, and new legislation such as the Freedom of Information Act of 1974 and the Privacy Act of 1974. However, they are relegated to a new and developing field of information policy, which is not the subject of this chapter. Here the subject is limited primarily to communication systems defined as the transmission of messages.

17

Many of these basic philosophical principles are imbedded in the substantive law—the Communications Act of 1934, which declares the purpose of the Act as:

> to make available, as far as possible, to all the people of the United States a rapid, efficient, Nationwide, and world-wide wire and radio communication service with adequate facilities at reasonable charges, for the purpose of national defense, for the purpose of promoting safety of life and property.... (Public Law 416 1934)

Communication policy as treated in this chapter is primarily structural and legal. This reflects the nature of government involvement in communication in the United States which, because of the prohibition of the First Amendment, is substantially inhibited from manipulating the content of messages. Regulation deals primarily with entry, market share, and tariffs, whereas the judiciary plays a far greater role than elsewhere in delineating the parameters of the marketplace of ideas.

Policy Promulgation

Communication policy decisions in the United States are driven by competition, controversy, and confrontation. There is no planning process in the U.S. government, no centralized forum for decisions. The process is consistent with the competitive environment of the marketplace and the adversarial proceedings of the legal system. It is assumed that there is no right and proper way of doing things, thus, whichever voice is stronger or more persuasive prevails. Arguments are put forward usually by lawyers representing corporate, public, and private interests. They are heard primarily in diverse locations such as administrative hearings, congressional hearings, or courtroom litigation. Policies are sometimes generated by public advisory groups, national commissions, or White House conferences. Even here the environment is confrontational, for the system selects the most highly visible proponents and opponents, and usually a national commission is not named until there is a heated controversy to be resolved. More rarely, new thoughts and ideas are put forward by policy analysts funded by government agencies or nonprofit foundations. But the former are more often ignored and the latter are most often successful when they enter the confrontational areas.

Decisions about the mass media are often forged in courtroom confrontations:

- sometimes by powerful corporations such as Mobil or Exxon;
- occasionally by individuals such as John Banzhaf, a law professor, who personally and individually carried his crusade against tobacco

advertising on television all the way to the Supreme Court;
- but most often by public spirited or concerned citizens banded together in voluntary organizations such as Action for Children's Television, Accuracy in Media, or the Citizen Communication Center.

Rarely is the arena for public policy legislative—but when it is, the forum may be a local city council or state legislature or the Congress of the United States. Since the independent authority of each is jealously guarded, the boundaries of jurisdiction are often assaulted. The new technologies tend not to recognize the language of lawyers, and it becomes difficult in transferring precedents from one historical circumstance to the next to determine, for example, whether an electronically dispatched, digitally encoded message is a "letter," to be sent only by the postal monopoly, not by telephone carriers or broadcasters, although the two latter are technically competent to do so. If it is a letter, the United States Postal Service would have jurisdiction; if it is a broadcast (e.g., teletext) by radio or television station, the Federal Communications Commission (FCC) would have jurisdiction. If sent by the public-switched telephone network on a local exchange (e.g., a voicegram or viewdata), a state public utility commission might have jurisdiction. If distributed by a cable television company as videotext, a local city council might have jurisdiction. Thus, much of U.S. communication policy involves jurisdictional disputes over which legal entity has effective operating authority.

This problem becomes further complicated when the message to be sent involves transfer of funds to and from banks at the federal level and others at the state level. The United States has no central national bank such as Barclay's or the Bank of Tokyo. Electronic funds transfer can be simultaneously a banking and a communication problem, with agencies that normally have nothing to do with each other both having substantial impact on policy. Such irreconcilable problems are often assigned to a special commission by Congress.

U.S. communication has never been addressed fully and completely as an integrated system by the executive branch, although there have been numerous efforts in recent years to set up a centralized agency for policy development. The first major effort was the so-called Rostow Report by the President's Task Force on Communications Policy (1967). This was directed primarily to the problem of international communication and particularly to the question of how the United States would transfer its satellite technology to the private sector, though its reach was far greater. This led in 1970 to the creation of an Office of Telecommunications Policy (OTP) whose major mandate was to address questions of U.S. participation in international communication policy (Zapple 1970). However, the interests of its first director crossed over to domestic policy, and the OTP participated regularly in FCC rulemaking proceedings, as the policy arm of the president. This penchant for interfering in domestic matters related to the content of commercial and public broad-casting as well as to the efforts to deregulate cable (Cabinet Committee on Cable Communication 1974), led to a massive lobbying effort by broadcasters. This activity culminated early in 1977 in the removal of the OTP from the White House to the Department of Commerce wherein resided the research support for OTP in both spectrum management and policy matters. Thus, a new National Telecommunications and Informa-tion Administration (NTIA) was organized with broad powers to address national telecommunications policy issues and limited resources. The first director, a former general counsel of the FCC, continued OTP's policy of intervening in FCC rulemaking proceedings as representative of the executive branch. The new director under the Reagan Administra-tion has announced the intention to dismantle the federal regulatory system altogether.

The Department of Commerce, except for historical purposes (the secretary administered the early licensing process for broadcasting), seems an illogical administrative home for NTIA. Being the least powerful of the executive departments, it offers less prestige than OTP had in the White House. It puts NTIA in a weak position with respect to disagreements over allocation of government frequencies that have been left to be resolved by the Executive Office of the President. It does not increase the influence over foreign negotiations with respect to communication, which is the primary responsibility of the State Department, and its only operational responsibility is over the facilities and satellite experiment projects, which were transferred from the Department of Health, Education, and Welfare to the new agency; thus its constituency for outside support is small. Consequently, there has been considerable sympathy for moving NTIA out of the Department of Commerce almost as soon as it was moved in. Under Reaganomics, the pressure for both deregulation and reduction in force seems likely to lead to considerable curtailment of NTIA activities if, indeed, the office is not abolished entirely.

When all other efforts to coordinate policy fail, a new method of coping has become popular. Following a procedure set up by the National Security Council for problems of national defense that did not neatly fit under any executive department of the agency's exclusive jurisdiction, the president's Domestic Policy staff sets up Domestic Policy Reviews (DPRs). These now number in the hundreds because life in a technologically advanced country has become increasingly complex while organizational and bureaucratic solutions lag behind. One of the most comprehensive studies of U.S. communication policy was initiated by the Domestic Council during the Ford administration and under the aegis of Nelson Rockefeller, then vice president, entitled *National Information Policy*. The report was published late in 1976 and fell between the cracks of the two administrations, although efforts to initiate privacy legislation did go forward. Other initiatives of the Domestic

Policy Council have been in issues of electronic mail, public broadcasting, privacy, computers, and common carriers. All of these internal review mechanisms culminate in a presidential message to Congress stating executive branch directives. Such a message is usually sent to Congress prior to any major legislative initiatives. In the absence of new legislation, telecommunications policy is decided usually in rulemaking proceedings at the Federal Communications Commission or in the courts. Since no major revision of the Communications Act of 1934 has successfully made its way through Congress for over a decade, there has been much agitation for a general rewrite. Many proposals were considered during the 1970s, though none successfully passed through the congressional obstacle course of committees and varied constituencies. As motion pictures, broadcasting, telephone, newspapers, and the postal system merge into one vast electronic confusion, federal regulators have to cope with defining teletext, viewdata, or videopublishing under legislation that is largely outmoded by the technological revolution that has engulfed the communication media.

The Print Media

The print media are ostensibly unregulated in the United States, but there exists a substantial infrastructure that has favored the development and proliferation of printed materials. Thus, the major policy disputes are not over licensing or censorship, both of which are prohibited by the First Amendment, but where the appropriate line should be drawn between public and private sector support of the print media.

The basic infrastructure includes:

- A commitment to public education which has assured a literacy rate of 98.8 percent, thus assuring access by all to the printed page. (Although 98.8% is the official figure cited, a Ford Foundation study suggests that as many as 64 million adults in the U.S. may be functionally illiterate [*Denver Post* 1979:23].)
- Public libraries in virtually all the cities and villages of the nation, so that no citizen is without reach of books, periodicals, and newspapers of general circulation.
- A strong copyright law which guarantees that both authors and publishers (but primarily the latter) shall receive the fruits of their labors—while at the same time providing for "fair use" copying by academics and commentators to provide and encourage free exchange of ideas and intellectual discourse.
- Postal subsidies that grant low fourth-class rates to books and subsidized second-class rates to newspapers and periodicals, which have encouraged a flourishing magazine subscription industry. Today there is a magazine for almost every special interest.

- A government printing office to publish and circulate reports by federal agencies.
- The franking privilege to members of Congress to permit free circulation of newsletters to their constituencies as well as publications such as "Baby Care" to new parents, as provided free by the Department of Health, Education, and Welfare (now Health and Human Services) to members of Congress.
- The Library of Congress, which has served as a national depository of printed materials as well as a rich resource for historians and other researchers.

There is no national agency responsible for newspaper policy such as the Federal Communications Commission for the electronic media. The basic philosophy, consistent with the First Amendment, has been to keep them as free from and as unfettered by government control as possible. Antitrust laws have been used to maintain a competitive marketplace despite a substantial trend toward mergers and acquisitions throughout the better part of this century (*Lorain Journal* v. *U.S.* 1951, *Times-Picayune* v. *U.S.* 1953, *Associated Press* v. *U.S.* 1945, *Citizens Publishing Co.* v. *U.S.* 1969). In colonial days numerous newspapers were published in the larger cities. By the late nineteenth century, almost every town or village could claim its community own voice. However, the economics of the marketplace, in an industry supported by a combination of subscription fees with advertising and without direct government subsidy, have found economic efficiency through what have in effect become one-paper towns owned by a small number of newspaper chains such as Harte-Hanks, Gannett, Newhouse, and Cox. Although these, as well as the big city newspapers such as the *New York Times*, the *Washington Post*, and *Los Angeles Times*, were primarily family owned, the trend toward monopolization has persisted. Today there are very few two-newspaper cities remaining—and many of these are sustained by an exception to the antitrust laws permitting (after extended congressional hearings) two newspapers in the same town to share printing facilities if one would go bankrupt otherwise (Newspaper Preservation Act 1970).

Newspapers are subject to normal taxation on earnings, and are the subject of environmental and safety regulations as well as equal opportunity laws. Efforts to except the classified ad sections from the latter failed in a situation in which two strong public policies—equality of opportunity and freedom of speech—clashed (*Pittsburgh Press Co.* v. *Pittsburgh* 1973).

The independence of editorial judgment is jealously guarded and the only recourse for alleged wrongs from publication of untrue or damaging information is through the courts *after* publication. For private individuals the recourse is a libel suit in which money damages may be obtained for untrue (libelous) statements for which demonstrable damage can be shown. The major policy effort has been to define a private personage—comment about public figures is held to be fair game unless malice aforethought can be shown. In a 1979 case, reporters were very disturbed to discover that their "state of mind" was admissible evidence of such malice. They feared this was an unmitigated invasion of their First Amendment rights and/or Fifth Amendment rights not to testify.

Efforts to obtain a judicially mandated reporters' privilege not to testify concerning their sources of information have not been recognized, although many states have enacted laws that protect a reporter from identifying sources of news and opinion. However, the confidentiality of sources is usually respected by the federal courts except where there is reason to believe a crime has been committed; in recent cases the federal courts approved police entry and search of *Stanford Daily* files—and have held in contempt reporters who refused to testify concerning their sources (*Stanford Daily* v. *Zurcher* 1978).

Other substantial controversies involve the right of newspapers to cover trials and the right of the government to prohibit publication of information that may imperil United States security. Both involve conflicting public policies—of the public's right to know versus the right of the accused to a fair trial or versus national security interests. In the first case the courts have favored protection of the accused from prejudicial publicity, but in the latter they have protected the public right to know over the government's desire for secrecy (*Sheppard* v. *Maxwell* 1966, *Nebraska Press Association* v. *Stuart* 1976, *New York Times* v. *U.S.* 1971).

Another recent policy initiative involved a right to reply through the pages of the newspaper similar to the fairness doctrine for broadcasters, which requires air time to be made available for response to a personal attack. The Florida state legislature enacted such a law requiring newspapers to make space available to the attacked—but the United States Supreme Court came down on the side of complete and unfettered editorial judgment (*Miami Herald Publishing Co.* v. *Tornillo* 1974).

For many years—indeed, as far back as the third term of President Franklin Roosevelt (FCC 1941)—rulemaking proceedings have been pending before the FCC concerning proposed prohibitions against newspapers being licensed to operate radio and television stations. President Roosevelt, who perceived the radio audience to be more accessible and supportive than the print media (most of whose conservative publishers opposed him), ordered the chairman of the FCC to get newspapers out of broadcasting. The courts soon decided that newspapers could not be excluded per se as applicants for broadcast licenses (*Stahlman* v. *FCC* 1942), but the FCC has continued for four decades to wrestle over the policy options of cross-ownership of the media. Once again in the 1970s the FCC initiated rulemaking proceedings seeking to bar newspapers from cross-ownership of radio and television stations (FCC 1970a). Despite strong opposition from both broadcasters and newspapers, the controversy has continued long enough to inhibit free investment across media lines, especially in the same market, where arguments against cross-ownership were strongest. The peak years for newspaper ownership were 1940 for radio (32.7%) and 1953 for television (69%) (Aspen Institute 1978). In 1975 the FCC finally reached a decision to order divestiture of existing newspaper-broadcast combinations in only sixteen cases (seven television and nine radio) where there was egregious evidence of monopoly control of local media, that is, where the only newspaper owned the only radio and/or television station. Such local combinations are prohibited for the future (FCC 1975). Newspaper ownership of cable systems in the same market has also been inhibited by similarly long, pending rulemaking, which lasted long enough to restrict a substantial flow of local funds from transferring into cable system development in local markets (FCC 1970b). These FCC rulemaking proceedings have been reinforced by antitrust rejection of proposed mergers.

The centralization of the newspaper interests in the United States has occurred despite the policy of local ownership and diversity. As publishing conglomerates were inhibited from cross-ownership in local markets, they exchanged properties and/or acquired them in other markets. Thus, the myth of a healthy local press in the United States has been displaced by an actuality of strong national chains—pooling financial resources and labor to publish what has become largely two national news services, AP and UPI, with syndicated columnists distributed by either the New York Times or Los Angeles Times-Washington Post syndication services. Thus, like movies and television programs, the news industry is substantially a national (but not nationalized) service. Only the Wall Street Journal purports to be a national journal, although the Gannett chain, which delivers news to its papers via satellite, has plans to publish a nationally distributed paper.

The Wall Street Journal claims that its circulation of 1,775,000 in 1979 was twice that of the New York Times, and three times that of the Washington Post. Publishing via satellite through regional printing plants in Florida, Washington, Colorado, Pennsylvania, Ohio, and Illinois, the Journal is also delivering news on demand to some 8,500 subscribers' computer terminals. It can claim to be the first fully electronic newspaper (Wall Street Journal 1980:13). Less than two million viewers for a network television program would assure its cancellation; but newspapers are more comparable to the local broadcaster who delivers the network signal just as the local newspapers deliver national services and syndicated columnists.

The New York Times, even its Sunday edition which has subscribers all over the nation, delivers two-thirds of its copies to metropolitan New York addresses. Certainly newspapers rely heavily upon local advertisers for support and to that extent differ substantially from motion pictures, which are designed for a national market of the consuming public, and network television programs, which are not only designed for a national audience but supported by national advertising. Not to be overlooked also are a thriving number of suburban "shoppers," which carry very local neighborhood news and very localized retail advertising.

Book publishing is also thriving, with paperbacks contributing a hefty two-thirds of the $35 per year spent on the average by United States readers. Cross-ownership in the book publishing industry is not forbidden under United States law. Both the New York Times Company and Time, Inc. have book publishing subsidiaries. Given that publishers such as McGraw-Hill have invested in broadcast licenses, and broadcasters like CBS have purchased publishing firms, there is substantially more horizontal integration than vertical in the print media, although Time, Inc. has major interests in Canadian timber.

The Motion Picture Industry

The motion picture industry in the United States is less regulated domestically than print, broadcasting, or common carrier services. It is also most successful internationally. Hollywood and Sunset Boulevard are known the world over. Their products are shared by the world's millions; Hollywood movie stars are as well known abroad as they are at home. Many movies have been made on foreign soil, and foreign artists are as readily accepted and provided dollar incomes as U.S. citizens. Thus, the motion picture industry has a genuine international flavor, has capitalized on free flow of information policies—in both directions—and has enjoyed a position of international acclaim as well as the fruits of the marketplace. To many critics this constitutes cultural imperialism (Smith 1980, Schiller 1976); but, if so, it is a voluntarily induced imperialism cultivated by the national television systems and movie theater distributors who buy the products on an open international market, not by any United States trade policy. And United States consumers who pay their own price of admission are victims of the cultural imperialism of Sunset Boulevard as much as their foreign counterparts.

United States movie attendance has dropped in number from the record 90 million per week in 1930 before television to 25 million in 1960 and a low of 16 million in 1971; and the number of theater seats decreased from a high of 12.1 million in 1931 to 6 million in 1972. This represents an even larger decrease in attendance since the population increased from 122 million in 1930 to 204 million in 1970 (Aspen Institute 1978). Today attendance is on the rise, with 22 million in 1978. However attendance figures are somewhat misleading since the television audience in the late afternoon and late evening, when movies dominate the screen, averages 28 million daily.

The outlets for viewing the product changed markedly with the advent of television. Now, with cable television, videodiscs, and prerecorded videotapes, "pay as you go" theater at home will offer more competition for the movie houses, which had already been decimated by television. For these reasons, many of the policy arguments in the United States about movies are over the distribution system.

The major regulatory impact has come from the antitrust laws, which were intended to break up the vertical integration of movie houses with motion picture companies. The Paramount case in 1948 required Paramount Pictures to divest control of its co-owned theaters at about the time that television was making its debut in the marketplace, and consent decrees with all the major production companies quickly followed the Paramount litigation (*U.S.* v. *Paramount Pictures* 1948).

Only a few will remember, forty-odd years later, that broadcasters promised during congressional hearings in the 1930s not to televise movies until after motion-picture theaters were closed—thus giving birth to what is now known as "the late, late movie." Today some television stations broadcast movies twenty-four hours a day—and theater owners no longer have much clout, but broadcasters were successful in hamstringing cable television systems from carrying first-run motion pictures except in competition with the theater during the first three years of release or after ten years when they were so old that television contracts had expired. This regulation was declared unconstitutional by the Supreme Court in 1978, thus freeing the cable industry to compete more fairly for distribution of motion pictures and giving investment in pay cable a new boost.

Motion-picture companies also have found a new outlet in made-for-television films. Many of the movies are pilots for series—many of which were never produced. Yet another art form—the television novel or miniseries—has become more popular in recent years. This uses the production capability of the motion-picture industry but not the distribution system of theaters originally designed for the purpose, since the fifteen to twenty hours required for such blockbusters as *Roots*, *Centennial*, *Holocaust*, *Wheels*, and *Shogun* cannot be viewed at one sitting. The entire nation may be captivated for an entire week as in the case of *Roots*, which was viewed in an estimated 31.9 million homes in January 1976, making it the third highest rated program ever after Part I (33.96 million homes) and Part II (33.75 million homes) of the motion picture, *Gone With the Wind* (*Broadcasting* 1977:19). Interestingly enough, this art form was pioneered by the Public Broadcasting System importing a British dramatization of the *The Forsythe Saga*; in the fall of 1979 an Australian television series, *Against the Wind*, was offered—all thirteen hours broadcast in a single week. Following the same pattern, *Shogun*, a joint venture filmed in Japan, was viewed during one week in September, 1980.

Much of the policy controversy concerning such made-for-television motion pictures has involved outrage on the part of U.S. authors' and writers' guilds that federal funds have been provided by the

Corporation for Public Broadcasting to subsidize such purchases as *Upstairs, Downstairs*, a British historical drama of Victorian and Edwardian England. Especially troublesome was the negotiation to provide advance financial participation for the British production of Shakespeare's plays, which U.S. actors and producers felt equally competent to produce. However, when the purchases are made entirely with private corporate funds, such as Mobil Corporation's funding of *Edward, the King* on a private network on commercial television, there is no mechanism for redress of grievances for the injured crafts and guilds—though the end result might be the same. The appropriate mechanism for redress does exist through export-import controls administered by the Department of Commerce that could be invoked to protect an endangered industry. There has been no such effort since the motion-picture industry has reaped great rewards from free international exchange. If U.S. performers have been shortchanged, it may be because of the failure of the United States Congress to recognize performers' rights as it has copyright—rewards to performers must be protected by individual contractual negotiations or union rules. Actors' guilds have developed elaborate mechanisms for measuring and collecting for performances, especially for reruns of commercials and television series. Such requirements are rigid, and failure to comply would result in expulsion from the union and/or refusal of other union members to work for the noncomplying company.

The motion-picture and television industries, though separate and distinct entities, have become more and more intertwined. Most of the major movie production houses have spawned television production divisions, including MGM, Twentieth Century-Fox, Paramount, and Walt Disney. Warner Brothers has also invested heavily in cable television systems. However, a multimillion dollar joint venture of the five major movie production houses with Getty Oil to form a pay cable service met with vociferous opposition from the cable industry and the Department of Justice, which successfully obtained an injunction on antitrust grounds. The actors and writers complain that the network censors inhibit their artistic freedom. Viewers, who have seen both theater and television versions of a movie, complain that the artistic integrity is jeopardized. Obscenities and explicit sex scenes are removed to meet the more stringent requirements of the broadcast code, and entire scenes are often removed to conform to time restrictions. Dramatic moments are often lost by the breaks for commercial messages. However, such decisions have been left to industry self-regulation by the rather general but unspecific requirements laid down by the FCC for television broadcasting. Sanctions are imposed by consumer acceptance and public outcry when standards of decency are contravened, and public interest advocates urge more stringent controls to protect children, particularly from obtrusive entry of objectionable material into the home environment—a consideration that in the eyes of the courts has justified a stricter standard than for movie houses. In the 1980s, a new movement called the Moral Majority has mounted a major public relations effort to clean up network television by threatening to boycott consumer goods advertised on offending programs. With the advent of cable television channels, which are funded by subscribers, the tension between artistic freedom of expression and the moral indignation of viewers is likely to increase.

The legal prohibitions on content in the Communications Act of 1934—"obscene, indecent or profane"—are substantially more restrictive for broadcast purposes than permitted for the motion-picture industry by the law of the land. For many years, motion pictures were deemed to be entertainment not subject to protection by the First Amendment. This permitted substantial regulation by states and banning from viewing where scenes did not pass the censor. After the Supreme Court held motion pictures to be protected by the First Amendment, censorship was replaced by a voluntary rating system that grades movies according to the level of nudity and explicit sex and violence portrayed, to which 99 percent of all U.S.-produced movies submit. Motion-picture producers who participate in the system display the appropriate symbols:

G—General Audiences
PG—Parental Guidance Suggested
R—Restricted, Children Under 17 Not Admitted Unless
    Accompanied by Parent or Adult Guardian
X—Under 17 Not Admitted

Hard-core pornography and some foreign producers do not participate in the rating system. In recent years there has been an explosion of film, pressing the limits of First Amendment protection to both film and the print media. Such offerings as *Deep Throat* and *The Devil in Miss Jones* were banned in many communities. Also banned was *Hustler* magazine, a more explicit exploitation of sex without the literary appeal of *Esquire*, which had been at the frontiers of First Amendment advocacy a generation ago. The Supreme Court abandoned the national standard for judgment about obscenity, which was based upon a subjective evaluation of "redeeming social value" to a new rule that permitted community standards of propriety to prevail (*Miller* v. *California* 1973). This is a very troublesome legal requirement for an industry that is national in scope, since it would be complex and costly to prepare regional versions of film and/or print. However, the hand of the judiciary has been very light, indeed, in recent years and the rule of the marketplace has prevailed.

The U.S. tax laws have had the greatest impact on the motion-picture industry because they have favored investment in production for many years. Capital has flowed freely into the industry and movies have been a favored tax shelter for the wealthy. This may have encouraged too many inferior films to be produced for the tax benefits rather than aesthetic merits, but the proliferation assured a large enough pool from which the audiences could pick and choose; and the odds were better than the horse races. *Star Wars*, the most financially successful movie to date, grossed $410 million in receipts (*New York Times* 1980a, Sec. 2:1). A 1976 change in the tax laws to restrict writeoffs may have contributed to the smaller number of films being produced—some ninety to one hundred a year compared to four to five hundred in earlier years.

By the 1930s, the industry, like every other mass medium, had evolved into a few large conglomerates—the Big Five: Warner Brothers (now a large communication conglomerate), Loew's Inc., RKO (part of the General Tire and Rubber family), Paramount, Twentieth Century-Fox; and the Little Three: Universal, Columbia, and United Artists (part of the Transamerica combine). These eight companies in the 1950s produced 95 percent of the films and controlled 70 percent of the first-run theaters in cities of over 100,000 population (Rivers, Peterson, and Jensen 1971). Distribution is no longer controlled, but 59 percent of the films are still produced by the Big Eight.

As in other areas, the drive toward amalgamation has been strong and the policy of keeping the door open for small independent producers difficult to maintain. More money is spent on advertising a single movie by the large companies than most independent producers can dream of funding for an entire production. There is little direct subsidy of production except the television drama series funded through the Corporation for Public Broadcasting and the Endowments for the Arts and Humanities.

Other ways in which national policy affects the motion-picture industry are in the application of copyright laws, safety regulations, and the equal opportunity regulations. Cable television, videodiscs, tapes, and other new technological opportunities are threatening to undermine the compensatory arrangements for viewing performances, and all of the companies are affected by both OSHA (safety of the employment environment) and EEOC (equal employment opportunities).

Unlike the print media, there is no government film producer comparable to the Government Printing Office nor an official depository of film comparable to the Library of Congress for the print media. There has been a substantial investment in government production of film. At the beginning of the Carter administration, a major effort was undertaken to identify all the funds spent on film production. The total sum was estimated to be $1,500 million annually. Policy has been directed toward transfer of this expenditure from in-house production dispersed among the many government agencies to independent producers under contract. However, rather than leaving decision making about individual producers highly dispersed as it was until the new study, it has been proposed that no contract film production be negotiated without the approval of a centralized office (whose locus is proposed to be the Department of Defense), a seeming anomaly except that the DOD has had the longest history of involvement and largest budgets to spend on film production for training personnel, recruitment, and other purposes. The DOD has also over the years provided substantial in-kind services to various filmmakers who needed such props as aircraft carriers, submarines, and tanks. A brief perusal of the films of the 1930s, 1940s, and 1950s will reveal a rather intimate relationship between strategic military interests and the films produced.

Broadcasting

Public policy concerning the broadcasting industry in the United States historically rested on the theory of scarcity of spectrum through which radio and television signals can be disseminated. As competitive technologies increase the availability of channels of communication, legal theory is coming to recognize that broadcasting is regulated because of its impact rather than its scarcity. Unlike the printed media, which is relatively free of regulation, the broadcasting industry has been highly regulated. The regulatory system was initiated originally in response to the chaotic competitive environment in which broadcasters found themselves in the early 1920s. Thus, the competitive marketplace, most cherished by U.S. policy, was abandoned by the competitors. If everyone spoke, no one could be heard. The resulting babble on interfering frequencies was intolerable (*National Broadcasting Co.* v. *U.S.* 1943).

Licensing

The legal philosophy of broadcasting regulation, established in the Radio Act of 1927 and later the Communications Act of 1934, is based on a theory of public ownership of the airwaves or electromagnetic spectrum through which the signals are broadcast, and the need for public management or allocation of the use of the spectrum. It was assumed that an equitable allocation of the use of such frequencies would guarantee that the ultimate owners (the public) would somehow be served through the establishment of a "public interest" standard. Licenses to use the spectrum are issued by the FCC, an independent agency headed by seven commissioners appointed by the president (with the consent of the Senate) for staggered seven-year terms. No more than four may be of the same political party. Licensees are thought to be "public trustees" serving as surrogates to pick and choose whatever news, public affairs, and entertainment will best serve the interests of the public. The principle was early established that broadcasting should not be permitted to become merely a medium of entertainment, and licensees were expected to schedule some minimal amount of the broadcast day in news or public affairs programming.

30

The commission has established a very complex weighting system. Applicants are assigned merit points to help the commission determine, on a comparative basis, which would best serve the public interest. These merit points cover such characteristics as local ownership and the amount of public-service programming proposed to be carried by the station. Once licensed, licensees are called upon every three years to justify their continued service to the public. Service for the past three years is reviewed and broadcasters make proposals for their continued public service over the next three-year period.

In early licensing proceedings, most of the qualifications reviewed were of an economic, financial, and technical nature to determine whether the licensee was qualified and adequately equipped to provide radio or television service. Representatives of the public have been permitted to intervene and participate in FCC proceedings only since 1966 (*Office of Communications of United Church of Christ* v. *FCC* 1966). Local groups now question the nature and quality of proposed and past service of the broadcasting entities to their local communities. "Ascertainment" requirements designate the manner in which each licensee should determine the problems, needs, and interests within the local community by interviewing community leaders and conducting community-wide surveys of the general public. An annual report on the ten most important public issues in the service area is required of licensees, and to show how they have addressed these issues through television programming, broadcasters must file an Annual Programming Report.

As a result of court decisions opening up the licensing process to public participation, religious groups such as the United Church of Christ and the National Council of Churches have helped many communities to organize local media lobbies or public interest groups. National media groups also have been spawned, including the Black Media Coalition, Action for Children's Television, the Gray Panthers Media Task Force, and the National Organization for Women Media Committee. Some have become a major force in developing communication policy in broadcasting particularly, and especially in pressuring stations to employ more women and minority personnel. The development of such groups has resulted in a great deal more litigation being pursued against broadcasters during the last decade than previously. Broadcasters have responded with a heavily funded lobbying effort to extend the period of licenses from three to five years and to establish a preferential system by which they might know what standard of performance would guarantee them continuation of their licenses. During the fall of 1981, this effort was successful in extending radio license permits to seven years and television licenses to five years. However, efforts to remove the "public interest" standard from the Communications Act have all failed to be enacted into law, although the prospects of passage under the Reagan Administration are considerably enhanced.

Content Regulation

Although there is much judicial rhetoric to prohibit control of content under the First Amendment, this principle is served more in the breach than in the observance. There are several ways in which content has been controlled by government regulation. Obscenity, however it might be defined, has never been protected by the First Amendment and is specifically forbidden to be broadcast by the United States Criminal Code (Title 18 U.S.C. §1464). The Criminal Code, which also forbids "profane and indecent" language, was recently upheld by the United States Supreme Court in the *Pacifica Foundation* case (*FCC* v. *Pacifica Foundation* 1978), affirming an FCC decision forbidding broadcast of "seven dirty words" during times when children are likely to be in the audience. This has led to much concern among First Amendment purists, because the decision rested on finding the language offensive to large numbers of the audience and especially on exposure of children to the indecent language. The current FCC commissioners eschew any intention to broaden the *Pacifica* holding or delve any deeper into content control; but the decision remains the law of the land.

A major problem has been how to handle controversial issues of public importance on the airwaves. One early and major thrust was to encourage the broadcast of news and public affairs rather than permit either radio or television to become exclusively an entertainment medium. This was achieved by establishing minimum percentages for each.

Presidential access to prime-time network television has been voluntary on the part of the networks, which negotiated appearances upon request. Time has rarely been denied, but the tenuous relationship is bound by the certainty that the executive has leverage in the form of licensing by a presidentially appointed commission. The complex interrelationship between the president and the broadcast media is fascinating and far more intricate than textbook coverage will intimate or the FCC regulations reveal. It rests upon a very personal contact of the president with broadcast journalists that has varied from Roosevelt's commanding use of radio in his "fireside chats," to a protective adulation and cultivation by Kennedy, to personal persuasion by Johnson, to intimidation and coercion by Nixon and Agnew.

There have been numerous efforts to establish a legally enforceable reply time to presidential addresses of an incumbent president, but none has succeeded—perhaps because the U.S. political system does not readily supply an easily identifiable individual upon whom such right of reply would devolve. Indeed, the trend has been in the opposite direction, to remove the presidential race from equal-time requirements even in a campaign. A proliferation of minor-party candidates made such demands upon television time that debates between the candidates of the Democratic and Republican parties was accomplished in 1960 and 1976 only by suspending the rule for the presidential candidates.

32

Political access to radio and television has been more difficult for congressional, state, and local candidates. Until 1972, licensees were not required to carry political messages except under general obligation to operate in the public interest. Under Section 315 of the 1934 Act, if they make time available for political purposes, either free or paid, they are required to make equal time available to all qualified candidates for the same office. This may make unreasonable demands on local broadcasters who serve large metropolitan areas that cover a multiplicity of congressional districts, state represented districts, and/or local city councils, as well as school boards and judicial districts that are in many states also popularly elected. However, some local radio stations of limited radius coverage find local elections a particularly rich source of revenue.

To protect against a prohibitively high rate to discourage political advertising during election years, Congress in 1972 enacted the Campaign Communications Reform Act (PL-92-225), which prohibits licensees from charging political candidates a higher rate than they have charged as discount rates to their most favored advertisers. Section 312 (a)(7) of the Communications Act was also amended to empower the FCC to revoke licenses for failure to make available reasonable access to candidates for federal office. Access to air time is also guaranteed under the "Fairness Doctrine" for other controversial issues of public importance. This policy made its debut as an administrative doctrine but was later added as an amendment to Section 315 of the Communications Act and was judicially affirmed (Red Lion v. FCC 1974).

Control of such coverage is guaranteed by the "public interest" standard, in that a license allegedly should not be renewed if no such issues were broadcast, but many licensees pass muster with virtually no performance. Where issues of controversy are broadcast, the choice of issue is legally under the control of the broadcaster with the proviso that no one side of the controversy may be favored. The choice of person or persons to voice the controversy is also left entirely to the broadcast licensee. Commercial networks have for many years required that all documentaries be produced by network personnel. This policy has been bitterly opposed by independent producers and also by public interest advocates, who, by and large, receive a great deal of air time in news coverage and "talk shows." But those whose opinions are ignored have no legal right of access and no judicial redress for their grievances, since existing unused frequencies are limited. They have to be interesting enough to attact broadcasters or affluent enough to go out and purchase a station or challenge a current licensee.

The Personal Attack Rule (47 C.F.R. §§73.123, 73.300, 73.598, 73.679), which is a refinement of the Fairness Doctrine, states the only circumstance other than equal time for political candidates in which a particular person or group has an absolute right of access to air time. When a broadcaster who is solely responsible for the content of broadcast messages permits the licensed channel to be used for the purpose of attacking the personal reputation of an identified person or group, that person or entity has an absolute right to obtain a transcript of the offending material and an opportunity to respond in order to explain or defend his or her reputation. This is a very explicit and limited right—rarely evoked but clearly available to offended parties and a deterrent to broadcast libel, for which damages as well as access to broadcast time would be available through the courts under common law practice (previously discussed in the section on the print media).

Regulation of content to protect children has been high on the agenda of both the FCC and the Federal Trade Commission (FTC). The debate at the FTC has been whether or not commercials should be eliminated for children who are too young to make consumer choices. Other items at issue in the FCC Task Force inquiry included the amount and time of children's programs as well as the content of messages.

Legal theory permits a protective attitude toward children, but marketplace realities deter regulation. There is very little programming on commercial television designed especially for preschool-age children, and studies of television viewing habits of school-age children indicate that they watch what adults watch. Thus, controlling commercial messages for children would ultimately involve controlling commercial messages for adults—a course the FCC and FTC would be loath to take. In addition, the financial supporters of children's programming (except for *Sesame Street*, *The Electric Company*, and *Mister Rogers' Neighborhood* on public broadcasting) are primarily producers of toys and food, whose dollars would be deleted were commercial messages curtailed. Therefore, there is a concern that the total amount of children's programming might decrease should advertising on children's programs be prohibited. Current policy appears to encourage new technologies to enrich program offerings for children. Nickelodeon, a children's channel on cable television, had attracted 5.6 million subscribers by late 1981.

The FCC has never specified the amount of commercial time that could be carried per broadcast hour, although the amount of commercial time is a factor in determining whether the licensee has served the public interest when the license is reviewed for renewal. The precise time permitted is set by a code of ethics promulgated by the National Association of Broadcasters. Currently, it is 9½ minutes per broadcast hour in prime time for network television affiliates, 12 minutes for independent stations, and 16 minutes for nonprime-time hours. FCC regulations do require commercials to be logged in and reported to the FCC on a composite week (seven different days picked at random) which is filed with the commission. FCC regulations also specify what must be reported as commercial time; for example, if the subject matter of the program is directly related to the commercial interests of the program's sponsor, the entire program must be logged in as a commercial.

The Public Access Movement

Because the spectrum was a scarce resource which, for the mass media, became largely a triple sole source of the same type of programming favored by national advertisers of consumer products, there arose a great outcry during the 1960s against the broadcasters who were said to monopolize the channels of communication with soap and perfume rather than with ideas and concerns of the citizens. And, because this network programming was exported worldwide, an outcry arose to the effect that U.S. cultural imperialism was selling a social system. United States cultural imperialism, as articulated in Third World pressures for a New World Information Order, is an issue difficult to address in U.S. communication policy, probably because there is no structural or legal way to deal with it. The underlying problems of control of the airwaves and ownership of broadcast facilities has preoccupied a major portion of FCC and judicial attention.

During the 1960s and early 1970s there was a strong movement to establish an absolute right of access to the broadcast media. This proceeded on several fronts—one was spearheaded by environmentalists who attempted to establish a right to "counter advertising." For example, if a commercial message contained messages of controversial public importance, then an opposing message was required under the Fairness Doctrine, they argued. According to the environmentalists, all commercial advertising did carry a social message, examples including (1) cigarette ads—opposed by nonsmokers who were reinforced by a report of the Surgeon General that cigarette smoking was hazardous to one's health; (2) automobile ads—gasoline-driven automobiles were said to be not only polluting the highways but destroying the air quality of most major cities; (3) food ads—nutritionists complained that these were contributing to public health problems by encouraging children to eat candy and sugarcoated cereals and adults to eat "junk foods" with little nutritional value.

The Court of Appeals held that there was an enforceable right to counter cigarette ads with public service messages exposing the health hazards of smoking. However, the FCC, after extensive hearings, declined to extend the concept to counter ads for all commerical advertising because the bulk of broadcast programming is supported by corporate advertising dollars which might be withdrawn if broadcasters were required to pay for the counter ads.

The second thrust for access to broadcast time came from the business community whose leaders felt that they were denied an opportunity to express their own views about public policy matters affecting their own businesses. They were concerned about the lack of coverage of issues they deemed important, as well as the antibusiness bias of the working broadcast journalists. Consequently, efforts were made by Mobil Corporation to purchase broadcast time to tell the oil industry's views of the energy crisis. Such efforts being refused by the networks, the issue was taken to the courts, which refused to establish a judicially enforced right to purchase time under the First Amendment in the absence of a legislative or administrative mandate to do so. Both the law and the administrative rulings favored complete broadcaster control of content (FCC 1974).

The same result ensued with the third thrust at establishing a right of access—this time from a combination of the Democratic National Committee (DNC) seeking a right to purchase air time for raising money and to reach voters with its political views, and a group of businessmen who opposed the Vietnam War and wanted to purchase air time to express their views to the American people (*Business Executives* . . . v. *FCC* 1971). After a negative FCC ruling, the Court of Appeals forged a new principle of public access to the public airwaves, which was then reversed by the Supreme Court. The Supreme Court did not completely close the door to a right of access, which might in the future be promulgated by the FCC and receive approval of the courts. However, the Supreme Court was reluctant to initiate such a policy contrary to the wisdom of the regulatory agency in whose hands its enforcement would ultimately rest (*CBS* v. *DNC* 1973).

Access has been encouraged in recent years more by structural changes than broadcast restriction, more minority ownership, more public broadcasting, fewer restrictions on cable television, and favoring competition in common carrier alternatives.

Ownership Restrictions

Much of U.S. policy has been directed toward ownership of the media, both multiple and across media modes. The natural tendency has been toward amalgamation of media interests and cross-investment of one medium into another. Thus, the large metropolitan newspapers made early investments in radio broadcasting and later in television. Some of the strongest stations were such co-owned entities in major markets as the *San Francisco Chronicle* and KRON-TV; the *Washington Post* and WTOP-AM, FM, and TV; the *Atlanta Journal* and WSB-AM, FM and TV. The controversy over combinations was long and protracted and (as discussed in the section on the print media) was resolved in a 1975 FCC rule prohibiting similar local cross-owned entities in the future. Over the decade that the proposal had been pending, many of the media companies had swapped or divested themselves of the co-owned stations. The *Washington Post*, for example, transferred its FM station to Howard University as a charitable contribution, thus providing a black-owned and operated station in the nation's capital, which is predominantly populated by blacks.

In this transfer, the *Washington Post* fulfilled three major policy directives: (1) to diversify ownership of the media; (2) to increase minority ownership of the media; and (3) to accomplish these ends by voluntary rather than obligatory means with private rather than public funds. This particular transaction is noted because it is illustrative of the complex interplay of public initiatives and private actions with which U.S. policy is both plagued and blessed. In another transfer, the *Washington Post* exchanged its locally owned television station with the locally owned television station of the *Detroit Free Press*. This transfer accomplished the purpose of the policy against cross-ownership of newspaper and television stations in local markets, but contravened the policy favoring local ownership and management of broadcast facilities.

Communication policy on ownership has been pursued more by what is called the "raised eyebrow" than concrete regulatory action. Communication lawyers find out which way FCC and FTC commissioners are leaning and advise their clients accordingly. Thus, potential mergers between broadcast and/or newspaper and cable interests have been stopped by the mere suggestion of activating a long-pending rulemaking proceeding, or of a suggestion of a protracted review by the FTC, or a threat of an antitrust suit by the Department of Justice. Horizontal integration of the cable industry was inhibited in this manner during the early 1970s.

Moreover, the progression of policy initiatives has followed a long-term continuum of keeping ownership of the broadcast media in as many hands as possible without upsetting the economic realities of the marketplace. By 1938 the FCC was concerned about network acquisition of stations that carried their program schedule, so that networks were prohibited early from owning all stations served by programming. The current rule permits a single entity to have licenses for no more than seven AM, seven FM, and seven TV stations (only five of which may be the more desirable VHF stations). The origin of the limit of seven was, interestingly enough, initiated when there were only seven hundred radio stations in the entire country, and was intended to limit a licensee to no more than 1 percent of the nation's radio stations. Now that ratio for television stations is about the same (1%), but with more than 8,000 radio stations, the restriction limits licensees of radio stations to less than one-tenth of 1 percent of the total number.

Another major problem in U.S. policy has been how to satisfy minority programming interests in a system that has been a predominantly mass medium. Basically, the thrust has been toward structural diversity rather than content control, a policy confirmed by the courts (*TV 9* v. *FCC* 1973). Recognizing the dead end that access rights had come to with the Nixon-appointed Supreme Court, the Carter administration made encouragement of minority ownership of broadcast facilities a major policy commitment. As late as 1977, the imbalance was such that only 41 commercial radio stations, 8 television stations, and 6 cable systems were minority owned and operated (Cable Communications Resource Center 1977). Applicants with minority participation were

37

given special consideration in license applications and renewal challenges. Efforts have been made to free funds for minority buyers by repealing the prohibition against use of funds by the Small Business Administration to finance broadcast interests. Also, distress sales to minority owners were permitted if licenses were challenged and the sale took place at less than 75 percent of the market value prior to the hearing (FCC 1979).

Other initiatives of the Carter administration were in the direction of completing the nationwide system of public broadcasting, extending service for commercial and public stations by translators or cable systems to rural areas, and otherwise a rather complete commitment to as unregulated a marketplace as possible to encourage the development of new technologies such as satellites, fiber optics, packet-switched data networks, and mixed media such as view data, teletext, and video-publishing.

Public Broadcasting

Public broadcasting enjoys a loyal and devoted audience, but rarely captures the attention of policymakers or industry leaders unless it captures more than 5 percent of the audience, or carries unusually controversial programs. Public broadcasting was perceived largely as an alternative to the commercial network system and as a panacea for the inadequacies of commercial broadcasters. The basic philosophy underlying the public system is one of localism. The original allocation of broadcast frequencies had been generously assigned to take care of the local communication needs of as many localities as possible within the limitations of spectrum interference, but commercial networks soon developed national sources of programming. One of the major driving forces of public broadcasters has been to keep programming control at the local level while trying to mobilize financial resources to produce quality programming that will be aired nationally.

As an alternative service to the commercialism of the networks serving mass audiences, the mandate of public broadcasting was too demanding. As an outlet for the views of the many minority interests that the commercial system could not accommodate, the burdens of the public broadcasters were too great. As if these internal conflicts concerning the basic service were not enough to contend with, public broadcasting has also been plagued with a divided system of governance that was intended to protect it from interference by government control of content and purpose, but has greatly complicated the management problem and clouded the policy function.

That public broadcasting has been as successful as it has over the last two decades is more a testimonial to the critical need for its existence than the ease with which policy can be made concerning its functions and funding. The original impetus for the development of a public system of broadcasting came from the educational establishment, which felt the need for a portion of the spectrum for pursuing its own instructional purposes. The original allocation in 1952 of VHF frequencies for educational use followed the setting aside in 1945 of twenty FM frequencies for use by educational institutions. There are very few AM stations operating as a part of the public system. The licensing of stations on reserved channels is strictly a function for the FCC as is policymaking concerning the practices which keep this restricted to noncommercial use. However, the funding of transmitters and equipment to make these stations operational has come, until recently, from the Department of Health, Education, and Welfare—consistent with the educational and nonprofit purpose of the stations. The facilities appropriation is now administered by the National Telecommunications and Information Administration (NTIA).

Encouraged by the report of the Carnegie Commission on Educational Television (1967), which led to the Public Broadcasting Act of 1967, a new type of television station known as a "community station" promoted a much broader concept of educational activity of the media than had originally been envisioned for the reserved channels. The 1967 Act established the Corporation for Public Broadcasting (CPB), which was to serve as the funding mechanism to insulate congressional funds to public television and radio stations from congressional pressure on program content. However, unlike the British BBC or the Japanese NHK, which have assured funding from license fees and more complete control over programming and delivery at the local stations, CPB has no operational control over the stations, which are licensed variously to nonprofit corporations, local school boards, state educational networks, and individual colleges and universities of both public, private, and religious inclination.

The ultimate choice of programming content is retained by the local station, and local control of the system is jealously guarded, although a national programming service is coordinated by the Public Broadcasting System (PBS) for the television side and National Public Radio (NPR) for the radio stations. PBS schedules and delivers service supplied by the producing television stations; and NPR actually produces as well as delivers radio programs to affiliated stations. NPR serves both as the trade organization representing the interests of public radio before state and federal agencies and as program producer, whereas public television recently created a new organization, the Association of Public Broadcasters, to provide representation, leaving PBS to concentrate on programming.

Much of the confusion in terminology with respect to the television stations derives from a policy decision that CPB should not and could not operate a "network." It was the intention of Congress, supported by the commercial networks, to avoid competition with the commercial networks and have the kind of very local service that had not been fully developed by the system of broadcasting prevalent in the United States at that time. To complicate matters further, the funding for public broadcasting comes from a large variety of sources: (1) direct contributions from the audiences who either watch or listen to the programs; (2) from major corporations such as Mobil, Exxon, Xerox, and IBM, which fund prestigious cultural programming on the national system; (3) federal agencies and national endowments; (4) private foundations; and (5) both state and regional networks that now provide programs related to state and regional needs. A new look at public broadcasting funding and structure was taken by a second Carnegie Commission in 1978. It recommended substantially increased federal funding and an endowment for programming to be set up within the CPB (Carnegie Commission . . . 1979). Another Carnegie Commission effort attempted to rationalize public investment in a pay cable channel for cultural programming (*New York Times* 1980b:C24).

Thus, there is no one centralized agency or entity to which one can go in the United States to find the ultimate authority or decision-making power concerning public broadcasting. It is a system divided unto and within itself. The miracle is that the system not only survives, but thrives. Perhaps its greatest strength for the future lies within the development of a satellite interconnection for both television and radio, which became operational for the television stations in the spring of 1978. Some twenty television stations cut the umbilical cord to the AT&T interconnection and initiated the first full-time delivery of television programming via satellite. This will ultimately permit delivery of four channels of programming for both television and radio at a cost no greater than that originally paid for connecting the single-channel service. Satellite service is projected to provide a great deal more opportunity for exchange of locally produced programs as well as delivery of programs of state and regional interest. However, as yet there is no mechanism in place for generating a fourfold increase in funding for the production of programs to fill all this channel space nor a plan for increasing the number of local public broadcasting stations to accommodate such an increase in programs. Initially the major advantage of the system may be in mere duplication of services for different times and places. Yet ultimately satellite delivery promises the resolution of the problem of conflict among the varying interest groups within the public broadcasting community that cry out for better service for their particular needs. However, the satellite may exacerbate the problem of the public broadcaster serving the local community, since it expedites the delivery of national programs.

Cable Television

Cable television is more widely prevalent in the United States than in most other countries of the world, with approximately four thousand systems. Originally, cable served primarily the small townships and rural villages of the United States that were beyond the reception areas of major television stations in metropolitan areas, but recently more and more systems have been built in the suburban residential neighborhoods of major metropolitan areas. Although cable currently passes about 55 percent of the nation's homes, still less than 28 percent are subscribers (21.9 million of 81.9 million). Nonetheless, this presents a competitive market for the delivery of television signals by alternative modes other than local broadcasting entities. After an enterprising independent UHF station, WTBS (Channel 17 in Atlanta), became a super station serving five million cable subscribers nationwide, its success was rapidly emulated by others in California, New York, and Chicago, delivering the signals of independent stations via satellite to cable systems all over the country. Satellites now serve cable systems with what has become an increasing number of programming entities; three religious services (Trinity, PTL, and the Christian Broadcasting Network), a Spanish language services (Galavision), two children's services (Nickelodeon and Calliope), the House of Representatives, two special sports services (Sports Program Network and Madison Square Garden), several movie channels, a community service network, Cable News Network, Home Box Office, and Showtime.

The number of earth-station applications before the FCC proliferated to such an extent that the FCC decided to deregulate earth stations, and it is no longer known how many are in service. Also, installation of a backyard satellite saucer had decreased in price to around $3,500 by early 1981, so proliferation of individual reception without compensation to subscription services was becoming a live issue.

The regulation of cable television by the FCC has been justified as ancillary to its broadcasting authority and because cable was deemed a threat to the economic viability of local broadcasting entities. The primary responsibility for regulation of cable television systems rested at the local level where authority was required for the use of city streets along which to string the cable. Since most cities did not want multiple telephone poles, it was necessary for the cable industry to develop an accommodation with the telephone companies. Much of the earlier anxiety of the industry came from seeking the aid of regulatory authorities to require a fair charge for use of telephone poles. In some states franchising was authorized by state legislatures, and in other states, public utility commissions claimed authority over cable regulation. In another group of states, the potential for alternative information services other than broadcasting plus the problem of the protection of consumers against unfair and inequitable rates led to legislation establishing state cable authorities. By late 1978 there were eleven states with comprehensive regulatory legislation, and many other states have enacted specialized legislation related to cable television (Kalba 1978).

Much of the public argument about regulation of the cable industry is involved with this tripartite division of responsibility among the local franchising authority, a state cable regulatory agency, and the FCC. Because Congress did not choose to clarify the authority of the FCC over cable television, the rationale rested upon an "ancillary to broadcasting" theory (*U.S.* v. *Midwest Video* 1972). The major thrust of the 1972 regulations was toward (1) setting the parameters for the carriage of distance signals, those beyond the normal range of local broadcasters; (2) the requirements of nonduplication of protected programs carried by local broadcasters; and (3) the obligatory requirement that cable television stations transmit all local signals. However, much of the regulatory theory was also based upon the projection that cable television had the potential to become a multichannel information system carrying a large variety of alternative services to broadcasting that would diversify the available marketplace of ideas. Therefore, a part of the FCC's concern in its regulations was that the local municipalities not charge too large a franchise fee and that cable television systems, when they were large enough to justify programming, begin to develop the alternative channel signals for which hope was promised. Thus, the FCC's very elaborate 1972 regulations not only set the parameters for signal carriage, nonduplication, and franchise maximums, but also required cable systems to offer local, live programming when they reached 3,500 subscribers and required that systems in the large metropolitan markets set aside a special channel each for municipal information, educational institutions, general public access, and leased services. Furthermore, in order to assure that the cable television system would be an interactive system, they required by 1976 that systems update their installations to provide a return communication channel.

As cable television systems suffered more than other industries in the economic recession of 1973 and 1974, they did not become a major source of income for local municipalities, nor did they develop their franchises in the major metropolitan areas. Pressure was put upon the FCC by the cable industry to weaken the 1972 rules. Ultimately most of the major mandates and prohibitions, including those which inhibited cable systems from carriage of live sports and recent movies, were thrown out by the courts as lying beyond the statutory power of the FCC (*Midwest Video* v. *U.S.* 1979). By 1978, Congress was proposing the deregulation of the cable industry in order to let it develop as the marketplace would respond, and the FCC was itself recommending the dismantling of its cable television bureau.

Another major policy issue confronting the cable industry was whether or not copyright royalties were payable for programs carried by the cable systems. This was resolved, first by a compromise in 1971 (orchestrated by the director of the Office of Telecommunications Policy) which permitted some carriage of broadcast signals in exchange for royalty payments; but this issue was treated by the Copyright Act of

1976, which mandated royalty payments by cable systems. This has not settled the issue satisfactorily to the broadcasters, who are agitating with NTIA support for a requirement for retransmission consent before cable can use the broadcaster's signal. Currently, the mood in the United States is toward deregulation of cable as well as radio, although leaders in the cable industry are less enthusiastic about deregulation if it means competition with the telephone industry. The original rewrite of the proposed Communications Act of 1978 (H.R. 13015) would have freed telephone companies from the present prohibition against offering cable television service within their own franchise areas, but the cable industry lobbied to have this prohibition reinstated in subsequent versions reintroduced into Congress in 1979 (H.R. 3333) and 1981 (S. 898 and H.R. 5158).

Common Carriers

Common carrier regulation in the United States is governed by Title II of the Communications Act of 1934. The underlying philosophy of the 1934 Act is to make available as far as possible to all the people in the United States, rapid, efficient, nationwide, and worldwide wire and radio communications for the defense and safety of life and property. By and large, access to the public switched telephone network for all the citizens of the United States has been achieved. Indeed, the United States, with only 6 percent of the world's population, uses one-third of the world's telephones.

Regulation of common carriers has been assured by various federal and state regulatory agencies, because it has been assumed that common carriers were a natural monopoly for which competition would be disruptive and wasteful since there were substantial fixed costs for service throughout the service area. Regulation is intended to provide universal access, just and reasonable carriage, and controlled entry into the industry through a fair and equitable allocation in the marketplace. Unlike other parts of the world where posts and telegraph and telecommunications are all amalgamated in an operational and policymaking entity, this has meant that the various telecommunications services in the United States have been carefully carved out and various private companies have been granted an exclusive domain for certain segments of the industry. Thus the telegraph services have been provided largely by the American Telephone & Telegraph (AT&T) affiliated companies, the General Telephone & Electronics Corporation (GTE), a large number of rural cooperatives, and many small telephone companies each serving its own geographically designated service area.

Regulation is divided between state public utility commissions, which govern intrastate services and tariffs, and the Federal Communications Commission, where interstate service is governed by Title II of the Communications Act of 1934. Much of the development of common carriers in the United States has also been governed by antitrust policy, which has prevented too much amalgamation of services of different kinds similar to the ministries of posts and telegraph in other countries. The telephone industry has been highly vertically integrated with AT&T ownership of Western Electric, which produces the instruments through which telephone service is delivered. GTE also has its own manufacturer of instruments.

Historical Development

It was not an accident of fate but conscious decision that led to postal, telegraph, and telephone services being provided by independent institutions rather than a unified government department or even a single company. Although authority to establish post roads and a postal service was given to the federal government in the Constitution, the electronic services were permitted to develop in an unfettered marketplace. Telecommunications and transportation were closely related and telegraph poles were initially established on the railway right-of-ways, which were often built on lands deeded by the federal government. There were clearly competitive railways and competitive telegraph companies, and only through market competition did the monopoly service of Western Union become established in telegraphy as AT&T became dominant in telephony. Monopolization led first to state regulation and then to federal laws regulating interstate commerce.

Part of the reason for diversified ownership of different forms of communication was lack of foresight on the part of existing service companies when new companies were developed; for example, Western Union turned down the opportunity to buy Bell's patents, which became the basis for the AT&T telephone empire. IBM similarly turned down the opportunity to develop Chester Carlson's new invention, xerography, which revolutionized facsimile transmission and spawned a strong competitor in communicating office products.

In 1912, when the British government assumed ownership of the British telephone system, the United States remained alone among the major countries with private companies providing all telephone service. In 1913, the United States Postmaster General started a debate over the nationalization of telegraph and telephone services under his department, urging that the use of wires for transmission was a natural extension of the constitutional authority to establish post offices and post roads. The telephone companies argued that a government monopoly of telephony and telegraphy would be unworkable because there would be no regulators to regulate the government monopoly. Nonetheless, President Wilson, under the pressure of wartime exigencies, nationalized the railways as well as telephone and telegraph services. The experiment in government ownership was short-lived, as the government was unable to operate without sharply raising rates when lower

44

rates had been promised. The public outcry was so great that less than a year later Congress proposed the immediate return of telegraph and telephone services to their private owners—and so ended public ownership of the monopoly common carriers (Brooks 1975:151-58).

Another important reason why services are provided by so many competitors is that antitrust policy has played a significant role in breaking up business organizations that appear to become too large or too integrated either vertically or horizontally. Originally, in 1879, Bell agreed to stay out of telegraphy and Western Union agreed to stay out of telephony in a private settlement over their respective patents. This agreement was circumvented, however, by incorporating the American Telephone & Telegraph Company (AT&T) to set up long lines to interconnect local telephone companies. By 1909, AT&T was able to buy control of Western Union and dream of a private empire over all United States telecommunications. This dream came to an abrupt end in 1913 under threat of federal antitrust action. In the so-called Kingsbury commitment (Brooks 1975:11, 136), AT&T agreed to abandon its interests in telegraphy. Not to be outdone, AT&T turned to radio telephony and acquired patent rights that led it into the broadcasting business and an alliance or cross-licensing agreement with General Electric and the Radio Corporation of America (RCA). However, Westinghouse was the first to put a broadcasting station on the air—KDKA in Pittsburgh in 1921—and it, too, became part of the private alliance that would have vertically integrated the broadcasting business but for the excesses of AT&T and the zeal of the Federal Trade Commission in compliance with its mandate to administer the antitrust laws. Although the concept of AT&T as a common carrier or "toll broadcasting service" did not meet with success in the marketplace (a harbinger of teleconferencing in the 1970s) (Barnouw 1966:43-46), AT&T controlled the voice-quality intercity telephone lines, which it refused to lease to other broadcasters. They were forced to use Western Union and postal telegraph lines that were inferior. AT&T, through its subsidiary, Western Electric, also began to manufacture and market radio sets in competition with its cross licensee, RCA. At the same time, the Federal Trade Commission launched an inquiry into the alleged collusion of the RCA-GE-AT&T-Westinghouse alliance in restraint of trade. Simultaneously, the members of the alliance were engaged in a secret review of their arrangement and an arbitration of their division of the market. While under threat of monopolization charges by the FTC, the various companies sorted out an orderly division of the market, with AT&T bowing out of broadcasting in exchange for the leasing of long lines for interconnection to the RCA-controlled broadcast network—the National Broadcasting Company.

Similarly, under another threat of antitrust litigation, AT&T entered a consent decree in 1956 that essentially has kept AT&T out of the data-processing business, which was then an unregulated infant industry spawned by the advent of computer technology in the late 1940s. The consent decree prohibited AT&T from engaging in unregulated communication services and limited it to tariffed services as regulated by the FCC. In another consent decree, the giant of the computer industry, International Business Machines (IBM), agreed not to engage in the provision of computer services except through an arm's-length subsidiary. However, some years later, in a private antitrust suit initiated by another computer manufacturer, the Control Data Company, IBM settled out of court by selling its domestic computer service bureau to Control Data and agreeing not to provide any competition to Control Data in the provision of computer services until 1979.

Thus, the antitrust laws have had a substantial impact upon the telecommunications and computer industries through both direct and indirect influence. Furthermore, the 1956 consent decree led the FCC into a lengthy series of regulatory inquiries in the 1960s and 1970s attempting to define the line between communication services, which were tariffed (and in which AT&T could participate), and data processing, which was to be provided by an unregulated and competitive marketplace.

As computer technology has become more and more intermeshed with communications, the regulators have become lost in a maze of legal distinctions which defy technological developments. The antitrust laws have served to rule IBM, as a manufacturer of computers, out of being a computer-service provider domestically (although it offers such service internationally) while also inhibiting AT&T, with its manufacturing subsidiary, Western Electric, from enthusiastically entering the race to make and sell computers, except as they can be marketed as an integral part of a regulated telecommunications system.

A long-pending antitrust suit against IBM was dismissed by the government in January 1982. On the same day, two proposed consent decrees were announced. One, in the government's pending antitrust suit against AT&T, would, if accepted by the court, require divestiture by AT&T of its twenty-two local operating companies. The other modifies the 1956 consent decree by freeing AT&T to compete in unregulated markets. However, current legislation requires that all interested parties be permitted to comment on proposed consent decrees. Both proposals have been consolidated in a District of Columbia court, but the final outcome may be delayed since appeals to higher courts may last for years.

Current Policies

One of the more interesting recent developments has been a general trend toward deregulation and competition in industry through a series of administrative decisions by the FCC. First, the FCC opened up competition in the equipment that could be attached to the basic telephone system in the Carterfone decision of 1968 (FCC 1968*a*), followed by a decision in the same year to permit MCI, Inc. (1968*b*) to establish a centralized common carrier service for interstate private line service via terrestrial microwave that would also be competitive with Bell's established interstate telephone service. The FCC also decided to open up domestic satellites to competition in what was called the "open skies" policy for domestic satellites. Rather than give the telephone companies the sole responsibility for domestic satellite telephone service, the FCC authorized Western Union and RCA to put up satellites that have now become operational. Although the FCC authorized AT&T and GTE to put up a satellite system, initially the satellite was not permitted to be leased for other than telephone service in order to permit the competitors an opportunity to build their competitive services. Satellite Business Systems (SBS), a partnership of COMSAT, Aetna, and IBM, was authorized by the FCC to offer a business satellite service, and the Xerox Corporation also filed for authority to establish a direct private line service, XTEN, using both microwave for intracity and satellite for intercity service. While the SBS satellite service became operational in 1980, the XTEN service ran into technical difficulties. COMSAT filed for authority to operate a direct broadcasting satellite service, precipitating the subsequent filing for authorization by a multiplicity of entities. Nine applications were accepted by the FCC for processing in the fall of 1981.

The public switched network is still maintained as a monopoly for the Bell System, GTE, and the smaller telephone companies. What is called the "local loop" service within the particular city also remains under monopoly control, but the trend toward competition may also open up the local service. Certainly cable television could provide an alternative local interactive voice as well as video service, although the tree-branch design of most cable systems does not favor a move in that direction.

The United States has a dynamic telecommunications environment. New technology has created the need for new regulations. Old regulations no longer make sense. Because of this, the federal government, states, industry, and users alike are participating in formulating new U.S. policies.

Activities leading to amendment or a rewrite of the Communications Act of 1934 are concerned with all aspects of telecommunications policies and issues in the United States as well as an organizational structure for regulatory bodies. In order to accomplish this, every aspect of telecommunications is being reviewed or has been reviewed by the appropriate congressional subcommittees. Hearings have been held that covered a wide span of the telecommunications industry, data processing industry, and users. In early 1982, bills H.R. 5158 and S. 898 were still pending in the Congress.

However, because the future of such legislative actions could not be foreseen, the FCC proceeded with its computer inquiry, and in April 1980 came out with a decision. According to the Chairman,

Today we have removed the barricades from the door to the information age. The supply of communications products and services will be limited only by the ingenuity of businessmen and scientists. Government will no longer be a barrier that prevents or delays the introduction of innovations in technology. (FCC 1980)

What the FCC did was to deregulate "enhanced telecommunications services"—those combining basic service (transmission capacity for the movement of information) with computer processing applications that provide additional, different, or restructured information. The FCC also unleashed AT&T and GTE to provide "enhanced services" so long as they did so through "arms-length" subsidiaries that would be required to offer all carrier transmission services under the same tariff as nonaffiliated competitors.

The FCC decision did not forestall the need for legislation, since appeals may be taken to determine whether the FCC can forego regulation voluntarily under Title II of the Communications Act of 1934; but its action is consistent with the stated policy of President Carter on 21 September 1979, which summarized the view of the Executive Branch as follows:

1. Technology has invalidated the old assumption that all aspects of telecommunications service are natural monopolies.
2. Innovation is hobbled by uncertainty and by the need to respond to artificial regulatory conditions instead of real consumer demand.
3. Competition is a fact of life in this industry—it should not be rolled back—and we should not allow it to continue developing haphazardly.
4. Competition should be encouraged and fully competitive markets should be deregulated. Some communication services such as local exchanges may remain regulated monopolies indefinitely.
5. Restrictions resulting from out-of-date definitions based on the distinction between telecommunications and data processing should be removed.
6. Rules that divide some communication services between domestic and international companies are outmoded and need change.
7. We need a new system that would be administered openly by public officials because these are important public policy decisions that should not be left solely to the industry.
8. Universal availability of basic telephone service at affordable rates must be maintained.
9. Extend to rural Americans the benefits of all the new communications technologies.
10. Rules that restrict rural telephone companies from offering cable television services should be removed.

11. Appropriate jurisdictional boundaries should be set between federal and state regulatory bodies.
12. The FCC should be given the authority to develop efficient means of assigning broadcast frequencies.
13. The technical quality of the telecommunications network should be protected.
14. Public participation in regulatory decision making should be encouraged.

This presidential message can be regarded as the official position of the executive branch concerning telecommunications policies, and is consistent with the long-established policy of encouraging competitive markets whenever and wherever possible. It represents the most progressive step toward integrating policy with respect to communication and computerized services. The policy has not changed under the Reagan Administration, since the Republicans are even more committed than the Democrats to deregulation of the industry. A bill passed the Senate in 1981 (S. 598) affirming the unleashing of what is endearingly called "Baby Bell," a company scheduled to take off in 1983 with modest assets of a mere $17 billion and 125,000 employees at its inception, more than half the size of IBM.

Under the January 1982 consent decree proposed in the government's antitrust suit against AT&T, the twenty-two Bell operating companies (representing about $80,000 million of Bell's $120,000 million in total assets) would be split off from AT&T, leaving the remaining combination of long lines, Western Electric, and Bell Laboratories free to compete in an open marketplace. Thus, the largest private company in the world, if current policy continues in the present direction, will be free to grow even larger in a rapidly growing field of telecommunications services.

What is clear is that the current trend is toward direct allocation of costs to particular services rendered, less internal cross-subsidy of services, and permitting AT&T to compete with newcomers but in a controlled environment in which competitive services must cover their allocable costs. How to encourage competition between regulated and unregulated industries is a major problem to be solved by policymakers as voice, video, and hard-copy services meld into a single service. The time-honored policy of allocating telephone service to AT&T, telegraph to Western Union, and letters to the United States Postal Service no longer makes sense technologically; policymakers have come to recognize that it makes no economic sense either.

Conclusions

Centralized planning of communication policy and management of communication facilities have been anathema for the U.S. government.

Only with great difficulty has the United States evolved a methodology for dealing with communication problems that transcend traditional media lines of authority or have international implications.

There has developed considerable controversy inside as well as outside the government concerning the role "Ma Bell" will play in the new competitive marketplace. While the Senate was completing legislation to approve the direction of FCC policy to date, the Department of Defense was arguing that the FCC had already gone too far in one direction, jeopardizing national defense by giving up the Bell system to too much competition in the long lines. Meanwhile, the Department of Justice was arguing that unleashing Bell to compete in data processing was anticompetitive and would likely lead to Bell domination of that market, and the Department of Commerce generally praised the entry of AT&T into new markets. The chairman of AT&T called the government a "three ring circus," insisting that all the telecommunications giant wanted was "a decent opportunity to compete" (*Washington Post* 1981:A20). Outside the government, the issue of AT&T competition is even more threatening, as the cable industry fights for congressional approval of FCC rules keeping telephone companies from providing cable television hookups in their service areas, and the newspaper lobby goes to court to obtain injunctions to keep AT&T from offering new electronic "yellow pages" via a television screen connected to a telephone. Seeing an erosion in advertising support of the print media, Robert Erburu, chief executive officer of the Times Mirror Co., publisher of the *Los Angeles Times*, recently defended its opposition to AT&T entry into electronic advertising by a simple statement of facts—AT&T is so big (1981). Far from being set in concrete, the boundaries between the regulated and competitive marketplace will continue for the foreseeable future to be a major focus of U.S. communication policy.

The attitude of the American people has waxed and waned with respect to federal investment in a communication infrastructure. During the early nineteenth century a centralized and nationalized postal service was established as well as a system of local publicly supported libraries, and a commitment to teach every citizen to read and write—an essentially 100 percent commitment to facilitate communication via the print media. This was and is a sine qua non of a democratic society. No such public commitment has been made with respect to telegraphy, telephones, broadcasting, or computers. All four have been developed essentially as a private-sector investment with the federal government's major role being that of watchdog to assure that competition would be promoted to the fullest extent. In broadcasting, an additional effort was made to license a limited spectrum available to qualified public trustees who would operate in the public interest, and the major thrust in common carrier services has been to assure that monopoly services were offered at a fair and equitable cost to the consuming public.

For telephony and broadcasting, nationwide coverage has been promoted through guaranteed loans to rural cooperatives and a subsidy of broadcasting facilities for educational nonprofit networks of both radio and television. No such effort is yet visible for data-processing services. Neither has there been a concerted effort to train the public in either broadcasting or computing, which require special skills comparable to reading and writing for the uninitiated.

If one dared to predict the direction of U.S. policy in the future, one would more likely suggest investment in communicative skills and nationwide availability of facilities for the masses than centralized telecommunications planning or a single federal agency with administrative responsibility over all communication entities. The recent breakdown in efforts to enact a comprehensive communications act is symptomatic of the difficulty of dealing with U.S. policy in omnibus legislation, and the proposed act did not even address the questions of the print media or postal delivery, as other committees of Congress have primary jurisdiction over these matters. The student who looks for neat solutions and easy answers to questions about U.S. communication policy will inevitably be disillusioned and disappointed. The marketplace of ideas to which the United States is unequivocally dedicated offers a potpourri of policy options none of which will ever be the unalterable and uncontroversial right one. To quote Learned Hand once again, ". . . right conclusions are more likely to be gathered out of a multitude of tongues, than through any kind of authoritative selection. To many this is, and always will be folly; but we have staked upon it our all" (*U.S.* v. *Associated Press* 1943).

References

Aspen Institute
1978   *The Mass Media*. New York and London: Praeger.

Associated Press v. U.S.
1945   326 U.S. 131.

Barnouw, Eric
1966   *A Tower of Babel*. New York: Oxford University Press.

Branscomb, Anne
1975   *The First Amendment as a Shield or as a Sword*. Santa Monica, CA: Rand Corp.

Broadcasting
1977   " 'Roots' Biggest Event in TV Entertainment History." 31 January, p. 19.

Brooks, John
1975   *The Telephone*. New York: Harper & Row.

Business Executives Move for Vietnam Peace v. FCC
1971   450 F2d. 642 (D.C. Cir.).

Cable Communications Resource Center
1977   *Report on Minority Ownership*. Washington, D.C.

Cabinet Committee on Cable Communication
1974   *Cable: Report to the President*. Washington, D.C.: U.S. Government Printing Office.

Campaign Communications Reform Act
1972   86 Stat. 3, 47 U.S. Code §312(a); §315(b).

Carnegie Commission on Educational Television
1967   *Public Television: A Program for Action*. New York: Harper & Row.

Carnegie Commission on the Future of Public Broadcasting
1979   *A Public Trust*. New York: Bantam Books.

CBS v. DNC
1973   412 U.S. 94.

Citizens Publishing Co. v. U.S.
1969   394 U.S. 131.

Communications Act
1934   48 Stat. 1064, 47 U.S. Code §151 ff.

Denver Post
1979   9 September.

Domestic Council Committee on the Right of Privacy
1976   *National Information Policy: A Report to the President of the United States.* Washington, D.C.: U.S. Government Printing Office.

Erburu, Robert
1981   Speech at Telecommunications Policy Research Conference, Annapolis, MD, 28 April.

Fairness Doctrine
1959   73 Stat. 557, 47 U.S. Code §315(a).

Federal Communications Commission
1941   Docket no. 6051, Order no. 79, 20 March, and 79-A, 1 July.

1968*a*   *Carterfone*, 13 FCC 2d. 420.

1968*b*   *MCI, Inc.*, 18 FCC 2d. 953.

1970*a*   *FCC Further Notice of Proposed Rulemaking*, Docket no. 18110, 22 FCC 2d. 339.

1970*b*   *Second Report and Order*, Docket no. 18397, 23 FCC 2d. 816.

1974   *Fairness Doctrine and Public Interest Standards*, 39 Fed. Reg. 139.

1975   *Second Report and Order*, Docket no. 18110, 50 FCC 2d. 1046, 31 January, recon. 53, FCC 2d. 598, affd., *FCC v. NCCB* (1977), 436 U.S. 775.

1979   *Minority Ownership of Broadcast Facilities*, December.

1980   Report no. 15650, 7 April.

FCC v. *Pacifica Foundation*
1978   438 U.S. 726.

Freedom of Information Act
1974   88 Stat. 1561.

Kalba, Kas
1978   *States, Stakeholders, and the Cable: The Evolution of Regulatory Policies*. Cambridge, MA: Harvard.

Lorain Journal v. *U.S.*
1951   342 U.S. 143.

Miami Herald Publishing Co. v. *Tornillo*
1974   418 U.S. 241.

Midwest Video v. *U.S.*
1979   440 U.S. 689.

Miller v. *California*
1973   413 U.S. 15.

National Broadcasting Co. v. *U.S.*
1943   319 U.S. 190.

Nebraska Press Association v. *Stuart*
1976   427 U.S. 539.

The Newspaper Preservation Act
1970   84 Stat. 466, 15 U.S. Code §1801 ff.

New York Times
1980a   18 May.

1980b   30 May.

New York Times v. *U.S.*
1971   403 U.S. 713.

Office of Communications of the United Church of Christ v. *FCC*
1966   359 F2d 994 (D.C. Cir.).

Pittsburgh Press Co. v. Pittsburgh
1973   Commission on Human Relations, 413 U.S. 376.

President's Task Force on Communications Policy
1967   *Final Report.*

Privacy Act of 1974
1974   88 Stat. 1561.

Radio Act of 1927
1927   44 Stat. 1166.

Red Lion v. FCC
1974   395 U.S. 367.

Rivers, William L.; Peterson, Theodore; and Jensen, Jay W.
1971   *The Mass Media and Modern Society.* San Francisco: Rinehard
                        Press.

Schiller, Herbert
1976   *Communications and Cultural Dominance.* New York: M.E.
                        Sharpe, Inc.

Sheppard v. *Maxwell*
1966   384 U.S. 333.

Smith, Anthony
1980   *The Geopolitics of Information: How Western Culture Dominates
                        the World.* London: Faber and Faber.

Stahlman v. *FCC*
1942   126 F. 2d 124 (D.C. Cir.).

Stanford Daily v. *Zurcher*
1978   436 U.S. 547.

TV 9 Inc., et al. v. *FCC*
1973   495 F 2d. 929 (D.C. Cir.).

Times-Picayune v. *U.S.*
1953   345 U.S. 594.

Title 18 U.S. Code
 1970   §1464.

U.S. v. Associated Press
 1943   52 F. Supp. 362 at 367 (S.D. N.Y.).

U.S. v. Midwest Video
 1972   406 U.S. 649.

U.S. v. Paramount Pictures
 1948   334 U.S. 131.

Wall Street Journal
 1980   7 January.

Zapple, Nicholas
 1976   Interview of (former Counsel for Communications to the Senate
                        Commerce Committee).

3

Communication Policy in the United Kingdom: A Culture Based on Makeshift Social Pluralism

Anthony Smith

Anthony Smith addresses the basic question of what a communication policy is and how it is developed and eventually recognized as policy. He discusses the advent of the printing press and the resulting new conceptions of the role and nature of government and the powers of the monarch and the state. He sees the development of the Stationers' Company as not dissimilar to the BBC, and he suggests that every new medium has been regulated in ways that are highly reminiscent of the Tudor system. Smith emphasizes that there are no basic propositions governing communication policy in the United Kingdom, only unconscious pieces of infrastructure that reflect the balance of political forces rather than any national outlook on communications. It is only by the aggregation of precedents and conflicts that the paradoxes of national policy can be derived; thus Smith sees national policies in communications as communications "cultures." Although no consistent philosophy or system of governance is perceptible, certain specifically British characteristics are present, in particular a peculiarly adept political stand-off; and so far communication institutions have remained sufficiently stable to be immune to the pressures of any single political administration.

Most of the people who spend their lives in Britain in the newspaper, broadcasting, publishing, telecommunications, and cinema industries would be as surprised to hear that they were part of a national communication policy as the character in Molière was when told he had been speaking prose all his life. All of these industries and the many others that are appended to them consider themselves discrete and mutually exogenous, even though there are links through joint ownership by conglomerate companies, through common interests in occasional proposals for law reform, and through common worries about the effects of the same economic downturns. These industries are responsible to or have relations with different ministries in Whitehall and undergo quite different forms of regulation. Moreover, their political linkages are different, and indeed, there exists no institution nor individual whose task it is to conceive of these industries as emanations of a national communication policy.

Functions such as telecommunications, for example, have resided hitherto within the compass of a single monopoly public authority. Others, like the radio and television media, are regulated through "quangos" (quasi nongovernmental organizations) which are governed by groups of independent individuals selected by a senior minister on the advice of experts who scour the country compiling lists of "the great and the good." Regulatory bodies like the British Board of Film Censors have been set up by the industry concerned at its own behest, whereas other bodies such as the Press Council have been set up by an industry following government insistence but without government intervention. The repertoire of governmental roles and guises is so multitudinous and varied as virtually to preclude the notion of overall national policy.

There is an extraordinarily diverse range of regulatory linkages between different sectors of communications, many of them accidental and resulting from historical quirks and the coincidence of personalities. In a society with as ancient and as continuous an administrative tradition as the United Kingdom, one must burrow very deep indeed to pick out the common factors that constitute policy of a general kind and at the same time one must be prepared to confront key involved individuals who deny vehemently that British society contains any common communication themes at all.

Yet a society has a communication policy as invariably as it has a foreign policy. This latter one might be defined as the society's totality of attitudes and responses toward the outside world, as these are expressed in official stances; foreign policy is composed positively as well as negatively, enshrined formally in a particular bureaucracy of diplomacy which constantly examines the society's responses and attitudes in order to encode them and generalize about them. Foreign policy has been made deliberately explicit over the centuries, although many an aspect of it remains implicit until the self-interests of the country are reinterpreted to encompass the previously unconscious element. Part of government has the function of formulating policy in foreign affairs, that is, making rationalizations that seem apposite to the society's needs. In communications, it may be said that implicit policies exist and are now perhaps just entering the process of being made explicit. The microprocessor and the technologies of advanced telecommunications are somehow forcing all information into a common condition of dependence upon common distribution services. In other words, a new branch of public policy appears to be emerging in the late twentieth century as a result of a technological shift and of the perceived social consequences of that shift. Nonetheless, in Britain at least, those most profoundly involved remain almost as profoundly unaware of the development.

We have, in a sense, been here before. The advent of the printing press at the time of the Renaissance brought with it new conceptions of the role and nature of government, new ideas about kingship and the powers naturally vested in the supreme authority in a state. The apparatus of censorship was imposed more to create order than to suppress, more as an act of industrial regulation than as an act of deliberate social control. Then, the communication policy emerged from an industrial policy, and to judge from the experience of France, Germany, and Japan, this is how things will move again in the late twentieth century.

Where governments had been content to proclaim laws from time to time, they now became aware that "law" existed as a universally comparable evolving body of social doctrine. Where specialist students had been taught the art of reading and writing largely in monastic institutions, they now became aware of the possibility of a new vernacular literature that was manufactured and broadly distributed through a society. Education too became a separable function. Childhood became separated out from the rest of life, as it were, and young people were isolated from society for their early years in order to acquire its special socially beneficial properties. It became clear that printing created a kind of physical extension of memory, in a way that writing had only partly achieved, since it was reproducible infinitely and deposited in identical form across a great land mass. Discussion could turn into schism; intellectual activity, conducted across a vast terrain, constituted in itself a surrogate form of politics. Public communication became subject to controls as a necessity of good governance. Complex systems of prior censorship emerged, in which church authorities made the intellectual decisions and state authorities carried them out by supplying the necessary force. Within a century of the development of the Gutenbergian press, the art of printing had spread very far indeed, creating an extraordinarily uniform response in community after community. In England, its arrival was slightly later than in Central and Western Europe but it became increasingly clear during the sixteenth and seventeenth centuries that the control of printing could be maintained only so long as the prerogative royal survived. It was impossible to find any agreed point of control outside the court itself. Printing was, according to one seventeenth century pamphleteer, "a flower of the Crown of England," so inextricable in its functioning from the necessary privileges of government that authority over it was as essential as maintaining the legitimacy of the prevailing dynasty itself.

Printing in England thus became the object of a "communication policy." The monarch handed out to trusted groups of subjects—all of them members of an ancient guild, the Stationers' Company—the right to make type, print works, and distribute them. The controls lasted only as long as the monarchy and collapsed with it. The civil war of the seventeenth century produced a wonderful flowering of journalistic literature of a most disordered kind and the return of Charles II brought a renewed and reinvigorated system of press licensing. The kingship came to depend for its very security upon a body of influential people—the public—who, after becoming aware of argument to the contrary, decided that it was in their interests and consistent with their convictions that a given dynasty should continue—and therefore the governments it chose. Thus there came an important turning point in cultural and political history, which resulted in a series of never-to-be-resolved dilemmas, all revolving around the question of how best to control the outpourings of a communications system that could no longer be physically controlled directly from the centers of power. Essentially, the authorities found themselves negotiating with the makers of opinion and, through them, with the people. It was possible to argue from period to period about the most appropriate measures to be taken to maintain social order while controlling and participating in the flow and counter-flow of doctrine, information, and argument.

With the coming of a market-oriented economy, it was natural that the press should develop, technologically and instrumentally, alongside other manufacturing industries. In the eighteenth-century press and later, control was maintained through a system of taxation that increased the price of publications to the point at which they could be concentrated within a small political class, and to this was added a labyrinth of laws protecting Parliament, the courts, and powerful individuals against "libel." Hired thugs were used to enforce the system upon unwilling printers. In the nineteenth century it became necessary to "free" the press for a broader interplay of market forces that has gradually produced, in the field of the newspaper and book publishing, a series of partly interconnected oligopolies; these have carved up the various markets among them, while leaving so much leverage and so much free play that they are far from constituting a real blockage. Currently, there is a universal feeling that a general individual freedom of publication exists, that information is widely accessible, and that the structures of the seventeenth and eighteenth centuries have given way finally, after long struggle, to the reign of intellectual liberty.

However, Britain has remained a monarchical society at its roots. Every new medium that has sprung into existence has been regulated in ways that are highly reminiscent of the Tudor system. The BBC is not at all dissimilar to the Stationers' Company. It was set up, after some debate, as an out-and-out monopoly which subsumed within itself all of the functions that constituted the early medium of broadcasting. It set out to colonize the society in the same way as had the established church, by rendering its products available and acceptable to all within the prevailing mores, while acknowledging the need for a cultural flexibility to the point at which its messages reached the vast majority of the audience. After some decades, fashions changed and the desire grew for a breaking up of the BBC monopoly, which had grown powerful on the basis of its exclusive hold over the revenue extracted from the receiver license fee. When commercial television finally appeared, it took a form very similar to the BBC—a public authority granting franchises to a network of companies neatly covering the whole of the territory of the United Kingdom by a system of carefully contrived adjacencies. This was not a system of commercial competition at all, but a new universal royal monopoly, this time not of the license fee revenue but of the total television commercial time of the society. Britain thus started along the road of creating a series of broadcasting monopolies, each broken in a sense by the other, but all of them essentially being monopolies over different things. This was exactly how publishing had been controlled from the sixteenth century onward.

The Post Office is another such monopoly, originally granted over the physical postal services, but then extended to encompass telegraph and telephone services, as well as a host of other social service functions. Today the Post Office has just been divided into two parts, and competition is to be permitted; but the basis of the new regulatory mechanism is, once again, a series of adjacent monopolies, with commercial competition operating in the sphere of attachments to the telephone, and the like. In communication policy, where industry and the regulation of mores meet, control systems consist of deeply entrenched analogues, each expressing some of the deepest responses of the society to its problems of internal order. Whatever the language of the argument that leads up to the system of regulation, there are bureaucratic atavisms at work which represent the barely conscious beliefs of a society about the appropriate terms of social order.

One must not make too much of this process of instinctual institutionalization, since it has been conducted, throughout the period since World War I at least, against the background of a continuous debate between Conservative and Labour parties about the role of the state. This debate has been the central issue in British politics. The various pieces of legislation relating to the mass media over the course of sixty years all bear the imprint of compromises worked out from time to time within a society in which the principal political concern has been whether state intervention can or cannot cure the social evils of the industrial system, inject growth into a declining economy, create the conditions in which investment will thrive. The mass media industries have all required new capital and thus have taken the direct brunt of the debate, since their institutionalization has entailed decisions about how this capital should be created and the resulting industry supervised.

The Conservatives have since 1950 looked for ways in which broadcasting can be opened up to private capital—though they have ended up by creating new or extensions of public authorities. The Labour Party has looked for ways to provide broadcasting out of public-sector funds under public-sector control, but has never attempted to remove the private capital from the medium once it has been permitted. The underlying compromise has been that the private capital has been placed under public authorities in two commercial channels and two score of commercial radio stations. Their boards have been decked with figures from the political left as well as the right in order to make the compromise stick at every level. Each enterprise has sought local and regional "roots." In the planning of telecommunications the same dual approach is visible, although the attempts to admit private capital have been very recent and relegated to nonnetwork elements. The chapter on Australia shows how a society very similar to Britain has revealed "a policy in the sense of a dominance of basic propositions, within broad limits" (Evans, Chapter 7). In Britain, however, no such propositions have emerged, only unconscious pieces of infrastructure. Comprehensive social philosophies have certainly been applied, but with results that reflect the balance of political forces much more than any national outlook on communications as such.

The contrast with France is most instructive. There, a major effort is being made by the government to advance the whole of the economy via telecommunications and microelectronics into a new industrial phase in which French capital will dominate certain aspects of Europe and create an alternative focal point of power in the West to North America. Britain is struggling to enter the same phase but cannot locate itself intellectually; it has treated the microprocessor as a threat to jobs or as a spur to industry. No public figure has drawn attention to the implications of the new technologies as communications devices. The creation of economic growth rather than the focusing of the society on a new set of objectives has been the main concern of politicians. The major universities contain no discussion at all of the social issue entailed in modern telecommunications. Activity is all at the fringes of the academic world and at the fringes of bureaucracy. Yet, it is surprising how much thinking and activity are taking place in Britain, but it has not yet begun to penetrate the central apparatus of the society as it has in the rest of the EEC, in Scandinavia, and in North America. When it does arrive it will certainly be through conflicting party approaches rather than as an area of national policymaking, and this in turn will place the emphasis once again on systems of governance—that is, on how eventually to place the responsibility for new ventures on the various forces in society asserting an interest in the field.

The U.K. Media

The United Kingdom has a population of 56 million and covers 244,000 square kilometers, with a population density of 230 persons per square kilometer. It has 18 million households and a gross national product of roughly US$5,000 per capita. Its 103 daily newspapers (national and regional titles combined—see Table 3-1) achieve a regular daily circulation of 20 million copies. It has 14 Sunday newspapers and 1,100 weekly papers, mainly with a local circulation, and all of these combined achieve a circulation of 37.5 million (see Table 3-2). The country contains 39 million radio receivers and 18 million television sets (thus presumably having reached the "perfect" spread of one set for every household and a radio set for every adult). In 1978, 324 new films were submitted to the British Board of Film Censors for certification for public release, but only 51 feature films over 72 minutes in length were actually made in Britain, which still has 1,500 cinemas that sold 126 million admissions in 1978—every inhabitant of the country making, on the average, three visits per year to a cinema.

Table 3-1

Number of National and Provincial Newspaper Titles and Periodical Titles, 1948, 1961, and 1976

Type of Newspaper/Periodical	1948	1961	1976
National daily newspapers	10	10	9
National Sunday newspapers	10	8	7
London evening newspapers	3	2	2
Provincial morning newspapers	28	21	19
Provincial evening newspapers	77	75	77
Provincial Sunday newspapers	6	5	6
Provincial weekly newspapers	1,300	1,223	1,072
General and leisure interest, trade, technical and professional periodicals	3,715	3,851	4,319

Source: *Newspaper Press Directory*, 1948, 1961, 1976.
Note: Since 1979 there have been 103 daily papers.

The Press

Despite the loss of a number of important newspaper titles in the generation since World War II, Britain's press has remained remarkably stable, compared with the newspaper industries of Western Europe. The great period of contraction of titles was before the war. Nonetheless, there have been a number of major public controversies in the 1960s and 1970s when important newspapers that supported the Labour and Liberal parties were obliged to cease circulation. The economics of the

Table 3-2
Circulation of National and London Evening Newspapers, 1961–1976
(thousands)

Newspapers	1961	1966	1970	1971	1972	1973	1974	1975	1976
Popular Dailies									
Daily Express	4,321	3,978	3,563	3,413	3,341	3,290	3,154	2,822	2,594
Daily Mail	2,649	2,318	1,890	1,798	1,702	1,730	1,753	1,726	1,755
Daily Mirror	4,578	5,132	4,570	4,384	4,280	4,292	4,205	3,968	3,851
Daily Sketch	991	857	785	—	—	—	—	—	—
The Sun/Daily Herald	1,407	1,238	1,615	2,293	2,699	2,966	3,380	3,446	3,708
Total	13,946	13,523	12,423	11,888	12,022	12,278	12,492	11,962	11,908
Quality Dailies									
The Daily Telegraph	1,248	1,353	1,409	1,446	1,434	1,420	1,406	1,331	1,308
The Guardian	240	281	304	332	339	346	359	319	306
Financial Times	132	152	170	170	188	195	195	181	174
The Times	257	282	388	340	341	345	345	319	310
Total	1,877	2,068	2,271	2,288	2,302	2,306	2,305	2,150	2,098
Total Dailies	15,823	15,591	14,694	14,176	14,324	14,584	14,797	14,112	14,006
Popular Sundays									
News of the World	6,689	6,152	6,229	6,129	5,996	5,944	5,824	5,479	5,138
Sunday Express	4,113	4,181	4,263	4,108	4,042	4,096	4,015	3,715	3,451
Sunday Mirror/Pictorial	5,320	5,219	4,826	4,683	4,497	4,543	4,576	4,251	4,101
Sunday People/The People	5,446	5,560	5,140	4,852	4,540	4,424	4,387	4,188	4,094
Total	21,568	21,112	20,458	19,772	19,075	19,007	18,802	17,633	16,784
Quality Sundays									
The Observer	722	881	830	799	794	796	819	730	670
Sunday Citizen/Reynolds News	318	216	—	—	—	—	—	—	—
Sunday Telegraph	688	650	764	755	767	775	777	752	759
The Sunday Times	994	1,363	1,439	1,418	1,455	1,517	1,478	1,380	1,382
Total	2,722	3,110	3,033	2,972	3,016	3,088	3,074	2,862	2,811
Total Sundays	24,290	24,222	23,491	22,744	22,091	22,095	21,876	20,495	19,595

Source: MacGregor 1977.

national newspaper (a phenomenon unique to Britain, though with an interesting analogue in Japan) necessitates a minimum circulation of two or more million daily for a paper circulating among the general working-class audience, although titles that depend upon more affluent readerships are able to flourish on lower figures. Thus Britain has acquired a sophisticated differentiated class pattern among its newspaper audiences and an important division has grown up between two quite separate newspaper cultures, the "populars" (normally tabloid, garish, exploiting sex very often, and selling on the basis of striking banner headlines) and the "qualities," intended for an educated middle and upper class audience and generating a very high proportion of revenue (over 80% in the case of the *Financial Times*) from advertising. The British newspaper reader has, in theory, an extremely wide choice every day among nine or more highly competitive papers, but in practice each of these concentrates on reaching a finely delineated social band of readers and surprisingly few change their newspaper habits more than once or twice during the course of their lives.

There have been three royal commissions on the press since 1945, each established as a result of parliamentary disquiet about the growth of concentration and monopoly. On each occasion a press council was recommended either to be set up or to be strengthened and plans for subsidies and subventions and other forms of direct governmental intervention were rejected, despite the relatively satisfactory experience of the rest of Western Europe with special press subsidies. Despite the growth of a handful of large press concerns, there have been constant shifts of ownership and control of the major chains on the death of the chief entrepreneurs, and the various commissions have all concluded that while further development toward monopoly would be undesirable, no present or avoidable threat to free expression is constituted by the prevailing level of concentration. Each commission has attempted to inhibit mergers through stronger monopolies legislation, but the Monopolies Commission, when impending mergers have been referred to it, has always permitted them. The real fear in Britain is simply that mergers could bring about a situation in which the Labour Party would cease to have a major daily paper supporting it, but this challenge to the party system of the country has never actually occurred at the moment of a general election, as Table 3-3 reveals. Despite the constant fears of Labour politicians and activists that the party could find itself stranded, opposed by the entire printed press, it has tended to enjoy a reasonable level of press support at election times, if total circulations rather than mere titles are counted. The whole evolution of governmental policy toward the press has had this political basis, and the fear, which has been expressed in one form or another ever since the 1920s (as the old party papers started to disappear in the face of competition from the newer "entertainment" papers), has influenced the whole of the institutional-ization of broadcasting as well.

Table 3-3
Newspaper Partisanship and Circulations, and Party Votes in General Elections, 1945-74

Newspaper	Circulation (In thousands) and Party Support									
	1945	1950	1951	1955	1959	1964	1966	1970	2/74	10/74
Daily Express	3,300 Con	4,099 Con	4,169 Con	4,036 Con	4,053 Con	4,190 Con	3,954 Con	3,607 Con	3,227 Con	3,081 Con
*Daily Herald/The Sun**	1,850 Lab	2,030 Lab	2,003 Lab	1,759 Lab	1,465 Lab	1,300† Lab	1,248 Lab	1,509 Lab	3,303 Con	3,457 All-Pty Coal.
Daily Mail	1,704 Con	2,215 Con	2,267 Con	2,068 Con	2,071 Con	2,400 Con	2,381 Con	1,916 Con	1,768 Con	1,738 Con/Lib Coal.
Daily Mirror	2,400 Lab	4,603 Lab	4,514 Lab	4,725 Lab	4,497 Lab	5,085 Lab	5,077 Lab	4,697 Lab	4,192 Lab	4,218 Lab
Daily Sketch/Daily Graphic‡	896 Con	777 Con	794 Con	950 Con	1,156 Con	847 Con	849 Con	806 Con	—	—
The Daily Telegraph	813 Con	984 Con	998 Con	1,055 Con	1,181 Con	1,324 Con	1,354 Con	1,402 Con	1,427 Con	1,385 Con
The (Manchester) Guardian§	83 Lib	141 Lib	139 Lib/Con	156 Lib/Con	183 Lab/Con	278 Lab	283 Lab/Lib	303 Lab/Lib	365 Balanced	354 More Lib Influence
News Chronicle‖	1,549 Lib	1,525 Lib	1,507 Lib	1,253 Lib	1,207 Lib	—	—	—	—	—
The Times	204 Lab	258 Con	232 Con	222 Con	254 Con	255 Con	273 ?/Lib	402 Con/Lib	351 Con/Lib	340 Con/Lib Coal.
Total Circulation	12,799	16,632	16,623	16,224	16,067	15,679	15,419	14,642	14,633	14,573

Total Conservative Circulation	6,713 (52%)	8,333 (50%)	8,599# (52%)	8,487# (52%)	8,715 (54%)	9,016 (57%)	8,538 (55%)	8,133# (55%)	10,441# (71%)	6,898# (47%)
Total Conservative Vote	9,578 (40%)	12,503 (43%)	13,718 (48%)	13,312 (50%)	13,750 (49%)	12,001 (43%)	11,418 (42%)	13,145 (46%)	11,872 (48%)	10,465 (36%)
Total Labour Circulation	4,454 (35%)	6,633 (40%)	6,517 (39%)	6,484 (40%)	6,145# (38%)	6,663# (42%)	6,608 (43%)	6,509# (44%)	4,557# (31%)	4,572# (31%)
Total Labour Vote	11,633 (48%)	13,267 (46%)	13,949 (49%)	12,405 (46%)	12,216 (44%)	12,206 (44%)	13,065 (48%)	12,178 (43%)	11,645 (37%)	11,457 (39%)
Total Liberal Circulation	1,632 (13%)	1,666 (10%)	1,646# (10%)	1,409# (9%)	1,390# (9%)	—	556# (4%)	705# (5%)	716# (5%)	2,432# (17%)
Total Liberal Vote	2,197 (9%)	2,622 (9%)	731 (2%)	722 (3%)	1,639 (6%)	3,093 (11%)	2,327 (8%)	2,117 (7%)	6,059 (19%)	5,347 (18%)

Source: "National Daily Papers and the Party System" in Studies on the Press, Working Paper Number 3-HMSO, 1977.
Notes: *Name changed to *The Sun* in 1964.

†Figure uncertain due to relaunching at that time.

‡Named *Daily Graphic*, 1946–52.

§"Manchester" dropped from title in 1959.

‖Ceased publication in 1960.

#Includes paper(s) with divided support, but omits *The Sun* in October 1974.

In the middle years of Mrs. Thatcher's administration, however, a major realignment of the main parties appears to be taking place. The new Social Democratic Party has attracted a large tranche of the national press, leaving the Labour Party's share, so to speak, to dwindle to nothing. Labour's movement to the left has obliged the press to jettison any remaining loyalty to the party which—in the last election—emerged as the principal party of Opposition. Should Labour ever return to power, it would inevitably be tempted to take fiscal measures that would have the effect of strengthening press support for the left.

One of the problems inhibiting the discussion of communication policy is that many of the apparent guidelines were laid down in the era of the development of the press. So many myths were created then, that it is difficult today to scrape away the shibboleths and accumulated verbiage—associated with the struggle for freedom of the press—that now encumber the discussion of the wider issues of communications. In Britain this problem is particularly acute. The press is and must remain the main forum through which the discussion of communication policy is filtered to the population as a whole, and yet it is precisely the press that feels it has already inherited the cultural mission and the total moral responsibility for the flow of information in society.

In Britain the struggle for freedom of the press took two forms: On the one hand it was a demand, from the late eighteenth century movement against the libel laws until the Great Reform Act agitation of 1830 (or the relaxation of the controls which Parliament and the courts exercised over the reporting of their affairs). On the other hand it was a battle conducted by newspaper proprietors for the freedom to establish their industry on a broader basis, without being encumbered by special taxes on paper, advertising, or cover prices. The paradox of press history is that both struggles were conducted ostensibly in the name of mass or general education and yet it was the working-class press, which existed plentifully but illegally under the worst of the controls, that was crushed when the press finally won its freedom. So long as newspapers were "stamped" and therefore expensive, the working class had to rely upon illegal unstamped and radical papers; with the gradual removal of the stamp duties (between 1836 and 1965) newspaper prices came down to rival those of the illegal papers, which were subsequently swept away. In the last third of the nineteenth century and the first third of the twentieth, there grew steadily a vast mass audience and an enormous press industry that came to rely more and more upon its entertainment content and style to attract its lucrative audience. The newspaper reached its peak as a form in the 1950s, when the advent of television and a change in the advertising flows significantly altered both the cultural and the economic roles of the newspaper industry.

There are dangers in the kind of generalizations that this chapter, with its broad compass, necessarily encourages. However, it is important to indicate the broad lines of the development of Britain's mass press, which has no comparable industry in any other country apart, perhaps, from Japan. The essence of the mass press was that a product of very high printing and picture quality as well as entertainment quality was distributed to every citizen of the country by eight in the morning, or earlier. The railway system was reorganized in the 1890s to cater to this need. The mass culture as a whole revolved around it. Profit was derived from selling each paper at cost or slightly below, while mass manufacturer-to-consumer advertising dominated the commercial management of the newspaper. Indeed, the mass newspaper and the mass distribution of groceries both emerged from the same technological innovation—the making of cheap paper from vegetable substances—and the two systems, communication and commerce, were entirely symbiotic. So long as it remained legal for manufacturers to determine the price at which their wrapped goods were sold at the counter (and to have legal sanctions against any who infringed on it by selling cheap), it was necessary and convenient for manufacturers rather than retailers to undertake the task of advertising. Their instrument, in the era of the new mass market, was the popular newspaper. Circulations rose to five million, even higher on occasion, and readership of a single Sunday newspaper could be as high as fourteen million (out of a population of about fifty million). In the aftermath of the Second World War, when newspapers had been thin because of the paper shortage, it became customary for families to take two or three newspapers every day. This practice sent total national circulations to their height in the mid-1950s. Many newspaper titles remained alive basically because each separate title was permitted an allocation of newsprint, and advertising was in constant search of space. With the freeing of newsprint from controls, newspapers thickened, circulations dropped, and titles disappeared.

In 1962, retail-price maintenance was made illegal, apart from books and newspapers, and manufacturers found there was no longer any point in taking newspaper space to advertise the prices of brand-name products, since price competition was now a factor of retailing rather than manufacturing. It was necessary for retailers to buy newspaper space and they had little interest in the mass press, since their market areas were circumscribed by the natural distribution areas of local stores. Local and regional newspapers enjoyed the benefit of the great increase in retail advertising and have continued to profit from the trend ever since. National papers found that a great deal of the advertising, whose existence underlay their own, simply dried up or drifted to the new medium of television. For those papers that circulated among the middle and upper classes the problem was not so great, since rising prosperity and a greater variety of goods meant that there were still many advertisers (retail and manufacturing) who needed privileged access to the wealthier social groups. For papers directed at working-class audiences, however, the problems were acute. Advertising shrunk steadily as a proportion of their total revenue. Those working-class newspapers, such as the *News Chronicle*, the *Daily Herald*, and the *Daily Mirror*, which had appealed to the more educated sections of their potential readership, were the hardest hit, and the first two disappeared, while the third has been experiencing increasing pressure. They all found that the ideal of attempting to give the audience high quality information in a very popular style (which is an expensive editorial policy) was increasingly difficult to live up to. Rupert Murdoch originally bought the renamed *Daily Herald*—the *Sun*—but found a way to make it popular by driving it "down market" and removing all those features designed to appeal to a vast class of autodidact mass readers that had slowly wasted away after the war years; the coming of further education to a large section of the population had moved this group toward the middle class "quality" papers.

Thus Murdoch's *Sun* discovered a successful formula for the time: to keep the cover price the lowest of all competitors for a given social group and to extend circulation by offering additional inducements to readers and to newsagents to the point at which a profit could be derived merely from the reader's revenue. Advertising came to represent a small and declining proportion of the *Sun*'s total revenue, and this in itself enabled the newspaper to lower its tone further and appeal to cruder and cruder tastes. No sooner had Murdoch dominated the mass market with this policy than another new newspaper entrepreneur entered the scene— Victor Matthews, who acquired the wasting Beaverbrook newspaper empire, and resuscitated it. In the course of restructuring the group he has introduced a new title, the *Star*, with a policy of appealing to a group of readers for whom the *Sun* is too demanding. The outcome of this phase of the age-old literary and commercial battle for the eyes of the mass newspaper reader of Britain is not yet finally known, but it would seem that the *Star*, like the *Sun* a decade earlier, is discovering that the market has a permanent gap—at the nethermost end.

It is obvious that such economic trends—and others not mentioned in this resume—lie behind the structural changes and crises that have bedevilled the British press. Government and opposition policy has concentrated upon devising measures to "save" one newspaper title after another, as they have vanished, faint from the incessant and viciously competitive struggle. In the cause of pursuing their intense rivalries, proprietors developed an extraordinarily paternalistic system of industrial relations. Enormous staffs were built up to help fight off rivals in Fleet Street morning by morning. But in the cost-conscious era of the 1970s the proprietors were left with excess staff, low and outdated investment in printing technology, and an industrial climate in which the trade unions had taken over complete power of hiring and firing. To be more precise, the unions had been given this power in the 1940s and 1950s in order to bribe workers to cut various corners in production and distribution. In the 1970s the inherited and accumulated practices were denounced by commentators and by proprietors (sometimes the heirs and successors of those who had actually mismanaged the papers in the first place) as industrial malpractices. For the workers, each acquired privilege was a piece of real estate that could be sacrificed only in exchange for very large sums of money. The economics of Fleet Street were exposed in one official report after another as an unmanageable shambles, culminating in 1978 with a twelve-month cessation of production at the *Times* itself, the most revered of British newspapers. The upshot of this long struggle has been that a certain measure of new technology may be admitted to the *Times*, at tremendous cost to its latest proprietors (the Murdoch group), but that no new technique may be used that removes the exclusive rights of typesetters over the task of setting type. Direct journalist input is not to be allowed, and this will be extremely damaging in modern economic conditions for a newspaper whose whole raison d'être is to provide its readers with a very large amount of text to read every day.

The economic issues that have controlled the evolution of British newspapers have been emphasized partly because they are normally overlooked in the examination of British communications. Emphasis is normally placed on the difficulties of industrial relations and upon the special restraints imposed in Britain on journalists through the strictness of the libel laws, the secrecy of government departments, and the strenuous rules concerning contempt of court and contempt of Parliament which inhibit the freedom of journalists. These are indeed important characteristics of the British media scene and account for some of its peculiarities—the ubiquity of lawyers in newspapers, the enormous fortunes to be made by people whose honor has been tainted in a legal sense by remarks made about them, the fear on the part of editors of the consequences of infringing these seemingly all-encompassing prohibitions. However, despite these regulations Britain has a lively press and somehow its many public scandals seem to erupt into the light of day, the more scandalizing perhaps by reason of the hoops through which the journalists and editors have to jump in order to get them into print. Nonetheless, it is the special culture of the society, its mass culture and its middle-class culture, that has influenced the shape and form and meaning of its newspaper industry, and this culture enjoys an interactive relationship with the special economic circumstances in which the newspaper industry has evolved. It is really not possible to develop a communication policy outside the social and economic nexus of the media as industrial concerns (see Table 3-4).

Publishing

In the field of communications there has never really existed a pure "private sector." Even in book publishing—the most detached, internationally minded, and "capitalistic" of the media industries—one-half of all production in Britain is ultimately purchased by the public

Table 3-4
The Largest Press Undertakings of the United Kingdom

Company	National M*	National E	National S	Regional M	Regional E	Regional S	Regional W	Total
Reed International	1	—	2	1	—	2	8	14
Beaverbrook Newspapers	1	1	1	—	—	—	7	10
Daily Mail & General Trust	1	1	—	1	13	—	36	52
Thomson Organisation	1	—	1	4	12	1	38	57
The Cowdray family's interests	1	—	—	1	10	—	97	109
Liverpool Daily Post & Echo	—	—	—	1	1	—	15	17
United Newspapers	—	—	—	2	6	—	31	39
D.C. Thomson & Co.	—	—	—	1	1	1	3	6
Daily Telegraph	1	—	1	—	—	—	—	2
News International	1	—	1	—	1	—	28	31
Guardian & Manchester Evening News	1	—	—	—	1	—	1	3
The Iliffe family's interests	—	—	—	1	3	1	17	22
Scottish & Universal Investments	—	—	—	1	2	—	20	23
Observer	—	—	1	—	—	—	—	1
Total	8	2	7	13	50	5	301	386

Source: The A/K Report, Federal Republic of Germany, 1977, p. 678.
*M = Morning; E = Evening; S = Sunday; W = Weekly.

sector. British teachers, unlike those of France and other European nations, rigorously protect their right of individual choice over the construction of courses and the selection of texts. Education authorities do not publish their own textbooks. Teachers' unions and publishers jointly insist that all purchasing be performed through bookshops, but a certain amount of direct supply does take place. This combination of the open market and public-sector power has the effect of making the publishing industry search for overseas outlets for the same basic investments. Half of all British book production is exported, unlike that of the publishing industry of the United States, which benefits from agreements over market spheres in the English-speaking world but does not rely very greatly upon exports. The problem of British publishers, therefore, is to maintain the economies acquired from the use of the same textbooks in the principal overseas markets. The latter are now increasingly subject to policies of indigenization of educational texts, though the hostile trend is concealed by the very rapid growth of the educational markets in the anglophone developing countries. However, as the multidisciplinary educational system of the United States gains ground throughout the English-speaking university world, it becomes harder and harder for British textbooks, directed to a completely different kind of tertiary education, to hold their market. On the one hand, therefore, the textbook industry is suffering from the tendency for the "Commonwealth edition" to fade away, while on the other the phenomenal growth in the use of the English language acts as a tremendous spur to production.

The government plays an extremely important role in the internal economy of the publishing industry. It permits a special book rate for overseas postal services, but not for domestic. It provides overseas aid to Third World countries in the form of book-purchase subsidies and supports the English Language Book Society, which distributes books at reduced prices in the developing world. The greatest involvement of the government, however, is in the area of taxation. In 1966–67 a new tax was invented by the Labour administration called SET (Selective Employment Tax), which was imposed on all forms of employment. Partly with the battle cries of the nineteenth-century battle against "taxes on knowledge" ringing in their ears, parliamentarians exempted books from the tax, which was in any case abandoned as a failure after some years; VAT (value added tax) was substituted, and was obligatory under the rules of the EEC, which Britain had joined. VAT is a tax imposed on every stage of the manufacture of a product; every collector of the tax is able to set outgoing VAT payments against the sum collected when the item is passed on to the next stage of manufacture, until it reaches the "ultimate customer," that is, the public who pays the basic price of the article plus a stated percentage, which finally is handed over to the Customs and Excise department. Publishers advanced successfully the argument that in the case of books there is no ultimate consumer and publishing is a distribution service in character, far more than a manufacturing process. The government was perhaps relieved to find the argument, and books were "zero-rated." That is, they were VAT taxed all along the line but at a rate of nil. This means that all VAT paid out by the the publisher for subsidiary materials and services can be recouped—an extremely valuable privilege extended to newspaper publishers with respect to both the price of the newspaper and the revenue from newspaper advertising. The exemption is technically in breach of EEC rules, but is ineradicably accepted in Britain, although if the use of English ever grew in Western Europe to the extent of the EEC becoming a major market for British books, it would be possible for French, German, or Dutch publishers to take Britain to the Community Court for unfair trading practices.

Another of the special trade regulations that helps to explain the special success of the British publishing industry is the Net Book Agreement. Until 1962 all forms of retail-price fixing were legal in Britain. Any manufacturer could insist that every retail outlet observe the recommended prices and, in return, the manufacturer felt secure in advertising goods nationally, in the knowledge that the advertised price would be universally charged. When retail-price maintenance was abolished, the Restrictive Practices Court upheld the request of the publishers to maintain the system through their Net Book Agreement, by which no member of the public may purchase a book at a sum less than the "net price." The argument advanced here was that it was in the public interest for bookshops to be encouraged to display the widest possible choice of books, and publishers could compete for the loyalty of the bookshops by granting any margins they wished as an inducement. This privilege is shared by the cement and gypsum industries, both of which require special geographical cartels with other extractive industries (cement requires a continuous supply of limestone) in order to offer the public the best bargain. The Net Book Agreement permits a kind of cartel between publisher and supplier in order to render the buying public a greater service. Thus flows the argument, and the Restrictive Practices Court could not now renege upon it unless it could claim that a material change in the nature of the publishing business had taken place. Certain exceptions are permitted to the agreement in the case of school texts, which may be sold direct to schools at non-net prices in certain circumstances.

The greatest fears within the British publishing industry relate to the possible implications of European trading policy. Already one-sixth of British books are physically manufactured overseas (in Eastern Europe, India, Pakistan, and Italy) where labor costs are lower than in Britain. Now that Europe has a nine-nation elected Parliament, it is possible that a "cultural policy" could emerge at any moment and overthrow the practices of decades. Already there are small signs that a policy is emerging: a European index of works of art is being proposed, in order to reduce theft; data are being collected on the internal operations of the auctions industry, for example. British publishers are most keen to see that no one starts to analyze publishing in the light of strict interpretation of the Treaty of Rome, which prohibits, among other things, the partitioning of the market, even with respect to cultural goods and works of art. (For example, it is difficult to maintain the British law that permits museums to prevent works of art from leaving the country even after being sold at auction.) The EEC has been regarded as an "open market" by U.S. and U.K. publishers because it has been an exiguous market; but that is now ceasing to be the case, and if the Treaty were strictly applied it would be impossible to prevent books legally sold by American publishers into Europe from passing into Britain, in breach of the agreement hallowed by time between publishers on both sides of the Atlantic. The whole rationale of British publishing thus hangs by a thread. There exist 700,000 outstanding contracts between U.S. and U.K. publishers and all of them are in breach of the Treaty of Rome. The current system is particularly damaging for best-sellers, and American publishers are avid to be able to dump an extra 50,000 copies of a high-selling work in the U.K. market at virtually no additional investment risk to themselves. Of course, all publishers are anxious to preserve copyright and to proceed only in a manner basically acceptable to the publishers of rival nations, for fear that seizure of a historic market could lead to rejection of the copyright system in retaliation. There are also clauses in the Treaty of Rome that can be used to protect the existing system, and so the battle could stretch out for many years.

These are by no means all of the ways in which government has become embroiled or potentially embroiled in the publishing business, but enough has been said to show that this element of the nation's communications system is by no means exempt from a constant dependence upon governmental aid. However, the agencies of government that perform these acts of protection are entirely unconnected with those that carry out broadcasting or telecommunications policy. It would be difficult to find ways in which, at the governmental level, connections are made between publishing and other media industries.

Film

In many European societies, the origins of communication policy (and of some of its contradictions) lie in the shock that was administered by the sudden domination of the cinema by the United States. The print medium, for example, is seen in Scandinavian countries as an indigenous medium, protected by language barriers against cultural domination from outside. The cinema and electronic media were, however, perceived in essence as imported industries, dependent upon technology and later upon content from outside. Despite the profound belief in the necessity of cultural freedom and free expression, which was mainly enshrined in attitudes toward the press, there grew, rapidly and powerfully, the feeling that the newer media were fit subjects for governmental intervention in order to protect the national culture against outsiders.

In Britain it has been possible for radio and television to retain powerful domestic bases, although domestic production is "helped" by public regulations. In the case of the cinema, however, Britain has found itself precisely in the position of the smaller European societies. Because of the common language with the United States, the film industry was virtually taken over when the talkies arrived. Even before that the cinema had been greatly dominated by France. Since the 1930s, Britain's own cinema has been felt to be slightly highbrow, addicted to adaptations of the classics, while the mass popular film has been entirely dominated by the American majors, who have also controlled the distribution and exhibition ends of the film business for long periods. American capital has sometimes been plentiful in Britain, providing sudden rushes of high employment for technicians, who have then been used to make essentially American films at cheaper rates. As soon as the terms of trade shifted, the capital was withdrawn and periods of high unemployment resulted. Even, as in the early 1970s, certain British "majors" have emerged (EMI in particular), and their capital has been employed in making American films for an American market. Britain has thus become a workshop for films, but, despite occasional flurries (such as in the early 1950s), has never contrived to create an indigenous film culture that would endure. Ever since the early 1930s, efforts have been made to create some kind of audience for indigenous films with the help of government money for educational projects, filmmaking activities, archival work, and latterly for production finance.

The great decline in cinema attendance that took place between 1950 (1,396 million seats sold) and 1960 (501 million seats sold) was the result of a new affluent society that turned to the home for diversion and entertainment. Television grew very rapidly, and a host of other gadgets poured into the average working-class home. The cinema reacted by making a series of giant blockbuster entertainment films and experimenting with technical innovations such as three-dimensional images, stereo, and wide screen. The number of cinema seats available dropped dramatically, as well as the number of attendances. Outside the large towns it became common for there to be no cinema at all for tens of miles. Individual productions grew more expensive and the total number of films produced dropped, on both sides of the Atlantic, because less capital was available and risks had to be spread further and further. Many production companies were forced out of business. The kinds of films that had been made and distributed in Britain—relatively low-budget features, horror films, and other mass entertainment that had little hope of large overseas markets—gradually faded away. Two of the three circuits of cinemas were merged, leaving only two that were large enough to return a profit on an indigenous film, and these two (Rank and ABC) were themselves linked to production and distribution companies. There was thus no longer any possibility of making a feature film in Britain and getting it shown to British audiences. The smaller cinemas, outside the two circuits, began to close, unable to find the product on which to survive, leaving the two giants with an ever higher proportion of the total cinema seats in the country. Then the shape of the cinema program began to change; the three-hour mixed diet of one major feature, a second feature, and some shorts disappeared in favor of a single full-length feature, and this change resulted in the elimination of the whole sector of the production industry that was used to train technicians and directors. Television provided the only training there was, apart from the nascent Experimental Film Fund of the British Film Institute.

The government brought about two significant and enduring forms of intervention in the early post-war years. In 1948 the government set up the National Film Finance Corporation in the wake of a major crisis in film

76

production in that year. The NFFC provided "end money" to producers—that is, the final cash advance to be repaid from eventual proceeds. Films were generally financed from a patchwork of advances from distributors, banks, and profits from previous attempts, and the NFFC began life as a kind of lender of last resort. At the same time, the Eady fund was set up. It was and still is a 7 percent tax on all cinema seats, the returns from which are distributed among British film producers in the form of a percentage of the distributors' gross receipts for their films. It is a system that rewards success and in the 1970s has come under great criticism, since much of the fund ends up in the pockets of the makers of pornographic films, who happen to qualify under the rules. In recent years the Eady levy has also resulted in contributions to the British Film Institute's Film Production Board, the successor to the Experimental Film Fund. These two forms of redistributive subsidy date from the time when the cinema was the major instrument of mass entertainment, when it was thought that British film production needed to be protected as a measure that would help staunch the flow of dollars out of the country. Today television has taken over the entertainment function and only a few thousand people are employed in Britain making films for the cinema, and many of these specialize in high-technology filmmaking (i.e., science fiction movies, special effects, etc.) to suit American requirements. As an industry, however, cinema still has some financial importance; it sells three to four times as many seats as the theater and five times as many as football league matches. It is a significant activity in its own right, despite its transformation from its position twenty to thirty years ago (see Table 3-5).

The NFFC has been provided over the years with a total capital of £12 million which has resulted in the making of two hundred or so films, mainly features. Its capital has been virtually used up and the government is unwilling to provide endless further advances, although it continues to qualify for over a million pounds annually, as a first call upon the funds from the Eady levy, which today brings in about £7 million a year in all—a figure that drops in real terms each year. It seems likely that these two devices will become a symbiotic support to indigenous production, with the NFFC attempting to operate as a kind of financing bank, recouping its investments where possible and enjoying a continuing flow of new resources. The British cinema also operates under a statutory quota system that obliges all cinemas to show a proportion of British films. In 1981, this was cut from 30 percent to 15 percent in order to help the exhibitors, but to the fury of technicians and producers in Britain, legislation has continued in the field of quotas since 1938. The Film Act of 1960 consolidated all of the legislation of the previous 22 years and remains in force.

The British Film Institute has already been referred to; it was created in essence in 1933 and was overhauled by an act of 1949. The BFI is now provided with nearly £6 million a year for the purpose of maintaining a

Table 3-5

Statistics on Cinemas in Britain

Year	Cinema Admissions (thousands)	Gross Box Office Receipts (£ thousands)	Number of Cinemas	Seating Capacity (thousands)	Average Price of Ticket (new pence)
1951	1,365,036	108,296	4,581	4,221	7.96
1952	1,312,077	109,856	4,568	4,200	8.39
1953	1,284,511	108,787	4,542	4,177	8.47
1954	1,275,776	109,992	4,509	4,156	8.73
1955	1,181,765	105,830	4,483	4,087	8.96
1956	1,100,794	104,217	4,391	4,026	9.19
1957	915,191	92,894	4,194	3,825	10.15
1958	754,651	83,391	3,996	3,664	11.05
1959	580,993	67,494	3,414	3,299	13.03
1960	500,789	63,641	3,034	2,960	12.88
1961	499,114	59,814	2,711	2,649	13.64
1962	394,963	56,889	2,421	2,420	14.46
1963	357,207	55,095	2,181	2,222	15.42
1964	342,780	57,533	2,057	2,104	16.79
1965	326,577	61,676	1,971	2,013	18.88
1966	288,841	59,400	1,847	1,883	20.58
1967	264,806	57,583	1,736	1,757	21.75
1968	237,281	57,677	1,631	1,627	24.29
1969	214,928	57,695	1,581	1,538	26.83
1970	193,027	59,041	1,529	1,466	30.58
1971	175,981	60,267	1,482	1,381	34.25
1972	156,640	59,371	1,450	1,198	37.90
1973	134,200	58,021	1,530	1,097	43.20
1974	138,455	69,338	1,535	973	50.10
1975	116,284	71,178	1,530	879	61.20
1976	103,865	75,829	1,525	827	73.00
1977	103,482	85,546	1,510	764	82.70
1978	126,100	118,200	1,519	738	93.70

Source: Statistics issued by the Department of Trade and Industry and published in "British Film Industry," BFI Information Guide no. 1, BFI, London, 1980.

National Film Archive, subsidizing a National Film Theatre in London and a series of regional film theaters throughout the country, and generally encouraging the development of a critical culture of the film. An Interim Action Committee, under the chairmanship of ex-Prime Minister Sir Harold Wilson, has been preparing plans for a further consolidation of existing legislation and institutions. It has advanced a plan for a British Film Authority that would absorb all of the administrative powers and functions, other than those of the British Film Institute. The BFA now seems extremely unlikely ever to be brought into being and the present rather haphazard system is likely to continue, unclear in its cultural purposes, unsure of its financial responsibilities, and inadequately funded to perform any single function to the full.

Broadcasting

To outsiders, the most interesting element in the British broadcasting system is the concept of the "authority," a chartered or statutory organization provided with a governing body of unpaid or almost unpaid individual citizens upon whom descends the complete power and responsibility for the broadcasting output of the organization. The BBC and the IBA (Independent Broadcasting Authority) are, to all intents, of the same genus, although the former runs its two television, four national radio, twenty local radio, and overseas broadcasting outlets on the basis of direct employment of all involved, while the latter acts as a regulatory and franchising body, providing licenses for private commercial companies to conduct television and radio broadcasting. At their most senior levels, both organizations consist of people chosen by the government of the day (although no accusation has ever been made of political bias in the selection) and both organizations have contained people at times who have been moved over from the other; yet the BBC and the IBA are in permanent deadly competition for audience and for public status. The competition is fierce and at times can even become litigious and personal, but there exists no financial basis for the rivalry since the BBC is furnished with the proceeds of a set-based license fee and the IBA-licensed companies have a monopoly of television advertising. In a new fourth television channel due to begin in November 1982, the IBA-licensed companies will still be permitted to collect advertising revenue (on a channel parallel with the one from which they derive their main revenue) but they will not have complete run of the channel in terms of programming. A separate board, subsidiary to the governing body of the IBA, will have control of the programming, while the IBA will mulct the companies of sufficient revenue to pay for the programs—£90 million in the first year of operation.

The powers of the IBA are thus, by international standards, rather odd. It decides which companies may broadcast (both radio and television) and over which areas of the country; it supervises the program content under the terms of the Broadcasting Acts, which have spelled out, in some detail, the controls over taste and political balance that the IBA must work within. At the same time, the IBA has to inspect the advertising for adherence to a complex set of rules, inspect the rate cards, and finally, inspect the profits of the companies, from which the government deducts 66 percent in a special levy that goes straight to the Exchequer and is followed by the normal taxes. The licensed companies are left with about 13 percent of their original balance, although when the fourth channel arrives they will pay further sums, prior to the levy, for the programming for this channel, some of which will pass back to them (in their capacity as program-making companies). It is a complex system which, to American and Australian eyes, is barely discernible as commercial at all.

However, it is an immensely lucrative system and has created in the course of a quarter century a number of important blocs of media capital. The IBA supervises all diversification on the part of the program companies or contractors, but it is today impossible to pry apart the world of commercial television from that of the press and the film industry, so inextricably interlocked have they become. A penumbra of independent program-making companies (independent, that is, from the "independent" companies of the "independent" commercial channel) has sprung up with investments in the United States and Europe, and there have been cases of these companies, whose ownership can be traced back to the IBA system, selling programs or coproduced programs to the BBC. Thus, Britain's television system is riddled with paradoxes and contradictions, although on paper it begins with two firmly rooted broadcasting "authorities" with enormously wide-ranging powers.

The organizational roots of this system lie in the founding moments of the BBC in the 1920s. The country was just recovering from a world war in which both sides had employed the most vicious forms of propaganda together with techniques of mass persuasion in order to engage in all-out warfare. The press barons, throughout Europe and America, were at the height of their power. In Britain, radio had been developed technically during the war and was now in urgent need of some structure in which to be housed permanently. The manufacturers required speed. The press required strict controls on radio's ability to enter into the territory they monopolized—public dissemination of general topical information. The government required safeguards against airtime being used by groups alien to the prevailing system and all political parties required an institution that would produce a stand-off among all contending parliamentary parties. The result was a commercial company set up by government but consisting of representatives of the industries responsible for the manufacture of radio equipment.

The Sykes Committee of 1923 created a British Broadcasting Company, under the leadership of John Reith, whose basic duty was to expand the sales of receivers. Each listener paid to the Post Office a fee for the right to operate a broadcasting "station" and the money thus collected was handed over, in part, to the new BBC. Within four years the outer commercial structure had been removed, at the instigation of the Crawford Committee, and the manufacturers were relegated in general status. In their place, a new form of public representation emerged. A group of individuals was chosen by the government of the day, presented with a royal charter, and set up as the supreme authority over a new British Broadcasting Corporation. Henceforth the power was to reside with them, but with the Home Secretary still holding the reserve power to intervene both positively and negatively in BBC programs. The governors of the BBC were chosen to represent the main blocks of the public in religious, social, and economic terms, but they were delegates from nowhere: one academic, one woman, one trade unionist, one industrialist, and so on.

As new social groupings became important, their *types* found representation among the governors (e.g., Blacks). The governors, however, were given no real executive opportunity to run the BBC; they were a final arbiter of taste, a defender of what the BBC had done within the Establishment, the blotting paper that soaked up the blood spilled in constant battle between broadcasters and politicians, a buffer state around the citadel of radio. They were, and are still, chosen not for any knowledge of the subject of their purview but as a kind of collective, iconic version of the society for whose broadcasting they take responsibility. The BBC was also stacked with advisory committees whose function was to carry the message of the BBC outward into their various constituencies and warn the BBC of any section of society that was becoming dangerously disaffected.

The central instrument of this system of governance was the BBC's charter, renewed from time to time by Parliament and enshrining all the principles of independence and all the prerogatives of the Home Secretary as these evolved through time. The General Strike of 1926 occurred at the very turning point from Company to Corporation, and the ambiguities of the BBC's independence in the course of those ten days have been debated by academics and broadcasting analysts ever since. It is by no means clear to what extent the attitudes of the BBC toward the duties of radio in a national crisis were independent, or forced upon it by force majeure, or jumped at in order to preempt that force majeure. The essential ambiguity has remained although the BBC, in the course of nearly sixty years, has developed certain elements of federalism, a certain willingness to play a repertoire of roles (especially since the birth of commerical competition in the 1950s). The growth of the BBC's freedom of maneuver, especially in the journalistic sphere, has been limited by its constant need to find a modus vivendi with each government and Parliament.

A dozen or more royal commissions and special committees of enquiry have been set up over the years to review its stewardship or decide whether it should take on board new channels or complete new media (television, teletext, the University of the Air, etc.). The license fees revenue system has remained virtually its sole source of finance (for domestic broadcasting) and it is unlikely, in the view of many now, that this funding system will survive a further decade of constant inflation, which divests the license fee of its capacity to offer broadcasting a long-term security. The fringe powers of government have grown considerably in the era of rapid inflation, since the BBC has had to return annually for governmental decisions to raise the fee. The internal social tensions of the last fifteen years—especially those arising from the situation in Northern Ireland—have made tremendous inroads into the freedom permitted BBC journalists in radio and television. It is surprising in a way that the BBC has survived the 1970s intact, still with its license fee, its vast spectrum of duties and activities in the cultural and political spheres, its command over the professional codes of all the specialist groups it employs, and its relative (to other industries) ability to command the industrial situation. The BBC's enormous cultural and artistic freedom, which might in the course of time be seen to have reached a kind of peak in the 1960s, was predicated upon its ability to manage the society, to placate and lead, to encourage some trends and repress others, to perform a constant sociocultural conjuring of its own authority. It was fortunate in many of its senior staff over the decades and in its collective acquired skill in self-maintenance.

In the 1980s it finds itself about to undergo a far more thoroughgoing commercial competition than in the past. Its two national television channels, which have hitherto had to command about 50 percent of the audience in competition against one commercial channel, will now have to face two such channels, competing in the mass and minority ends of the television market. In radio it retains a monopoly of national broadcasting, but the country is becoming thickly covered with local commercial stations. The license fee, which was always slightly ahead of the BBC's total needs, is now a wasting asset, while advertising has leapt ahead, endowing the BBC's competitors with a far higher income, despite a smaller range of responsibilities. Far higher rates of pay in the commercial sector are drawing much talent out of the BBC. Political displeasure is exhausting its executives and causing them sometimes to falter in their public symbolic acts of autonomy. If the BBC should ever fail to maintain its position, either financially or politically, then the whole notion of governance that lies behind it would be discredited. A major tool of British national communication policy would have been broken; its essence lies in the use of nonmarket and nonelective sources for the social power of which radio and television consist.

With the breaking up of the concept of the central monarchical privilege, of which the BBC is the modern exemplar, there would depart from British society the very guarantee of its cultural homogeneity and, therefore, the possibility of a nonpoliticized or depoliticized culture. Britain would slip into the position of France, Germany, and Italy, where cultural power is treated as a version of or substitute for political power and either subdivided among contending groups or subsumed into the state as an indispensable aspect of the supreme authority of the society. The BBC was a latterday counterpart of the established church, an attempt to separate the institutions of moral power from those bearing political power and to create a concordat between the two at the top of the society. The BBC was then left to nourish the power that lay at its roots. There is therefore a severe danger in the 1980s and 1990s that the rifts within British society will lose the instrument that papered them over and could therefore begin to demand cultural (i.e., broadcasting) power of their own.

Until now only religion and the political parties have been able to claim any broadcasting time of their own. The various acts that govern the BBC and its commerical counterpart, the IBA, have obliged it to provide time for the main and subsidiary religions of the kingdom and also to provide time for party political broadcasts between elections and special party election broadcasts during campaigns. Ministers have been permitted the right to broadcast across all channels simultaneously, but their opposition counterparts have always been permitted to reply on the basis of equal time. With those exceptions, editorial power has always remained de facto with the two broadcasting authorities. The break-up of that part of the national consensus which nourished the BBC as an institution could lead to a proliferation of demands from political, trade union, and social groups for the direct use of broadcasting time. With such demands would come an implicit demand to dethrone the broadcasting professions from their position of autonomy.

The quasi-professional status of broadcasters has been used hitherto as a buttress for the special power of the BBC; the exposure of that status to pressures from outside is part of the process by which the central autonomy of the BBC and the IBA over their respective halves of the industry is being subjected to perhaps terminal tensions. In Britain the fate of the new media—pay television, cable, satellite television, and so on—is still undecided. They are operated, if at all, experimentally only, directly from the Home Office. It is possible that the pressures which play upon the BBC could shift in time to the new media, leaving the traditional broadcasting institutions presiding over intact structures but guarding decaying media. In this way, the social issue would be resolved without open challenge to the structural assumptions of the BBC and the IBA. That would be a typically British resolution of the problem. The question of the new media, now under far more active discussion in other European societies than in Britain, is really a question of what kind of private sector will be permitted—and will become viable—in Britain, where the very success of broadcasting in cultural terms has been an important factor in the laggardness of other private sector media to develop.

Telecommunications

The advent of new technology and new conceptions of the role of public authorities in industry are having a profound impact in the l980s on national thinking about telecommunications in Britain. In a sense, the Post Office, with its double monopoly over postal and telecommunications services, was the first nationalized industry. It has always suffered from a tension between its purely commerical identity and its close connection with government. For centuries the chief executive of the Post Office was always a minister in the government, sometimes in the Cabinet. But in 1969 the functions of the Ministry of Posts and Telecommunications were finally separated from those of the Post Office, and the latter became an ordinary nationalized industry pursuing its own independent commercial destinies, while the former was later merged into the Department of Trade and Industry (DTI).

The Post Office has thus emerged as a monopolist of message services by two competing methods. It also provided a range of money services, which compete with those of the normal commercial banks but complement the other over-the-counter services of the postal organization. Unlike the postal services of many other countries, the British Post Office is also a carrier of small packages and in this it competes with a variety of other publicly provided services (e.g., the railway) and other private carriers. Finally, the Post Office has played a crucial role within the welfare state as the provider of over-the-counter moneys to senior citizens and various underprivileged or handicapped groups. In more recent years the Post Office has also extended its monopolistic purview into data-processing, and in this field it is still working out the relationships between itself and the private sector. It is by no means clear whether the Post Office, in the interests of pursuing its statutory obligation to break even and not be a charge upon the taxpayer, may enter into any nonmonopolistic service. Thus, there exists no obligation for the Post Office to run a full-scale parcel service, although there does exist a firm obligation for it to operate an extraordinary range of telecommunications services, which could be run competitively in the private sector but are not (so far). It is this telecommunications arm which has now been severed and reestablished as British Telecom, a separate entity.

The terms of the Post Office telecommunications monopoly are impressive. It has, throughout the British Isles, "the exclusive privilege of running systems for the conveyance, through the agency of electric, magnetic, electro-magnetic, electro-chemical or electro-mechanical energy, of speech, music and other sounds, visual images, signals serving for the impartation of any matter otherwise than in the form of sound or images, and signals for the actuation or control of machinery or apparatus." The whole policy of the new Thatcher administration in Britain is to whittle away this vast apparatus of accumulated privilege by hiving off profitable subsystems and dividing the postal from the telecommunications elements. In this policy it is largely supported by the recommendations of a committee of enquiry (the Carter Report of 1977) commissioned by the previous administration.

In order to develop its broad range of activities the Post Office has consumed a very high proportion of total new invested capital— something like one-fifth of all new investment in manufacturing industries. The habit of total monopoly dies hard and many of the new services it is pioneering, in order to make the best of its existing networks, are being cast in the traditional totalistic mold. Thus the viewdata or videotex service (called Prestel), a field in which Britain is an important pioneer, is to consume a great deal of capital throughout the early 1980s, although the popularization of the system will depend upon other pieces of capital invested in the private sector, among manufacturers and information providers. It is by no means clear that the two areas of investment are adequately complementary or being properly coordinated.

In this and other new media, success depends upon a relationship that is relatively new between public and private elements: the Post Office has long indulged in the belief that it can safely dominate in any relationship with an outside body, for example by dictating terms to manufacturers who are suppliers of its equipment. It is, and behaves like, a monopoly. With the advent of the new media, the Post Office is having to enter a competitive field, in which its statutory prerogatives are not able to offer it full commercial protection. It is uncertain whether the Post Office has yet comprehended the nature of the change to its status that the new technologies are bringing about. It is even less certain that it has the will or the special skills necessary today to use public capital in ways that are normal with private capital. The Post Office, with its massive debt burden and mixture of profitable and subsidized services, is therefore at the first stage of a profound crisis of identity and purpose. This has aroused the concern of public enquiries, which have raised the whole question of how British telecommunications policy should in the future be conducted. Again and again the Post Office has moved into a new area of research (e.g., waveguide systems) without realizing that it could no longer impose technologies on the national system by its own fiat.

The Post Office, even more than other British public institutions, enjoys a tradition of extreme secrecy in its planning and policymaking. It has, in recent years, been extremely difficult even for the government to pry from the Post Office information concerning its investment in switching systems, its policies toward international spectrum regulation, and so forth. The Carter Report of July 1977 argued that the Post Office has a positive duty to disclose its proposals for discussion and argument among representatives of the different outside interests, and that Post Office planning should take into account the needs of the customer and of the supplying industries. The report argued for the establishment of a Council on Post Office and Telecommunications Affairs that would give "strong and well-informed advice" to the secretary of state (for industry), who retains ultimate authority over the conduct of all nationalized industries. The council would consist of six independent members with the requisite variety of expertise, in addition to representatives of relevant government departments and of the Post Office and Telecommunications corporations themselves (presuming these to be separated).

Two economists at Cambridge University's Department of Applied Economics, have, however, issued an influential riposte to the Carter

Report (Cripps and Godley 1978) and argue that the proposed council should encompass a much wider range of interests and should concern itself with the interests of the national economy as a whole. In a sense, this document argues for the same breadth of concern as the Nora Minc report in France. The crucial decisions are how and when new techniques should be introduced into the national network, since it is from these that the specific strategies of new services flow, as do the problems arising from the phasing of orders.

The role of telecommunications in national economic planning in the 1980s will be on a scale similar to that of North Sea oil. Already a quarter of a million people are directly employed in Post Office telecommunications (now British Telecom) alone and are responsible for 2 percent of the total national output. By 1976 Post Office annual investment was half that of oil and double that of steel. The investment program of the Post Office can thus exercise a dramatic influence on the British balance of payments and over economic development as a whole. Already British suppliers have lost an enormous share of the world telecommunications market and the specifications and timing of Post Office strategies can greatly influence the ability of domestic manufacturers to make equipment compatible with foreign systems. There has been in recent years a severe danger that the British equipment market could slip into the hands of German, Swedish, Japanese, and American competitors, and in the course of time these rivals are bound to direct their energies more specifically at the British market.

The whole question of relationships between the Post Office and private manufacturing industry has become a crucial issue within British economic strategy: the Post Office has traditionally seen itself as the principal partner, but the needs of the economy suggest that there is a wider social and economic need for the Post Office to help domestic industry design equipment for an international market. Where the Post Office has dictated terms it should perhaps begin to explain its needs and permit industry to supply them in ways most conducive to employment and growth. The Post Office has in the recent past tended to overload the manufacturing system and then cut back drastically, causing appalling problems among those employed.

System X has been a case in point. Britain's new secret highly advanced switching system has been on the drawing board for many years. The system is so advanced that it will take two decades to phase into service, once it is fully operational, and it is already some years late. It is arguable, however, that the network requires a more evolutionary system, since an excessively innovative technology tends to hold up the development and introduction of individual types of equipment which, in any case, must remain compatible with the rest of the network until the more complete transformation has been achieved. The combination of secrecy, international jealousy, and a kind of institutionalized self-defeating pride has provided Britain with an advanced system that will arrive in place toward the end of the century, while manufacturers and the public complain increasingly bitterly about the declining quality of the existing service. As the Cripps-Godley report (1978) put it, "the question whether a more evolutionary approach should be adopted is probably the most crucial strategic issue of all."

The main problem with the Post Office and therefore with current British telecommunications planning is one of historical heritage: the Post Office is organized to run certain services on an exclusive basis, but it is not clear that it is organized in such a way as to serve the best interests of the society. Britain has to find a system of national planning that will broaden the range of considerations to such matters as employment, the continuity of technological development, and of industrial strategy and macroeconomic policy in general. But the need goes much further: so wide are the implications of telecommunications development that the decisions taken by telecommunications planners are really decisions about the kind of society a given nation wishes to build. It is clear that Britain has a very long way to go before it works out the precise kind of forum necessary and finds the way to educate its masters—its politicians and civil servants—to realize the priority that now lies in the territory of communication policy.

Conclusions

Several of the chapters in this volume emphasize the lack of coherent and overall policy or philosophy carried across the communications landscape. It has perhaps become clear from this contribution also that a future-oriented policy is impossible where connections have clearly not been made between the disparate elements of a national communications system. In all cases the writers have had to look for consistencies that are vague and unconscious rather than deliberately sited. Each society has built its communications industries one upon the other, shaping each according to the convenience of preexisting factors and institutions. It is only from this piling up of precedents and conflicts that the paradoxes of national policy can be derived. And at that point one sees that they are not policies at all, but rather communications *cultures*.

There is the heavy centralism and state monopolism of France, the almost obsessive libertarianism of Sweden, the makeshift social pluralism of Britain, the frantic capitalism of the United States. Though they might to some extent be founded upon talk of policy, these are not policies but national colorations, administrative practices endemic in given societies.

However, there are certain important categories into which these national communications cultures can be placed. There is a primary division in the twentieth-century world between providing and receiving countries and between policies directed at particular media that have been either provided or received. In Scandinavia, for example, the press is an indigenous medium, but cinema, radio, television, and modern computer-driven media are all essentially imports, the deployment of which necessitates various forms of national economic, industrial, and cultural protection. A society that rigidly opposes state intervention in the content of the newspaper may well have accepted such intervention eagerly in the case of the cinema in the days where American domination first threatened the homogeneity of many of the new European nations in the post-Versailles era—just as it threatens the cultural integrity of so many Third World countries today. Thus, a bifurcated communications culture has grown up in many European societies, with ramifications that seem quite normal to the inhabitants, though extremely perplexing to North American observers for whom there exists the possibility of only one First Amendment made to the regulation of free media. The contrast therefore between those countries in which the electronic media have been received (either in technology or in content) and those in which it has been autochthonously developed is an extremely far reaching one. Britain, however, exists somewhere in the middle, as both provider and receiver, the victim of American invasion of its cinema, but a major exporter of systems and content in its own right.

Much of the unconsciousness of British policymaking in this area stems from this conflict. France has also experienced something of this same phenomenon, as an important supplier to the francophone world, but on a smaller scale than Britain to the anglophone. Britain's view of its communications role throughout the present century has been that of a systems-builder: Reuters is still a major supplier of foreign news throughout the world. The BBC's programs are retransmitted even today in many Third World countries and its television documentary work is exported in increasing quantities. Britain's publishers continue to dominate the schools and university libraries of many other nations. Yet there is a considerable fear of "Americanization," which has influenced the regulatory systems of the country's domestic media. This fear has created the structures that today surround commercial radio and television in Britain, and has created systems in which the power of transmission has been maintained within the state monopoly, unlike most other societies with private capital in their broadcasting systems. There are controls on the total quantity of imported television material and cinema films, controls which are now confronted with a paradox: the society is attempting to Europeanize its culture but can find no way to permit a flow of foreign language or translated material while still trying to staunch the inward flow of American material. Britain is drawn, in the telecommunications field also, toward the idea of European consortia and cooperative ventures even though the American link is always more convenient, cheaper, and less politically vexatious in the medium term.

Perhaps the most problematic issue dominating this field, one that has to be cleared away before communication policy can ever become a recognized branch of national governance, is that of state intervention. The state has been involved in the provision of the majority of the communications content of British society's media since the birth of mass state education in the 1870s. The power to commission is the greatest power of all and since Parliament was from the start the focus of the national debate over the religious question in education and latterly over the secularization of culture and the attempts to make education more scientific, Parliament and the executive have both greatly influenced the educational content and therefore the production of materials. Yet the newspaper press simultaneously has implanted upon the national mind the idea of state intervention in media content as an evil. Unlike other societies of Europe, Britain has never really resolved the problem of how to get round the overt fear of state involvement.

France has allocated important educational, telecommunications, and other roles to the state since the Press Law of 1881, upon which press freedom in France has been built. Germany has escaped the dilemma by making the *Land* the focus of cultural policy rather than the federal government. The Scandinavian societies have given the state the task of ensuring that a range of indigenously controlled print media continue to exist, and their newspaper revenue support systems are designed to ensure that the state guarantees political plurality to the newspaper system, as well as diversity of ownership. Britain, however, has evolved between systems, torn between the market capitalism of America and the cultural protectionism of Western Europe. This is partly why Britain's press policy betrays such schizophrenia. All the postwar royal commissions have spoken disapprovingly of state involvement in the press and, in the case of the MacGregor Commission (1977), all forms of state subsidy were ruled out, for the same traditional reasons.

Yet Britain alone, of the countries of Western Europe, provides the press with the privilege of zero rating value added tax with respect to both the sale price of each paper and the sales of advertising space, a privilege which lifts the newspaper out of the same nexus of costs and tensions as other industries and services. The press thus has secured a privilege of considerable pecuniary value and one that in practice helps the larger newspapers to compete with the smaller ones; a blanket subsidy or nonselective privilege always helps the strong against the weak. In practice, this means that in Britain the state plays a vital regulatory role within the realm of the press in regard to the value added tax.

There are many other instances of privilege in press regulation in Britain. The lobby system in Parliament, by which the political correspondents of a number of publications are permitted access to the inner recesses of the building, to the exclusion of the representatives of other publications, is one such instance, affecting a completely different aspect of policy. The system has the effect of turning the inner group of political writers in Britain into a semiprofessional clique, not eager to offend politicians, among whom the investigative approach is rare. We have already seen how the political parties represented in Parliament are given the boon of free broadcasting time between and during election campaigns, while other political groupings that have not fought for their particular creed or philosophy in parliamentary terms are excluded from this semistatutory privilege. Thus, Britain regulates the media through the distribution and reception of small "free gifts"—tokens exchanged between media and political estates—while in the arena of formal debate, and in the context of royal commission reports, debates, or Acts of Parliament, all suggestion of state intervention is eschewed.

This raises the whole question of what the "state" means in the context of the media. Clearly the privileges mentioned are not confined to any specific government. They arise from Parliament itself as an institution rather than from the executive. There is no Ministry of Information with full purview of the whole media scene, still less the whole communications scene. There is no clear division between governmental institutions and media institutions in the case of broadcasting, the cinema, and education. Furthermore, there is a growing convergence between these and the media of print as industrial giants proceed to gobble up one another's assets, and franchises are handed out to industrial concerns that contain newspaper and entertainment interests. In Britain there is a variety of agencies that regard themselves as protective of the society against the "state," while being perceived by most citizens as part of the state themselves, ranging from the judiciary to the ombudsman or parliamentary commissioner.

The contrast with Sweden is therefore almost complete. Göran Hedebro (Chapter 5) has said that

> State interventions have up to now had a clearly defensive character. . . . The state is trying to maintain a diversified and pluralistic media arrangement in a market that would otherwise be dominated by strong capital interests, creating oligopolistic conditions.

In Britain proposals for such forms of intervention have come from the far left almost entirely and have therefore been ruled out for reasons of presumed motive. Although intervention occurs on a considerable scale, it is conducted by a wide variety of agencies. The character of the broadcasting organizations, which today have the power to manipulate the whole of the rest of the media (through commissioning power, cross-ownership, career structure), is such as to make it hard to decide whether they are state institutions or not. They are clearly not governmental institutions, being less subject to ministerial control than the broad range of nationalized corporations.

Throughout this broad terrain, certain specifically British political characteristics are present, even though no consistent philosophy or system of governance is perceptible. At the heart of every one of the institutions or media systems is a peculiarly adept political stand-off. The press is not wholeheartedly partisan as it is in parts of Europe and certainly not wedded to the notional objectivity of American journalism. At elections certain newspapers adopt extraordinarily fierce political poses, but few operate under the eye of political agents as in other countries with party presses. In broadcasting a complex web of personal and institutional relationships operates to soften the political impact of the content, through the gentle pressuring of individuals during the long course of their careers; through the permanent "coopting" pressure that passes through the broadcasting authorities; through the constant opening up of new potential for private capital in radio and television; through the constant rearrangement of personalities in executive positions and on governing bodies. Within broadcasting itself, a nonpartisan cushion of bureaucracy separates the day-to-day pressures from the long-term political maneuvering and, so far, institutions have remained sufficiently stable to be immune to the pressures of any single political administration. In cinema, it is very rare indeed that any real political content reaches the status of general release. The decision of the Conservative Party to advertise on cinema screens during the run-up to the 1979 General Election was an extraordinary oddity; political advertising is banned on television and sat strangely on the large screen among commercials for local restaurants, soft drinks, and cigarettes. The techniques of political stand-off are basic to Britain's media culture. Communication policy has been subjected so much to the political dogfight that institutions can survive only if they promise both sides of Parliament that change would bring more trouble than stasis. The phenomenon is a familiar one throughout the public life of Britain.

References

Annan, Lord, chr.
1977   *Report of the Committee on the Future of Broadcasting.* Cmnd.
                     6753 (March). London: Her Majesty's Stationery Office.

Blumler, J.C., and McQuail, D.
1968   *Television in Politics.* London: Faber & Faber.

Bradbury, M.
1971   *The Social Context of Modern English Literature.* Oxford:
                     Blackwell.

Briggs, A.
1979   *Governing the BBC.* London: Oxford University Press.

Burns, T.
1977   *The BBC: Public Institution and Private World.* London:
                     Macmillan.

Cripps, F., and Godley, W.
1978   *The Planning of Telecommunications in the United Kingdom.*
                     Cambridge: Department of Applied Economics, University of
                     Cambridge.

Fadiman, W.
1973   *Hollywood Now.* London: Thames & Hudson.

Hirsch, F., and Gordon, D.
1975   *Newspaper Money: Fleet Street and the Search for the Affluent
                     Reader.* London: Hutchinson.

Houston, P.
1963   *Contemporary Cinema.* London: Penguin.

Katz, E.
1977   *Social Research on Broadcasting: Proposals for Further Devel-
                     opment.* London: BBC.

Lewis, P.
1978   *Whose Media? The Annan Report and After.* London: Consu-
                     mers' Association.

MacGregor, Lord, chr.
1977   *Report of the Royal Commission on the Press*. Cmnd. 6810
                     (July). London: Her Majesty's Stationery Office.

Seymore-Ure, C.
1974   *The Political Impact of Mass Media*. London: Constable.

Smith, A.
1978   *The Politics of Information: Problems on Policy in Modern Media*.
                     London: Macmillan.

Smith, A., ed.
1974   *The British Press since the War: A Book of Documents*. Newton
                     Abbott, Devon: David & Charles.

1979   *Television and Political Life: Studies of Six European Societies*.
                     London: Macmillan.

Tracey, M.
1978   *The Production of Political Television*. London: Routledge.

Tunstall, J.
1971   *Journalists at Work*. London: Constable.

1977   *The Media Are American*. London: Constable.

Wintour, C.
1973   *Pressures on the Press*. London: Andre Deutsch.

Wyndham Goldie, G.
1977   *Facing the Nation: Television and Politics 1936–76*. London:
                     Bodley Head.

4

Communication Policy in Canada: Development within Overwhelming Constraints

Jean McNulty
Gail M. Martin

Jean McNulty and Gail Martin discuss the issue of implicit and explicit policies and examine the British and American influences on the development of Canadian communication policies and the contradictory pulls between two different philosophies. The constitutional tensions between federal and provincial governments, the nature of the population (including the large French sector), and the geographical distribution of that population are also seen as important influences on policy formation that generally result in a curious marriage of private enterprise and public support. Canada has developed expensive hardware and distribution capabilities to overcome her geographical disadvantages and is today the most technologically advanced nation in communications. It spends more per capita than any other country on communications hardware, although this emphasis has been at the expense of production and programming. The major problem of proximity to the United States has been exacerbated by the tensions between urban and rural areas and between English Canadians and other ethnic groups. The efforts to develop programming on a level competitive with that of the American networks has drained resources from other areas and caused complaint from those who do not want their American programming interfered with. The nagging question facing the authors is whether, in the face of such odds, it would have been possible for Canadian systems to have developed differently.

There are two distinct and sometimes apparently unrelated sources from which to study a nation's communication policy. One consists of official statements about goals and means embodied in legislation, regulations, reports, of commissions and committees, Parliamentary speeches, regulatory decisions, and the like. The other consists of the observable results of communications decisions and practices. From the perceived functioning of communications systems it may be possible to infer the social, economic, and political policies of the society that gave rise to the practices. Not unexpectedly, such analysis often reveals major discrepancies between the goals embraced in official policy statements and decisions and the ends actually attained by the aggregate of decisions and practices in a society over time. Often there is no apparent fit between explicit and implicit communication policies. In this chapter, we have taken the term "communications" to mean the systems and institutions which provide newspapers, books and magazines, film, radio and television, cable television, and telecommunications services. We will examine each of these areas within Canadian policy.

In probing the implicit federal policies underlying the development of communications practices in Canada, the heritage from the mother country, Great Britain, is encountered side by side with equally powerful and sometimes contradictory influences from the neighboring United States.

In discussing communication policy in the United Kingdom (see Chapter 3), Anthony Smith has commented that the British have been more hesitant than other European countries such as France, Italy, and Germany to develop explicit communication policy statements. Yet as his paper eloquently demonstrates, Britain's communications systems developed under the direction of clear and powerful, if unspoken, policies of the society. Smith suggests that these are rooted in feudalism, class distinctions, and political and economic arrangements surrounding the press since industrialization, as well as more recent accretions such as the elitist niche accorded to professional and publicly subsidized broadcasters. Smith's paper strongly suggests, although it does not spell out, the value to a society with strong traditional arrangements for allocating power and protecting wealth, of ensuring that information channels fit well into those traditions and reinforce them. There is no reason to make such policies explicit, since their maintenance is ensured by what Smith calls "bureaucratic atavisms" well embodied in the society.

However, the current acceleration of technological developments in communications presents new policy problems. Customarily, no one in Britain is allowed to constitute a direct threat to established interests. This is handled in two ways. First, official bodies make no statements about such developments; they are ignored, as videotext was recently by the Annan Committee on Broadcasting (Annan 1977). Second, there is much commissioning of consultative reports from industry and universities in an effort to understand fully the new technology and its implications, but these are intended for internal bureaucratic consumption rather than public enlightenment.

In the United States, by contrast, two other traditions contradict the British ones. Since their successful revolt against Britain, the Americans have placed great faith in explicit, written constitutions, laws, and rules as a means of avoiding the inequalities embedded in older systems. By ensuring that rules are written down and available to all, everyone knows his or her rights and has access to judicial process for redress of grievances. A second major distinguishing factor is the American insistence on strict separation of press and state. Government ownership of or participation in newspapers, broadcasting, and publishing has been and remains anathema in the majority American view of the role of journalists and broadcasters as the guardians of liberty and watchdogs of democracy. The role of government in American communication policy is purportedly only that of a strictly hands-off referee arbitrating among the interests of competing groups. As the chapter by Anne Branscomb on the United States demonstrates, the American government is neither expected nor allowed to engage in formulating national or public interest policies for communications systems to guide their development.

The evolution of Canada's communication policy and practices can be understood only if these dual and conflicting influences are kept in mind. On the one hand, Canada is a parliamentary democracy modeled on Britain and continues similar unspoken mechanisms for maintaining power and privilege among the few. While Canada has existed as a federal state only since 1867, it was building upon older traditions in English Canada and Quebec, both of which had evolved patterns of social structure quite unlike the American version of a democratic society. Similarly, Canadians have never adopted the American distaste for government involvement in broadcasting. Indeed, publicly owned radio and television and explicit government statements about the role of communications systems in achieving "national unity" and equity between Canadians have been accepted practice since the early part of this century.

On the other hand, a large part of the Canadian population is not of British descent. Besides Quebec's French majority, the other provinces have been settled by significant numbers of immigrants from Europe and smaller numbers from Asia. The attitudes of many Canadians have been and are being shaped by proximity to the United States and its communications media. Private broadcasting interests in Canada can count on Canadian sympathizers when they invoke American ideals such as First Amendment freedom of the press and "the free marketplace of ideas" in their protests against Canadian regulation of the privileged position of the public broadcasting corporation.

Major Factors Affecting Communication Policy

The traditional allocation of powers between the federal and provincial governments has been a source of active debate over the past decade and is heating up over the issue of ownership and pricing of natural resources such as oil. Jurisdiction over communications has been part of that debate, with Quebec vociferous in demanding autonomy in communications matters as a means of protecting its cultural distinctiveness. This tension between the provincial and federal governments has been a continuing and significant factor in the development of Canadian communication policy since the late 1960s.

Currently, significant levers of economic power in Canada are shifting from the manufacturing provinces of Ontario and Quebec to the oil- and resource-rich provinces of Alberta, Saskatchewan, British Columbia, and, most recently, Newfoundland. This disruption of the historical power and wealth relationships within the country is altering all other societal arrangements and will significantly affect the disposition and control of communications media, possibly in ways unforeseen at present.

Constitutional tensions exist between centralization of policymaking and control of communications by the federal government and the interests of the provincial governments to allow for regional or local differences (see, for example, Quebec 1973). The Canadian confederation, established under the British North America Act of 1867 (the BNA Act), provides for a distribution of powers between the federal government and the provincial governments. Initially there were four provinces; since 1949 there have been ten provinces and two northern territories administered by the federal government. Jurisdictional disputes in a federal state are fairly common and Canada is certainly no exception to this rule. In 1980–81, lively and at times acrimonious debate occurred in Canada about the "patriation" of the Canadian constitution (the BNA Act) from Britain, the approval mechanisms to be used for future constitutional amendments, and the explicit guarantee of civil rights to be written into the constitution. Regardless of how these matters were finally settled with regard to the BNA Act, uncertainties will remain about the limits of federal and provincial powers in matters of communications that cannot easily be resolved by reference to a statute written in 1867; these uncertainties and lack of national consensus have impeded and confused developments from time to time.

Another factor that contributes to the complexity of policy formulation in Canada is the nature of its population, which was almost 23 million at the time of the 1976 census; in 1981, it was over 24 million (Statistics Canada 1979 and 1982). This makes the Canadian population about 10 percent of the U.S. figure, a proportion that has remained fairly steady for at least thirty years. The distribution of people across Canada is heavily concentrated in southern Ontario and Quebec. Between them, these two provinces—often referred to as Central Canada—had about 14.5 million people in 1976, or about 63 percent of the country's total. The remainder is spread over four western provinces, four eastern provinces, and two northern territories. The total land area of Canada is 9.2 million square kilometers, which gave an average population density in 1976 of 2.49 persons per square kilometer. Even excluding the vast northern territories, the density of the provinces was only 4.21 persons per square kilometer in 1976 (Statistics Canada 1981).

Historically, the Canadian nation is viewed as having evolved from two founding nations, the French and the British. The number of indigenous peoples has always been relatively small and they have rarely been in a position to influence the cultural ethos of Canadian settlements. In 1971, it was estimated that there were about 300,000 native Indian people in Canada; in addition, there were about 18,000 Inuit people (formerly known as Eskimos), mostly in the Northwest Territories. Most of the Canadians of French origin now live in Quebec where their ancestors settled more than two hundred years ago. French settlements have not flourished in other parts of Canada as they have in Quebec (Statistics Canada 1976).

At the time of the 1976 census, 25.6 percent of Canadians claimed French as their mother tongue and 61.4 percent claimed English. The distribution of anglophones and francophones is very uneven, especially between Quebec and other provinces. Eighty percent of Quebecers speak French as their mother tongue, compared to only 5.6 percent of Ontario residents. In all provinces, except Quebec and New Brunswick, the percentage of residents whose mother tongue is French is less than 6 percent. New Brunswick is about 66 percent English and 33 percent French, the latter being mostly people of Acadian descent.

Leaving aside language differences (and the cultural differences that go with them), Canadians have come from a wide variety of ethnic origins, whether recently or long ago. The last census to record the ethnicity of Canadians was in 1971. At that time, 44.6 percent were of British origin and 28.7 percent were French. Other European countries provided 23 percent of Canadians, the most numerous groups being German (6.1%), Italian (3.4%), and Ukranian (2.7%). Asian peoples represent only 1.3 percent of the total population, with Inuit and indigenous Indians making up 1.5 percent. While those of British origin constitute the largest single group, they do represent all four ethnic groups within Britain—and a considerable drop from the 57 percent which the British made up in Canada at the turn of the century. The French percentage has dropped only slightly during the same period, while the European nations have increased their share from 8.5 percent to 23 percent. In 1971, slightly less than 85 percent of the population had been born in Canada, reflecting the high levels of recent immigration, especially in the early 1950s. About 8 percent of the 1971 population was born in continental Europe (Statistics Canada 1981).

Perhaps because of the complex mixture of people living in Canada, and consequently the lack of an established consensus on many issues related to communications, it has been the practice of the federal government—and more recently of some provincial governments—to encourage public discussion and comment about certain issues.

The process by which federal communication policies become explicit is usually conducted partly in the public arena and allows for participation by a variety of people and institutions. For example, under the procedures of the Canadian Radio-television and Telecommunications Commission (CRTC), matters concerning policy questions, license renewals or conditions and rate structures for federally regulated common carriers are all considered at public hearings, in which the public can participate if they wish.

The Minister of Communications or the Secretary of State (depending on the subject) may issue Green Papers to encourage public discussion of a proposed policy. White Papers are sometimes issued to indicate government policy made explicit—on satellite communications, for example. On a number of occasions over the past ten years, task forces and special committees have been set up to examine specific problems and issues, and their reports have been made public. Since 1928, indeed, it has been the practice of the federal government to employ the inquiry process of royal commissions and parliamentary committees on many occasions to examine aspects of broadcasting development and to obtain public comment.

This public involvement, as well as the more usual consultations with industry associations and within the government itself, provides the federal government with considerable information from which to draw in establishing policies. Of course, the number of members of the general public who participate is often not high but the opportunity to participate is there, unlike the situation in most other countries.

Proximity to the United States, coupled with a large land mass and relatively small, scattered population, has been another major factor in the evolution of Canadian communications systems, as can be seen, for example, in the history of radio in Canada. By 1928, virtually all of the radio broadcast frequencies then available for the North American continent had been claimed by American broadcasters. Nearly everywhere along the Canadian border—where most of the population has always lived and most of the cities are located—it was possible to receive American radio programs. Almost nowhere outside the largest cities of Montreal and Toronto was it possible to receive Canadian radio programming until explicit policy and government action led to the creation creation of a Canada-wide service.

In the ensuing fifty years, this proximity to the United States has been a major factor influencing the development of Canadian communication policy on radio, television, satellites, and computer networks. The problem is not just one of proximity but also of relative size and economic strength. The Canadian land mass is greater than that of the United States but its current population of 24 million people is only a tenth of that of its neighbor. Three-quarters of the Canadian population live in an uneven string from Newfoundland to British Columbia within about 200 kilometers of the U.S. border. Of necessity, in the early days of communications development, Canada had to give priority to very real and very expensive problems of distribution.

Covering the country with a network of radio stations and later of television stations has been the preoccupation of communications planners and policymakers. Canada today is thus said to be technologically the most advanced nation in communications, spending more per capita on communications hardware than any other country. Critics within the country have pointed out frequently that this emphasis on hardware and distribution capability has been at the expense of production and programming capability—that is, the content which these expensive systems carry.

This combination of proximity to the American giant and internal problems of long distances and small population gave rise to another aspect of Canadian communication policy, which was first adopted as a solution and has remained as a continuing source of problems—the attempted mixture of public and private broadcasting within one national system. At the same time as Canada's British heritage predisposed it to accept the commitment to public broadcasting of the European nations—specifically, the model of the BBC—it was faced with the practical recognition that providing domestic broadcasting to a majority of the scattered population could probably not be accomplished through private enterprise and would call for some form of public support. However, the public support provided through Parliament was never sufficient to allow the creation of a fully public system (Weir 1965). Therefore we have witnessed in Canada the evolution of the Canadian Broadcasting Corporation (CBC), supported primarily by public funds, existing side by side and in a number of varying cooperative arrangements with privately owned broadcasting stations and later television networks (Peers 1969 and 1979). The development of the telephone system, the transcontinental microwave networks, and most recently the operation of the ANIK satellites continue this curious marriage of private enterprise and public support.

All these factors will recur as underlying themes in the following discussions on the press, publishing, film, radio and television, cable television, and telecommunications.

The Press

The newspaper industry in Canada consists of three elements: the French-language press, the English-language press, and the ethnic press. The third element until recently has been insignificant in its share of the advertising pie. In recent years, newspapers published weekly or biweekly for suburban areas or in smaller towns have gained increased strength, unlike the daily press. The total circulation of weeklies (including the ethnic press) is probably about 9 million copies, whereas the total circulation of dailies had fallen to about 5 million by 1975 and has not kept pace with the growth in total households. It is estimated that more than one-quarter of Canadian households do not purchase a daily newspaper at all. By comparison, magazine circulation was over 16 million by 1976, and rising.

Traditionally, Canadian daily newspapers have been Canadian owned, but domestic ownership has not been enforced by legislation or statutory regulation—unlike other media industries. The reasons for the strength of Canadian ownership are not self-evident, but seem to depend on three things. First, Canadian daily newspapers have historically had close ties with political parties, and these ties could not be readily carried on by foreign owners, particularly Americans whose political system is so different. Second, the principal newspapers have been owned by families or family trusts, not by shareholders whose shares could be purchased on public stock exchanges. Takeover bids, then, depend on reaching private agreement with the previous owners and acquisitions usually cannot be achieved by surprise or covert share purchases. So far, it appears that Canadian owners prefer to sell to other Canadians. Third, the practice for failing newspapers seems to have been to close down, rather than to have been bought up by new publishers.

The trend since the early 1950s has been for many local city markets to have only one daily newspaper published there. This is highly advantageous for the surviving-newspaper owners. It also makes it costly for a new newspaper to start up later in competition. Even in markets where two newspapers exist, they customarily have arrived at a modus vivendi of having one morning and one evening publication. In Vancouver, for example, the two newspapers share a printing facility, as well as distribution and advertising services, even though they were owned until recently by different newspaper chains. A recent study concluded that there are now only seven Canadian cities where local competition for newspaper readers exists between newspapers not owned by the same company: Edmonton, Calgary, Winnipeg, Toronto, French-speaking Montreal, Quebec City, and St. John's. These seven communities have 49 percent of the daily newspaper circulation in Canada, in French and English.

In 1980, public concern about the increased concentration of ownership in daily newspapers was heightened when Thomson Newspapers took over FP Publications. This move gave the Thomson organization the second largest share of Canadian daily circulation, the largest being that of Southam. Shortly after the Thomson-FP takeover, Thomson closed down the *Ottawa Journal* (one of two English-language dailies in the city) and Southam closed down the *Winnipeg Tribune* (one of two dailies in that city) on the same date. Other exchanges or sales of newspaper properties between the two companies also occurred at this time, leaving both Vancouver papers owned by one company and both Victoria papers to be merged into one. This sudden drop in the availability of choice at the local level caused concern, notably in Ottawa, where federal politicians were made aware of the loss of a newspaper on their own doorstep.

Consequently, a Royal Commission on Newspapers was established under the leadership of Tom Kent, a former public servant and newspaper editor, and currently dean of administrative studies at Dalhousie University. The commission's report was submitted to the federal government in July 1981, but no response has been made by the cabinet yet (Kent 1981). The reaction to the commission's analysis and recommendations from newspaper editors and publishers has been almost entirely hostile, since the commission has called for actions ranging from the ordering of certain divestitures by major companies and mechanisms to provide greater freedom to newspaper editors from owner control. It remains to be seen if the federal government will undertake the tough action recommended by the Kent Commission—especially, if, as has been pointed out, some action may be intruding upon the powers of provincial governments.

Historically, newspaper owners in all industrialized countries have played a leading role in forming or guiding public opinion of industrial workers settling in urban areas. They played this role in Canada in the late nineteenth and early twentieth centuries (Kesterton 1967). After the First World War, they found themselves threatened by the development of radio broadcasting, originally in the United States and later in Canada. The threat was partly to their influence on popular opinion but more seriously to their advertising revenue. In the United States, the commercialization of the radio proceeded rapidly, with the acquiescence of the federal government. However, in Canada, because of the lively Canadian nationalism of the 1920s, there was public concern about more Americanization of Canadian society if commercial radio of the American type were to be developed. After considerable discussion in government circles and a royal commission report (Aird 1929), it was decided that the Canadian public should fund a national broadcasting service to link Canadians across the land and to provide Canadian programming.

Newspaper publishers, among others, favored this idea because it was assumed that the national service, modeled loosely on the BBC, would not carry advertising. However, the Canadian Radio Broadcasting Commission and its successor, the Canadian Broadcasting Corporation, were not funded adequately by the federal government, and radio advertising quickly became necessary for continuing operation. This displeased the newspaper owners considerably. The solution proved to be to get involved themselves (directly or indirectly through subsidiary companies) in the ownership of private radio stations. Later, in the late 1950s and early 1960s, they also became engaged in the ownership of television stations.

At present, the major newspaper chains are all involved in the ownership of private radio and television and, to a lesser extent, cable television through subsidiary holdings. The principal companies in

English Canada are Southam, Thomson Newspapers, and the Sun Group. In Quebec, Paul Desmarais's Gesca Ltée. and Pierre Peladeau's Quebecor Inc. have considerable holdings in newspapers and broadcasting. A major corporation in several of the mass media is Maclean-Hunter, which did not own any daily newspapers until 1978 but has long held a dominant position in the publication of magazines and trade journals in English and French; it is involved in radio, television, cable television, and printing of all kinds. During the development of radio and television service in Canada, several other large corporations have emerged with significant holdings in broadcasting. For example, Argus Corporation, which controls Massey Ferguson, Hollinger Mines, and Domtar, also has interests in radio and television through Standard Broadcasting and Bushnell Communications. Companies such as Rogers Cablesystems, Moffat Communications, and Western Broadcasting have risen to prominence in broadcasting without the base of a newspaper empire. These last-named companies have no particular interest in protecting the advertising revenues of the print press.

Before the Second World War, unionization of the journalists was virtually unknown on Canadian newspapers, and it took over a decade for most major newspapers and the electronic media to acquiesce in collective union agreements for their staff (Rutherford 1977). The Newspaper Guild of the United States is the journalists' union in English Canada; Le Syndicat des Journalistes performs the same function for the French-language press, mostly in Quebec. The latter union has been much more active in expressing concern about media concentration and has also been much more interested in gaining control over the content of their newspapers. Codes of ethics and agreements that delineate the limits of management authority are not uncommon in the Quebec press, although they do not reach the extent of journalistic authority actively pursued in some European countries. The professionalism of journalists in the English-language press is still in the process of formation and their ability to influence the management or the owners remains slight in many cases (Stewart 1980). So far, journalists working for Canadian Press (CP) have remained ununionized.

The key role of CP needs some explanation. Canadian Press is a cooperatively owned agency funded by the major newspapers across Canada. Its job is to collect and disseminate news from all across the country to all its subscriber newspapers. This news is provided in English- and French-language versions. CP also uses foreign news agencies to supply its subscribers with international news. The principal foreign agency used is Associated Press (AP), supplemented by Reuters and Agence France-Presse—especially for the French-language CP service. (CP also provides selected news services called Broadcast News to almost all radio and television stations in Canada.) The widespread use of CP copy in most daily and weekly newspapers across the country tends to make them very similar in content and style. Although Canadian

Press is not the only newswire service in Canada, it is by far the most widely used.

In 1970, the Special Senate Committee on Mass Media (the Davey Committee) voiced concern about the degree to which CP depended for its foreign news on the Associated Press, Agence France-Presse, and Reuters rather than on its own reporters (Davey 1970). In 1977, the CRTC's Committee of Inquiry into the National Broadcasting Service commented on the overwhelming preponderance of Associated Press items that were selected by CP to provide all foreign news to CP subscriber newspapers (CRTC 1977). For Canadian news, the committee noted the predominance in the CP wire service of items from a handful of places—Toronto and Ottawa predominate in the English-language service; Montreal and, to a lesser extent, Quebec City dominate the French-language service. Most recently, the Kent Commission repeated the Davey Committee's criticism of CP's poor record in obtaining news from outside Canada other than by using other (foreign) wire service reports. CP staff located abroad is now reduced to two correspondents in London, one in New York, and one in Washington—a coverage even lower than that which the Davey Committee thought abysmal. As with earlier reports, the Kent Commission was critical of CP's efforts to provide adequate coverage about and for French Canada and of its treatment of news from areas of Canada outside the Toronto-Montreal population corridor.

Aside from these problems of balance and perspective, use of CP-collected material by most newspapers and broadcast stations tends to provide the same sort of newsworthy information across different media. The Davey Committee put the blame for this uniformity in newspaper content squarely on the newspaper publishers who choose to rely on CP as heavily as they do (Davey 1970). The diversity of locally available information is seriously reduced as a result of this practice.

Cross-ownership between broadcasting and newspapers is very widespread. The Davey Committee, which issued its three-volume report in 1970, devoted a great deal of space to a review of the ownership groups then existing in the Canadian mass media. The cross-ownership of newspaper and broadcasting holdings as well as the concentration of ownership in the mass media generally has increased considerably since then, despite the committee's clearly expressed concerns that these forms of ownership and control are usually against the public interest, since they reduce the diversity of information and opinion made available to the general public.

Since its establishment in 1968, the Canadian Radio and Television Commission (renamed the Canadian Radio-television and Telecommunications Commission in 1976) has tried to exercise some control over the degree of ownership concentration. However, it cannot exercise any direct supervision over newspaper owners who hold no licenses for their publications. The CRTC can only prevent excessive concentration by refusing to permit a broadcasting licensee corporation (which may be controlled by a newspaper chain) to acquire additional broadcasting licenses. Generally, the commission has attempted to prevent one corporation from controlling all the broadcasting licenses (radio, television, cable television) in one local area. Joint ownership of the television station and cable television system in one location is usually forbidden. However, the commission treats each application for acquisition of a licensed company on its own merits and there are no rules whereby it can be determined in advance that an application would be refused on clearly established grounds.

Publishing

While the problems and issues of newspaper publishing have been those of concentration of ownership and of limitations in the range of information and viewpoints provided through the press, these difficulties can be seen as internal to Canada, problems to which internal solutions might be found. However, the situation is quite different for the book publishing and film industries, both of which try to exist in an internationalized mass-market, mass-culture environment. In magazine and book publishing, as in feature film productions, Canadians have maintained a somewhat uneasy truce between two conflicting pressures: one is to achieve the development of cultural expression by Canadian artists in a medium that is dominated by multinational corporation merchandising; the other is to establish entrepreneur-based, economically viable industry structures that can produce mass-market products to compete internationally (and domestically) for a share of the world market.

Whether pushing either of these directions can satisfy the goals of a wide range of people and institutions in Canada is a matter for debate, as is the question of whether either direction is in the interests of Canadian society as a whole. Artistic goals frequently clash with those of the private entrepreneur, while the governments (usually federal) attempt on behalf of the public to provide assistance where and when needed. No one is fully satisfied with the ways in which Canadian publishing has developed, and no satisfactory policy framework has yet been devised (Crean 1976).

Since the establishment of the Canada Council in the early 1950s, there has been public recognition that the periodic support of artistic work (and of artists) is a laudable goal of federal government policy. Although some MPs and private individuals grumble about specific artistic works supported by the council, in general the principle is not in dispute. However, even when authors receive grants to help them while writing, it is still necessary to find a publisher and to distribute the book or magazine article across Canada and abroad. Without those later actions taking place, a writer cannot reach the public. Thus, it has come about that much attention by writers and others in Canada has been given to the economics of publishing Canadian work. Although it may seem in the following pages that economics is the *sole* concern, this is not the case. Nevertheless, it has come to loom large in policy discussions because there are many economic difficulties in the production and distribution of books and magazines intended primarily for the Canadian public.

At this point in a discussion, the argument about "art" as an international activity or as an expression of cultural individuality almost invariably arises. Much of the debate about whether or not Canadian writers should strive to be more "international" and less "provincial" is already loaded (semantically and otherwise) in favor of the viewpoint that to look beyond the bounds of one's own cultural framework is more modern and, therefore, better. However, a contrary argument can be made that no writer can escape his or her own cultural background and cultural experience, and some Canadian writers see the "international" argument as a thinly disguised push for acceptance of American (or British or French) cultural perspectives. To be a Canadian writer, however, does not mean the writer seeks to reach only a domestic audience or that his or her writings can be of interest only to Canadians. In order to reach people outside Canada, the writer becomes even more entangled in the worldwide distribution systems for English- or French-language publications. For domestic or foreign distribution, a Canadian writer must choose between Canadian-owned and foreign-owned, usually branch-plant, publishing companies.

Regarding the ownership of book publishing companies in Canada, for a number of reasons (including costs of distribution across the continent), Canadian publishing houses owned by Canadians have never been either numerous or strong. Before the Second World War, Canadian publishing was dominated largely by subsidiaries of the well-known British houses, such as Oxford University Press and the Macmillan Company. Then during the 1960s a dozen new American publishing houses set up branch plants in Canada. These foreign competitors undercut Canadian operations in two ways:

1. By acting as distributors for foreign books, these outsiders took away from Canadian houses valuable profits that could have been used to subsidize Canadian works.
2. By representing larger houses, the outsiders proved to be better able to cope with the educational market, which changes rapidly since textbook decisions are made by individual school districts, not by the provincial departments of education.

Canadian-owned publishing operations have seldom been large or profitable enough to undertake the considerable and expensive research and development needed to produce textbooks. Foreign houses, particularly American ones, can simply adapt textbooks already developed by them for a large market and then use the more extensive selling and promotional activities required to market them.

By 1970, two of Canada's major domestic publishing companies had to sell out to Americans. When a third announced it would have to go the same route, an Ontario royal commission on publishing investigated the English-language industry, much of which is in Ontario. Following the commission's report recommendations (Rohmer 1972), the Ontario government began a program of government subsidy with a $900,000 low-interest, long-term loan. Since then, the Ontario government has combined the resources of the provincial lottery system to sponsor a "Half-Back" scheme whereby lottery ticket buyers can use losing tickets (costing $2) to save one dollar on the price of a Canadian book.

Many small publishing companies owned by Canadians and dedicated to publishing Canadian materials spring up each year. Some survive in a marginal way, others disappear. They are subject to the same kind of unequal economic competition battle that Canada is faced with in the production of broadcasting material. The Canadian border is open to importation of books from the south, apart from a 10 percent tariff on American books. Ninety percent of the books bought by Canadians are foreign produced, either by publishers outside the country's boundaries or by foreign-owned publishing companies operating within Canada. One American-controlled company operating in Toronto is as large as all the members of the Association of Canadian Publishers combined.

The situation in Canada is not unlike that in South America where Spanish publishers predominate, and in India and Africa where English publishing houses hold sway. The doctrine of the free flow of information, which historically has favored strong nations at the expense of weaker ones, is repeatedly invoked against those who would do something to protect the Canadian cultural industries. Ambivalence on a number of levels seems to have kept legislators and government officials from taking any effective action to protect Canadian publishing. It has been demonstrated in the courts by suits brought by noted Canadian authors that the existing Canadian copyright law, for example, seems to give greater protection to American authors than it does to native ones. Ontario is the only province to have developed a scheme of guaranteed loans helping Ontario publishing companies to obtain financing for their high-risk, low-yield, capital-intensive industry. During the 1970s, on many occasions, Canadian nationalist publishers called for six major types of action; none of them has been carried out on a broad scale at the time of this writing. They are:

1. An improved copyright act;
2. Control of distribution channels and the introduction of Canadian quotas—particularly with paperbacks and book clubs;
3. Prevention of foreign takeovers and introduction of new branch plants;

4. Licensing of Canadian publishers to act as agents for foreign publishers;
5. Mandatory increase in Canadian content and Canadian publishing of textbooks for schools and universities;
6. Financial aid to Canadian publishers through loans and perhaps tax allowances.

Canadian book publishing shares with the Canadian magazine industry, particularly when it comes to paperbacks, a major problem in distribution. Once again, the trouble is that the distribution channels are American dominated (Litvak and Maule 1975). The magazine distributors operate by contract with wholesalers, mostly American owned, who set up an entire selection of titles, all of which must be accepted by the distributor. The easiest, most efficient, and most profitable thing for the distributors to do is simply to deal with the American material supplied them. Adding Canadian titles from small houses and distributors only adds a considerable amount to their trouble and very little to their profit. In self-defense, the Canadian magazine publishers formed an association and in the mid-1970s set up their own distribution system for the densely populated areas of southern Ontario. Even there, the undertaking has proved expensive and has required subsidy.

One piece of protective legislation was passed by the Canadian Parliament in 1976. Through an amendment to the Income Tax Act, it removed the tax exemption for Canadian companies placing advertising in foreign-owned magazines, including *Time Canada* and *Readers' Digest*. At the last moment before enactment, however, *Readers' Digest* (which like *Time* maintained an editorial office in Canada) was able to convince the responsible authorities that the Canadian edition of *Readers' Digest* was indeed distinctive enough to merit its exclusion from the new protective bill, so Canadian advertising in that publication remains tax deductible. The removal of tax exempt status from *Time* magazine resulted in its withdrawal from the country and subsequently in the remarkable strengthening of the Canadian news magazine, *Maclean's*, which has been able to go from a monthly publication to a weekly one, with expanded staff, size, and coverage. Canada now has a national news weekly for the first time.

In discussions of policy initiatives for the protection of national publishing industries, it is interesting to note the American example. The strong American publishing industry was built with the aid of two major policies:

1. Contrary to the doctrine of the free flow of information (much invoked to protect American interests abroad today), the United States has had, and enforced for years, an embargo against books manufactured in any other country in numbers over 1,500.

109

2. Both magazine circulation and book-publishing industries in the United States were built up between 1925 and 1950 by publishing, without respect to copyright or payment of royalties to authors, the works of British and Canadian writers.

This latter practice resulted in Canadian writers having to move south of the Canada-United States border to obtain any kind of copyright protection. It also resulted in British books manufactured in the United States being dumped on the Canadian market because Canadian publishers who were party to an imperial copyright agreement with Britain were obliged to pay a 12½ percent royalty, while the Americans were not. These two combined American practices nearly destroyed Canadian book publishing, and indeed weakened it to the point where the foreign takeover was, in effect, almost unstoppable.

Film

The indigenous Canadian feature film industry has fared no better either domestically or abroad than the country's television programming and book publishing industries, for similar reasons. Despite attempts since the 1920s to set up a film industry, Canada remains an importer of feature films, rather than an exporter. In 1967, Parliament established a Canadian Film Development Corporation (CFDC) to try to remedy this situation. Canadians were spending $200 million a year at theater box offices, and of that almost a third was being taken out of Canada by major U.S. distributors. The purpose of the CFDC was to help raise sufficient investment capital to underwrite feature film production in Canada. The Department of the Secretary of State drew up a list of stipulations that would determine whether a film was indeed Canadian in content and production. The corporation then attempted to require applicants for CFDC loans to have already obtained a valid distribution contract, preferably with a financial commitment for at least 50 percent of the budget. In this they ran headlong into one of the major hurdles to Canadian film production—all the major Canadian theater chains were foreign owned. It took several years of negotiation and organization before Canadian filmmaking companies could begin to get preproduction guarantees of distribution. By 1973 to 1975, the CFDC had achieved a return of 32 percent on its investment and had two box office successes—*The Apprenticeship of Duddy Kravitz* and *Black Christmas*.

The federal government has signed coproduction treaties with Italy, France, and Great Britain to try to stimulate Canadian production activity. It has also introduced a provision under the appropriate income-tax regulations to allow 100 percent of capital cost write-offs to investors in certified feature films. (Originally 100 percent in any one year, the write-offs were reduced by the minister of finance to 50 percent in his November 1981 budget.) This last measure seems to have had a notice-

110

able effect, and the number of Canadian films, especially English-language ones, achieving box-office success is making a slow but steady increase.

The story of how Canada came to this unenviable position in the world film industry can be enlightening reading. Canada, unlike virtually every other country in the world, has never imposed any quotas on the importation of foreign films, nor are there any special tariffs on imported films, nor is there any language barrier separating English Canadians from the great Hollywood production mill. English Canada in fact is treated as part of the American domestic film market and has taken no effective steps to change this situation. Yet in 1948, when, because the vertical integration was operating in restraint of trade, a United States antitrust case against the film industry required film production companies to divest themselves of their theater holdings, the ruling did not apply to Canada. The result is that, today, three out of four theaters in major Canadian cities are owned by Famous Players, which is 51 percent owned by Paramount Pictures (which in turn is owned by Gulf and Western, a multinational conglomerate based in the United States). The pattern of vertical integration between producers, distributors, and exhibitors remains undisturbed in Canada, so that independent film producers have inadequate access to exhibition circuits in their own country (Crean 1976).

The Canadian television industry, which is increasingly providing a market for films, has not improved the lot of the Canadian film producer. Canadian television networks have chosen to emulate the American networks and acquire their films from major film distributors, selecting what has already shown itself to be popular in the theaters. Canadian film misses out in the second round because it did not get a chance to get into the first one. Increasingly, film production companies in Canada look to the introduction of pay television as their salvation. Whether or not it enables them to obtain better distribution and whether or not that leads to financial returns sufficient to encourage the industry to grow and prosper are matters for debate.

Perhaps the most interesting example of all time—of how not to promote a domestic communications industry—occurred in the 1940s under the rubric of the Canadian Co-operation Project. Canada was experiencing serious trade deficits with the United States, and in order to forestall the imposition of a quota on feature films, or of requirements for Hollywood to spend some revenues on Canadian film production, the Motion Picture Association of America persuaded the Canadian government to settle for increased references to Canada in Hollywood movies. Unbelievable as it may seem today, the Canadian government agreed and a project representative from Canada was sent to Hollywood where he supervised changes of dialogue in American films. Instead of "they caught Louis Engleday in Detroit," the Hollywood film would now say "they caught Louis Engleday on his way to Canada." The idea apparently was that such references would increase tourism to Canada and thus remedy the balance of payments problem more effectively than direct action against the American film industry.

The one area in filmmaking where Canada has achieved worldwide recognition is in the work of the government-sponsored National Film Board. Founded by John Grierson in 1939, the board began by producing propaganda films during the Second World War and went on to achieve a substantial world reputation for Canada in the field of documentary film. At one time, thought was given to expanding the operations of the National Film Board to include full length feature films, but that development was stopped primarily by lack of adequate public funding to undertake such an expensive activity. For many years, private companies engaged in film and video production in Canada have sought to reduce the NFB's prime position as filmmaker for government departments, declaring that such work should be open to private entrepreneurs. In 1981, the private producers got their way, and it is now government policy that the majority of government contracts for film work should be given to the private sector, not the NFB. Because it is now limited to a minor role, the NFB's future looks bleak even though its artists continue to win many awards for their less numerous film productions.

Radio and Television Broadcasting

Policy regarding radio broadcasting, from its earliest days in Canada, was developed on the basis of the regulation needed to allow the best use of a limited resource, the radio spectrum. In the 1920s, it was accepted that there was only a small number of radio frequencies available for use in Canada and that therefore use of such frequencies would have to be licensed. It soon became apparent that there had to be some government action to develop broadcasting service for all Canadians, not merely those who were easily reached from major population centers. It was also apparent that conscious effort would be needed to produce informational and entertaining programming in Canada, otherwise there would be a tendency to use already easily available American programs and American formats. As was succinctly written by the Fowler Committee on Broadcasting in 1965, "The only thing that really matters in broadcasting is program content; all the rest is housekeeping" (Fowler 1965). Despite that observation, much energy has gone into the housekeeping side.

Since the establishment of the first royal commission into broadcasting in 1928, the federal government has regularly returned to the establishment of commissions or special parliamentary committees as a chief instrument for policy formulation in the broadcasting field. The 1932 Radio Reference case was heard by the Judicial Committee of the British Privy Council, which established that the federal government had *exclusive* jurisdiction over radio communication in Canada (*Dominion*

Law Review 1932). The recommendations of these bodies have been more or less faithfully reflected in the several Broadcasting Acts by which the Canadian Parliament sets out general goals and overall structure for the broadcast system within Canada. Ongoing supervision of the performance of broadcasting stations and networks is left to an appointed body responsible for the translation of the general provisions of the Broadcasting Act into day-to-day regulation and practice. Problems and issues in Canadian broadcasting have been such that thirteen special investigating policy commissions were found necessary between 1928 and 1978. There have been five revisions of the various broadcasting acts, and three different organizations charged with supervision on a day-to-day basis.

Originally, the board responsible for directing the public broadcasting network was the Canadian Broadcasting Commission (after a short-lived Canadian Radio Broadcasting Commission from 1932 to 1936). In addition to providing a public broadcasting service, the corporation was charged with the responsibility of supervising the private stations, which had been made affiliate members of the first radio broadcasting network (Parliament of Canada 1932 and 1936). By 1945, private broadcasters began to object strenuously to this subjection to, as the private broadcasters put it, being licensed and controlled by their competitor. During the 1950s, neither the Massey Commission of 1951 nor the Fowler Commission accepted the argument of the private broadcasters (Massey 1951; Fowler 1957).

The Fowler Commission stressed its view of Canadian broadcasting as "a single system" and disagreed that the public and private sectors were separate and competing elements. That commission did grant, however, that there was some confusion between the two roles of the CBC Board of Governors:

1. As regulator of all broadcasting licensees; and
2. As executive officers of the CBC itself.

Therefore, they proposed that the regulatory role be split off from the CBC and given to a new board. The commission made recommendations as to how this split could be made without creating serious problems in the overall policy direction of the broadcasting system.

Without heeding both the warning and the careful recommendations, the Progressive Conservative government of John Diefenbaker drafted a new Broadcasting Act, which Parliament passed into law in 1958 (Parliament of Canada 1958). It established a regulatory body separate from the CBC, called the Board of Broadcast Governors (BBG). This arrangement soon functioned in such a way that the CBC—the public system—was regulated and controlled essentially by its own board, while the private broadcasters were regulated by the BBG. This change occurred just as television was developing on a major scale across Canada and it was not long before the new board approved a private English-language network, called the CTV, or Canadian Television Network, to cover the country. We thus had the spectacle (which we still have) of parallel public and private television broadcasting services functioning independently and in competition with one another. The competition has been made more intense by the licensing of third television stations in some cities, by the introduction of other regional networks, and by the extension of American television networks' reception via cable television.

The overall result has been a Canadian broadcasting system in which the private networks operate very much along the American model, financed totally by advertising and therefore subject to competition for audiences in order to get satisfactory ratings. The public service, the CBC, which has never received adequate funding from Parliament, must also depend on advertising for a significant part of its television revenues. For its radio networks (which carry no direct advertising) and its television networks, the CBC is caught in the same ratings competition for audience gain as the private networks. As the provider of the national broadcasting service, the CBC is under a good deal of political pressure to serve national policy goals. On occasion, the CBC has been subjected to special inquiries to determine if it is performing according to Parliament's or the governing party's view of its mandate (CRTC 1977).

The history of Canadian broadcasting policy has thus been marked since 1928 by what appears to be a dichotomy between thought and action. Each commission and each of the broadcasting acts have asserted the importance of a publicly owned national broadcasting service, modeled on the British one, for the achievement of national broadcasting goals—cultural identity, national unity, and equity of service for all Canadians. But in practical day-to-day decision making and under the pressure of finances and competition, the power and influence of the national service has been eroded by the pressures of the marketplace approach that has directed American broadcasting policy from the beginning (Hindley, Martin, and McNulty 1977).

In the development of radio service, and later of television, the Canadian government has paid a great deal of attention to the provision of service to people living outside the main urban centers. Attention has also been given to ensuring that Canadians were able to receive a broadcasting service in either French or English, and more recently both official languages. Generally, the French-language networks are centered in Montreal, while the English-language networks are centered in Toronto and extend east and west from there. Almost all television stations are affiliated with a national or regional network, while the majority of radio stations are not. Until recently, only the CBC was permitted to establish permanent networks of radio stations (which could be made up of public and private stations).

In March 1981, there were 704 originating broadcasting stations in Canada; a further 1,795 were rebroadcasting stations (CRTC 1981). While some of the originating stations were independent, the vast majority were affiliated with one of the 32 licensed networks. Of the 704 originating stations, there were 390 AM radio stations, 197 FM radio stations, and 117 television stations. Almost all are French- or English-language stations but there are 23 multilingual radio stations, as well as five multilingual television stations. These stations have been licensed by the CRTC to allow for the broadcasting of 40 percent or more of their programming in languages other than French and English. Such stations usually exist in urban centers where there are sufficient numbers of recent immigrants to support the stations either indirectly through advertising or directly by subscriptions and voluntary assistance.

The noncommercial multilingual radio stations are really part of a broader movement toward community radio that has been going on in Canada since the early 1970s. Community radio stations are owned and operated by local associations who are the licensees. The stations depend on voluntary staff, donations, and listeners' subscriptions to the association in order to survive financially. The conditions of their licenses state that they are not permitted to carry direct advertising, but they can have limited sponsorship of programs. The principal idea behind the movement for community radio was to permit people to have access to the airwaves, and to provide an alternative outlet for opinion, information, and entertainment to those outlets operated by commercial radio or by the CBC (McNulty 1979). The same idea of community access was applied to cable television—but not broadcast television—as we will discuss later on.

Almost all the approximately fifty community radio stations are operating in rural areas or in the Northwest Territories. This type of local service in northern settlements is of special value to the indigenous peoples, who can produce live programming in their own dialects and languages. Most northern settlements receive the CBC radio Northern Service which is a mixture of the CBC's AM network programming and programs prepared in the five regional stations in the north, exchanged between them, or locally distributed only. The several native languages together with English usually make up the language mix, which varies from one northern subregion to another. The Northern Service has been provided by the CBC to isolated areas since 1958. During the 1970s, its reception was extended to all northern communities with 500 people or more; this accelerated coverage plan was made possible by special funding approved by the federal government and by the use of satellite technology (CRTC 1974a). The Canadian satellites have also been used to provide a television service to the north, but this has been much less advantageous to northern people because almost none of the programs are produced in the north or with special attention to the interests of northern people (Feaver 1976). The linkage between broadcasting and satellites is more fully discussed in the section on telecommunications.

A major problem for all of Canadian broadcasting, especially television, is the production of Canadian programming—usually called Canadian content, or Cancon. The problem is exacerbated by the proximity of American radio and television stations. In some Canadian cities, usually less than 100 km from the U.S. border, householders with a good rooftop antenna can receive the three major American television networks from stations in the neighboring cities to the south. By the mid-1960s, cable television companies had developed in most of the major Canadian cities; for a small monthly payment of about $5, Canadians could receive three or more U.S. stations with great clarity and reliability.

Today, Canadians live in the most cabled country per capita in the world, with every Canadian living in a small or large city able to receive three or four American commercial stations and the one public broadcasting or educational station with the same clarity that they receive the two or three Canadian ones. The audience has become accustomed to high-budget star system productions punctuated by advertising. People object vociferously at CRTC public hearings and in letters to newspapers against any attempt to control the reception of American television or radio in Canada or to increase Canadian programming content quotas on the national networks.

The problem of the importation of American programming into Canada is a two-headed one. Not only are American programs received in Canadian homes directly over the border through cable television systems or antennae, but the Canadian stations themselves, forced into a competitive battle for audience ratings, buy American programs and put them into their own prime-time scheduling slots. The economics of the matter are simple. Typically, American programs cost Canadian networks about ten to twenty thousand dollars per hour. Making the original program could have cost the American producers around one hundred thousand dollars. The American producers, having recovered most or all of their costs on one American network sale, are then able to sell the programs around the world at nominal cost. Canada is the prime foreign market; program sales and prices for Canadian showings are kept high by competition between the Canadian networks for the most popular programs. A Canadian station producing an hour of Canadian written, acted, and produced programming pays up to ten times as much as what it pays for the American programming. In addition, advertisers in Canada pay more heavily for time during the American programs because they get higher audience ratings. As a result, the Canadian station owners receive 60 percent of their returns from American programming that costs only 40 percent of their outlay. There is no economic incentive to increase Canadian productions or increase Canadian content in the schedule (Babe 1979).

116

In an attempt to counter the flood threatening to drown out Canadian television productions altogether, the BBG in 1959 introduced a regulation requiring a minimum of 55 percent Canadian content on Canadian television stations (Parliament of Canada 1959). This requirement was refined and built upon by the CRTC, the supervisory body that succeeded to the role of the BBG after the new Broadcasting Act of 1968 (Parliament of Canada 1968). The CRTC has emphasized public hearings and public participation in its granting and renewal of licenses and the development of regulatory practices concerning the broadcasting system. This, however, has not served to make Canadian content regulations popular with either the public or the broadcasters themselves. Because Canadian broadcasters were putting their Canadian content in nonprime-time hours, in 1974 the CRTC had to direct that the CBC broadcast Canadian programming at least between the hours of 8 and 9 p.m.

For public broadcasters, particularly since the establishment of the CTV network, the political and social goals of Canadian broadcasting have been assumed to be the business of the public broadcasting network, the CBC. The private stations have felt themselves free to pursue the purpose of their enterprise—profit-making through minimizing all expenses including program expenses. The CRTC's imposition on private broadcasters of the obligation to provide a minimum of Canadian programming is generally regarded as an irksome burden—a situation that has not produced creative and inspired Canadian programming in the past and does not seem likely to do so in the future. There is not much on the horizon to suggest that Canada will move from its position as an importer of television programming into the ranks of the exporters like Great Britain and the United States. As with the film industry, the introduction of pay television is seen by some independent producers as the solution to the problems in Canadian television production.

Cable Television

Cable television systems, as was indicated above, have been intimately connected with the development of broadcasting and broadcasting policy in Canada. They also, however, possess unique characteristics and future application potentials that ally them more closely to telecommunications systems such as the telephone and computer data networks. In large part because of this dual nature of cable systems, and in anticipation of future data and information transmission activities they may engage in, the Canadian Radio-Television Commission was reconstituted in 1976 as the Canadian Radio-television and Telecommunications Commission (Parliament of Canada 1975). The functions of the broadcasting regulatory body (the CRTC) were linked with some responsibilities of the Canadian Transport Commission, which had been responsible for telecommunications regulation—certain telephone companies, the telegraph networks, communications satellites, and so on. The new enlarged commission is still referred to as the CRTC.

Since 1968, cable television systems have been regulated by the CRTC as part of the "single system of Canadian broadcasting" by identifying them under the provisions of the Broadcasting Act as "broadcasting receiving undertakings" (CRTC 1969 and 1971). This interpretation has been questioned from time to time, particularly by the provinces of Canada, which claim that since no over-the-air broadcasting is involved and the wiring is entirely within provinces, cable systems resemble closed-circuit television operations and thus could come within provincial jurisdiction. This suggests another area of tension within Canadian communications regulation and policy—the one between federal and provincial authority. These matters are at present under negotiation as part of the larger issue in Canada of a renegotiation of the constitution, particularly with a revision and elaboration of the respective powers of the provinces and the federal government within confederation (Woodrow et al. 1980). Cable television is expected to be one of the areas that will be allocated to the provincial governments more than has been the case in the past.

The main interest of the CRTC in cable, as "broadcast receiving undertakings," has been to integrate it into the broadcasting industry in such a way as to cause minimal damage to the objectives of Canadian programming. Early attempts were made to forbid a cable system using a microwave link to bring a signal from the U.S. border up to cities that could not receive American signals with one simple mountain-top or other well-placed antenna. Public objection was so strong that the ruling was rescinded and now Canadian cities more than 500 km from the border can receive American stations through cable company leased microwave links. Licensing decisions by the CRTC in the late 1970s attempted to implement an informal rule referred to as the "3 plus 1" restriction on certain cable system operators that would mean they could carry only three American commercial stations, plus one educational or public broadcasting American station on their basic service. Again, public opposition to this suggestion has been vociferous, through interventions to the commission, letters to newspapers, and members of Parliament. It remains to be seen whether it can be implemented when more and more cable systems, especially in urban areas, provide their customers with what is called a converter service—with the addition of a small electronic switcher, the home television set will be able to receive thirty or more channels.

One area where CRTC policy has met with financial success and approval from the broadcasters and little or no objection from a public that either remains oblivious to it or is unconcerned about it is called program substitution. The provisions of this regulation allow television broadcasters to apply to cable operators in their reception area to substitute a program, complete with its Canadian advertising, for the same program broadcast at the same time by an American station that is carried on cable. The net effect of this substitution is to increase the revenues to the Canadian broadcaster, the intent of the CRTC being that those revenues will be funneled into Canadian productions. On the whole, the public stations of the CBC network take little advantage of this regulatory provision. The private stations of the CTV network do so to a greater degree. The ones who need and profit from it most seem to be the independent private television stations that have been added in major Canadian cities in the last five to ten years.

The addition of these independent stations was a matter of some controversy at the time they were licensed by the CRTC. Obviously, they could contribute to an even greater fragmentation of the Canadian audience, which is enormous as it is. The CRTC thinking, however, seemed to be that new creative efforts and additional competition might prod Canadian programming production into a more creative and imaginative set of ventures than it had demonstrated itself willing to undertake under just the parallel system of private and public networks that existed at the time. There is some evidence to indicate that, at least in the area of regional and local programming about the concerns of the metropolitan and surrounding areas served by the new stations, the CRTC policy has had some beneficial effect.

Because of its strong emphasis on integrating cable television into the broadcasting system, the CRTC has paid relatively little attention to the rate structure of the cable-television industry. While all fees charged to subscribers have to be authorized by the commission, and even though it has been argued that cable television is a natural monopoly like the telephone system, the method of rate regulation used by the CRTC has been rather ill defined (Babe 1975). Rate of return regulation, such as is used for public utilities and common carriers in North America generally, is not used by the CRTC to control or review rate increases by cable-television operators. So long as the cable-television service provided was a simple one of supplementing off-air reception of television signals, a simple form of rate regulation could be maintained, on some established criteria of service quality. However, as the services offered become more complex and as more optional services are made available, the simple rate structure will disappear; another method of rate regulation will become essential if the new services are provided only through the cable-television monopoly service.

One other policy that the CRTC has pursued with cable television has to do with the community channel. In the early 1970s, the commission began to encourage cable-television operators to set aside one television channel for the community in which each cable-television system existed. A community channel is now required by regulation of all cable-television licensees.

119

The idea behind the community channel was that this would be a service provided by the licensees, for which they would not charge subscribers directly, and the community-channel programming produced would be the cable-television industry's contribution to Canadian program production (CRTC 1974b). The opportunity for people in the area to appear in community programs, or to be involved in producing programs, was and remains a very important feature of the community channel. However, the success in involving local people in the community channel tends to vary widely from one area to another, depending on the nature of the "community" itself and on the efforts made by the operator or program staff. Typically, the community channel obtains a very small percentage of the potential audience, though audience size is not considered by the CRTC to be a criterion of success for the channel. The difficulty of attracting large audiences to a little-watched channel can be frustrating for the volunteer programmers, especially when they feel they have an important message to get across to local people. Clearly, access to a television channel (one of many available) is not in itself a sufficient condition for people to be able to use the airwaves effectively; an audience is essential too.

In addition to their controversial role in fragmenting the Canadian audience for the existing Canadian television system, the larger cable companies have been pressing for permission to exploit their role as closed-circuit television systems by selling movies and other television materials on either a subscription or fee-per-item basis. These types of services are usually referred to as pay television. Cable-system operators wish to participate in one or more Canadian distribution networks of feature films, documentaries, sports events, and informational programs by making these available to the subscribers on their particular system on one or more of the many channels becoming available under the new extended services. As mentioned earlier, many Canadian cable systems are upgrading their capacities to thirty and more channels which individual subscribers would be able to receive on their existing television sets with the addition of the converter and by payment of more subscriber fees. The development of pay television entertainment services in the United States, distributed mostly via satellite and cable television, has been watched with envy by Canadian cable operators. Some Canadian companies have become involved in American pay television through the acquisition of cable franchises in the United States; this experience has further reinforced their belief that pay television would be profitable in Canada.

In the search for profit-making ventures to fill these channels, cable companies have for some time been looking into the possibilities of programming services such as the one just described, as well as data transmitting systems, fire and burglar alarm services, teleshopping, and videotex services of various kinds. Until 1979, the CRTC had declined the application of the cable systems to provide pay-television services to private homes on the grounds that this would probably contribute to further fragmentation of Canadian audiences and do little to increase Canadian production in either the film or the television industries. In this stance, the commission had the support of the private broadcasters and the CBC, although some wavering occurred over time. The problems of the Canadian film industry, which the cable systems indicated they could alleviate, have come increasingly to the fore as one rationale for Canadian pay television. In 1980, the question of pay television (whether by cable television, satellite, over-air, or some combination of these means) was reexamined by the CRTC in the context of improving all television services to rural and remote areas of the country.

Following a series of hearings in 1980, the CRTC's Committee on Extension of Service to Northern and Remote Communities submitted a report which recommended, among other things, that there be no structural or institutional link made between pay television and services to isolated communities. The Therrien Committee urged that priority be given to the latter before any further CRTC hearings were held on pay television (Therrien 1980); unfortunately, the two subjects remain entangled in the minds of many people, including broadcasters, probably because both will use satellite distribution and will charge some type of direct fee to receiving households. Leaving aside the satellite-television linkage (discussed toward the end of the following section), the connections between pay television, cable television, and satellite will be complex and have been the subject of much policy discussion in Canada.

In April 1981, the CRTC announced it would hold hearings to consider which pay television services might be offered to Canadians so as to achieve the dual objectives of minimal damage to over-air broadcasting and opportunities for the development of a Canadian program production industry (really a combination of existing and future video and film production companies). Applications for national, regional, and special programming pay television licenses were heard in October 1981. Decisions on the licenses were not expected until spring 1982, and services could be available for reception by 1983. The impact of these services on the goals established by the CRTC may not be assessable until 1985 or later.

Although much of their effort has been expended on getting approval for pay television, cable companies would also like to be able to offer informational computer-mediated services to their subscribers; in this field, though, they may have to compete with the telephone systems (Babe 1975). Because the telephone networks, with their intricate switching capability, seem to offer greater suitability for the tasks required in offering an interactive information service to Canadian households, they are in a strong position to enter this field ahead of cable television operators. A discussion of interactive services is more appropriately dealt with in the following section.

Telecommunications

For most Canadians, telephone service is provided by one of sixteen major private companies or government-owned telephone companies or corporations. Of about eight hundred systems in Canada, nearly seven hundred are small rural cooperatives in Saskatchewan. The telephone industry has a complex system of mixed public and private ownership, with the two largest entities being Bell Telephone (serving most of Ontario and Quebec) and British Columbia Telephone (serving the western province of British Columbia). The three largest public companies operate in the three prairie provinces, the area where distances between subscribers are great and initial costs of the distribution network hardware were high. Since its beginning in the 1840s, the telegraph industry in Canada has been under federal government control. Regulation of telegraph and telephone rates and service was deemed necessary for protection of the public interest because of the companies' operation of natural monopolies—that is, only one system can provide service in any one area.

This regulation of rates can occur either at the provincial level or at the federal level, depending on historical and jurisdictional circumstances (English 1973). The major telephone systems on the prairies are owned and controlled by the individual province concerned. The two large privately owned systems mentioned previously, Bell and B.C. Tel, are both regulated federally. To carry on the pattern of public-private symmetry observed in Canadian broadcasting, transnational telegraph (and more recently, data communications) services are provided by joint efforts of a public agency, Canadian National, and the privately owned Canadian Pacific, both of which are railway companies with telecommunications subsidiaries.

Problems of system interconnection, ensuring compatible equipment between provinces and different telephone companies, have been solved by nongovernmental means; a voluntary organization called the Trans-Canada Telephone System (TCTS) is an arrangement among ten major common carriers across the continent. Through agreements with the smaller telephone companies, TCTS can provide telephone links from coast to coast and from the southern border to the far north. The telephone companies also provide most of the transmission links for the carriage of television signals; they provide much of the cross-country distribution network for the CBC and CTV television networks.

While telephone and telegraph companies are regulated by Canadian authorities, and most companies are owned and controlled by Canadians, the equipment used throughout most of the systems may be manufactured in Canada or elsewhere. The manufacturing capability as well as the ability to innovate from within the telephone industry is an important policy consideration.

The selection of the "chosen instrument" company or companies to produce needed technological innovation and manufacture equipment has occurred in several European countries, either through state monopolies or through agreements between the governments and multinational corporations based there. In Canada, however, the designation as a chosen instrument of Northern Telecom, a manufacturing company associated with the Bell Telephone system and its research arm Bell Northern Research, is not generally accepted. There are those who argue that Bell should have an arm's length relationship to Northern Telecom and should be required to purchase telephone equipment from whatever company can supply it cheapest. This dispute must be resolved as part of the overall effort of Canada's government to develop a coherent policy toward research and development of high technology in Canada.

The dispute also relates to the "foreign attachments" issue of whether or not manufacturers of telephone attachments (including telephone sets and computer terminals) can be allowed to sell to consumers in competition against the telephone companies themselves. Until recently, the telephone companies insisted that all attachments had to be bought or leased from them only. This corporate policy may have to be dropped if the regulatory authorities decide it is in the public interest to have competition in the attachments business.

While there is a strong industrial strategy argument to be made in favor of vertical integration, within private telephone companies it has presented an effective obstacle to government regulation of service rates. It is exceedingly hard for the regulating agencies to determine whether a rate increase is fair to the public and needed by the company unless it has the means and authority to check whether charges made by the equipment supplying companies, also part of the telephone conglomerate, are themselves fair and reasonable, or simply a vehicle for hiding excessive profits. Regulating the rates and level of service of Canadian telephone companies is further complicated by their being owned and controlled by larger companies. The outstanding example of this is the situation of B.C. Tel (federally regulated) and Quebec Tel (provincially regulated) which are both controlled through majority share ownership by General Telephone and Electronics International of New York.

The basis for governmental control over a telephone company in Canada is much the same as in the United States: regulation as a public utility with a view to ensuring that "just and reasonable" rates are charged to customers. At the federal level, the CRTC is responsible for regulating all broadcasting and for the rates of the federally regulated carriers including Telesat Canada, the satellite corporation. The CRTC was responsible only for broadcasting until April 1976. At that time, it was given additional responsibilities for telecommunications by the transfer of authority over telephone and other common carrier rates from the

Canadian Transport Commission. However, having broadcasting and common carrier regulation within one body does not mean there is an overall telecommunications policy at the federal level. Further legislative changes are needed, in the form of a telecommunications act, to provide unified policy framework.

Attempts were made by the federal minister of communications to develop a national communication policy but these efforts were rejected by the provinces for various reasons (Canada Minister of Communications 1973a). Aside from whatever legislative changes may occur at the federal level, and however the authority for regulation may become divided between the federal and provincial levels, major questions have to be answered soon in Canada about the direction in which new and emerging communications technologies are developed. The increasing urgency for these directions in the late 1970s led to proposals for a royal commission of inquiry and to other ideas for examining alternatives in a public forum. Because an inquiry conducted by a royal commission or similar body could take up to two years to complete, the then minister of communications preferred to choose a different method of seeking recommendations for action.

In November 1978, the Honorable Jeanne Sauve appointed the Consultative Committee on the Implications of Telecommunications for Canadian Sovereignty, since known as the Clyne Committee. The Commitee was asked:

1. To produce specific recommendations on a strategy to restructure the Canadian telecommunications system to contribute more effectively to the safeguarding of Canada's sovereignty.
2. To make recommendations on the future of the Canadian telecommunications system in relation to new technologies and the need for Canadian software and hardware resources to meet foreign competition, with particular reference to the role of broadcasting in contributing to the preservation of the sovereignty of Canada, including:

   a. The best use of communications satellites to the greatest advantage of Canada.
   b. The status of the cable companies in relation to broadcasting and to the common carriers in the provision of new services.
   c. The importation of foreign programming.
   d. The framework and timing for the introduction of pay television nationally.

The committee took as its definition of sovereignty "the ability of Canadians (both in government and in the private sector) to exercise control over the . . . direction of economic, social, cultural, and political change." Like many other groups that have studied one or the other aspects of telecommunications or broadcasting in Canada, the committee saw the parallels for Canada between the nineteenth-century development of railway networks and the twentieth-century development of communications networks in ensuring the ultimate prosperity and sovereignty of Canada. In these ideas, there is for Canadians a strong awareness of the economic strength of the American marketplace and its influence on the much smaller Canadian market. For this reason, the Clyne Committee followed along a familiar path when it said:

> In approaching telecommunications we should realize that its importance demands we view it in a special way. Telecommunications, as the foundation of the future society, cannot always be left to the vagaries of the market; principles that we might care to assert in other fields, such as totally free competition, may not be applicable in this crucial sphere. We must look at it freshly, without preconceived ideas. (Clyne 1979)

Thus, it is generally assumed as a cornerstone of telecommunications policy that some government direction is required. Where the arguments arise within Canada is on the extent to which government should interfere with commercial or corporate decision making about the exploitation of technical innovations to meet future consumer demands. The Clyne Committee's recommendations on the action needed by the federal government were favorably or unfavorably received by the various communications industries according to how they might be affected by the proposed actions. Because the Committee's report was published in March 1979, only two months before the change of government from Liberal to Progressive Conservative, no action resulted directly from its work. In February 1980, the Liberal Party again returned to power.

One of the topics the Clyne Committee attempted to deal with was what it called "informatics," or computer communications. The advancement of industrialized countries toward computerization and the information economy has been widely predicted since the early 1970s, and many of them have developed industrial strategies to respond to the information age. In Canada, the initial awareness of the potential benefits and dangers of computer communications came through the work of a federal government task force known as the Telecommission, which was established within the newly formed Department of Communications in 1969. The work of the Telecommission was focused on the current state and future prospects of telecommunications in Canada and its results were published in a series of over forty studies and in a summary book called *Instant World* (Telecommission 1971).

Other studies on computer communications and on the impact of computers on the privacy of individuals and institutions followed. The federal government issued a Green Paper on computer communications in 1973 but no formal policy has been announced since then (Canada

Minister of Communications 1973b). Despite the head start which Canada had, in the early 1970s, in considering the consequences and policy alternatives facing the country in the information society of the future, this lead has not been fully exploited by federal or provincial governments to establish specific policies that would guide industrial and commercial developments related to computerization although much discussion has occurred (see, for example, Science Council of Canada 1979).

The development of videotex technologies has increased the complexity of the decisions that have to be made. Researchers at the Communications Research Centre of the federal Department of Communications developed a prototype interactive information technology system known as Telidon (Madden 1979). Since 1978, the federal Department of Communications has promoted the idea that there would be considerable advantage for Canada if this system were to be adopted by other countries, and if its standards were to be used as international standards for such systems. It has been argued that the economic advantages in terms of manufacturing and sales of electronic equipment would give a major boost to Canada's industrial base. It would also mean that the system used in Canada to provide information would be designed to respond to domestic conditions and could be set up to contain a great deal of Canadian software and Canadian information (Godfrey and Parkhill 1980). However, the adoption of technical standards compatible with the Telidon software does not ensure a new marketplace for Canadian videotex equipment. Nor does the existence of Canadian equipment connected to telecommunications networks (or cable television systems) provide any funding or support for the creation of Canadian data banks or Canadian information resources to be made available through a videotex system—despite some writers' enthusiasm for a future information marketplace that is to provide opportunities for new entrepreneurs (Thompson 1979).

Concerns about Canadians being able to exercise control over Canadian information are a broader problem than simply that of Telidon. Transborder data flow is, for Canada, a major problem with business data because data banks maintained by parent companies of Canadian industry tend to be located outside the country, usually in the United States (Cundiff and Reid 1979). Access to information about Canadian industry and business transactions can become a policy issue when computer networks are controlled from outside the country. Beyond this point of principle, major employment and manufacturing opportunities for Canadians may be lost if data banks and computer facilities of all kinds are not maintained within the country (Serafini and Andrieu 1981).

The federal government itself is a major user of data banks for its own purposes and public concern about these is focused on the protection of individual privacy and the discovery of what kinds of information about an individual one or more government departments may have. The

126

accuracy of the information is also of concern to individuals whose employment or financial credit rating is hurt by inaccurate or outdated information about them. To respond to these concerns, the federal government in 1977 introduced into Parliament the Human Rights Act, which is designed to protect the rights of individuals named in federal government data banks (Parliament of Canada 1977). In 1978, the first privacy ombudsman was appointed. Similar laws exist in several provinces. A freedom of information bill that would extend the individual's access to information (with specific exceptions for national security) to all records that are under the control of the federal government—not just stored in data banks—was introduced into Parliament by the Progressive Conservative government in October 1979 but was not passed into law before the government fell.

In the field of satellite communications systems, Canada has been a pioneer, particularly to provide services in the north where terrestrial radio communication is very difficult because of climate and atmospheric conditions. In 1962, Canada launched a scientific satellite, ALOUETTE I, followed by ALOUETTE II in 1965. In 1964, Canada joined INTELSAT and thus collaborated in the launching of Early Bird, the European–North American experiment. Later on, Canada was also involved with the United States in a series of experimental satellites known as the ISIS Series, studying the ionosphere.

Until 1969, Canadian satellite development was in the hands of the Canadian Overseas Telecommunications Corporation (COTC), a federal crown corporation responsible for coordinating Canada's external communications with international agencies. After some internal discussion in the mid-1960s, a White Paper on satellite policy was issued by the federal government under the auspices of the minister of industry (Drury 1968). Subsequently, an Act of Parliament formed Telesat Canada with an exclusive mandate to operate commercial satellite telecommunications within Canada (Parliament of Canada 1969). Its first satellite was launched in 1972. Telesat Canada was financed by an equity share issue of which 50 percent is owned by the government and 50 percent by the major telecommunications carriers. In 1981, Telesat had four geosynchronous communications satellites, located at fixed points in space over the equator. They have been used for the carriage of telephone and data communications traffic as well as for color television and radio broadcasting signals. Three satellites are all of the type known as ANIK A, with twelve transponders each, while a fourth known as ANIK B is a hybrid with capacity to operate in both the 6/4 GHz and 14/12 GHz bands. Another series of satellites begins operation in 1982 to replace the fading A series satellites and to provide more 14/12 GHz capacity (Telesat Canada 1980).

In seeking to ensure that all Canadians have equal access opportunities to communications services, it must be remembered that approximately six million people, or about one-quarter of Canada's population, live in rural areas and remote settlements. For reasons of social equity, both federal and provincial governments have long favored the improvement of communications services (principally broadcasting and telephone) for people outside the urban centers. There is clear recognition that the differential costs of providing service between urban and rural areas can only be overcome if special technical and financial resources are used in a concerted effort to extend service beyond the normal economic limits. Because of its capability to provide linkages over long distances and to overcome poor atmospheric conditions, the communications satellite has been perceived as the answer to the communications problems of northern Canada. Before the first ANIK satellite was launched in 1972, it was claimed that not only would signals be sent between southern Canada and the north, but also there could be better communications between northern settlements.

The use of satellite linkages to provide broadcasting services to rural and remote areas has been pioneered in Canada through the work of the federal Department of Communications, Telesat Canada, and the Canadian Broadcasting Corporation (CBC). Since 1972, a number of small communities in northern Canada, many of them inhabited by indigenous peoples, have been provided with television reception through the ANIK satellite and the installation of ground stations linked to low-power rebroadcasters in the communities concerned. Clearly, the use of the satellite to provide high quality television signals for local distribution is vastly superior to the previously available method of taped television program packages. The distribution facility works well, although it is costly for the numbers served compared to the cost of the conventional television transmitter used to reach large populations in a southern city. The economic cost of this service, however, was expected by the federal government to be balanced against the social benefits of reducing the isolation of people in the north from the mainstream of Canadian life.

Due to the prohibitive costs involved, the capability for television transmission from the north to the south or between places in the north has been almost nil. The result of this extension of broadcasting service has, thus, been limited to better quality and more immediate reception of television programs from outside the north; it has not allowed the people in the north to respond effectively to what they receive. Nor has the satellite linkage so far allowed people in the south—almost all of Canada's population—to become more familiar with what the north and its people are like. Because of limitations in its production budget, the CBC has been able to do very little programming for its Northern Television Service, especially for or about the north; the result is that almost all the programming is either from southern Canada or from foreign sources, mostly American. According to many spokesmen for the indigenous people, the effect of this television content on them, especially their children, has been extremely detrimental. The two aspects most frequently cited are the effect on children's behavior and the effect on community life and involvement caused by excessive hours of television watching.

Although communications satellites are not new in Canada, their widespread use for the provision of broadcasting-type services is a new idea. Until the fall of 1979, the ANIK satellites of Telesat Canada had been used in only a limited way for the distribution of television and radio signals. Except for the provision of CBC signals to a number of isolated northern communities via a local rebroadcaster, the satellite linkages have been used primarily by the CBC for network purposes of sending programs to the different time zones across the country. Occasionally, several of the private broadcasting television networks have used satellite distribution, but they generally rely on microwaves for network transmission. The ground reception of signals from the satellites has been by Telesat-owned and more recently broadcaster-owned earth station equipment.

However, since about 1978, with the lower priced earth stations becoming available in North America for purchase, numerous communities in the northern half of Canada have acquired earth stations and are illegally receiving signals off American domestic satellites that carry about thirty television signals, including pay-television services. The illegality has mainly to do with the reception of signals from a foreign satellite, in violation of the INTELSAT Agreement as well as an agreement in the form of an exchange of letters between Canada and the United States. Because there has been no television network on the Canadian satellites other than CBC's, it is apparently irresistible for the northerners to turn to other available satellites and receive a wider choice of television programs. While the problem of illegal reception of American satellite-carried signals is confined to small northern communities, it could remain a minor headache for the federal government. However, earth stations may soon be acquired by southerners and there remains a lack of Canadian material via satellite from which to choose for reception.

In the fall of 1979, the federal Department of Communications began to experiment with the provision of small earth stations to a few households and small cable-television systems in northern Ontario to provide reception of CBC television and of the Ontario educational television network known as TV Ontario. Other experiments of this type are being considered in other provinces. However, the choice of television signals on the Canadian satellites remains limited, and in order to make this type of reception attractive, there are now plans to provide a package of television signals through the ANIK satellites to be made available to all Canadians within reach of an earth-station hook-up (probably via the local cable-television system). In order to make this package attractive to viewers—and to the cable television operators—

consideration is being given to proposals for carriage of Canadian pay-television services that would consist of original programming previously unseen by viewers.

This idea of a satellite package was followed by the Therrien Committee in 1980 when it recommended action to improve the choice of television and radio service for Canadians in northern and remote communities. In that year, the CRTC heard applications from a number of companies anxious to provide such services and, in April 1981, a network license was issued to Canadian Satellite Communications, Inc. (CANCOM) to provide up to four television and six radio signals to unserved communities for a fee per household of $4 per month. In late 1981, the CRTC was still proceeding with applications for local redistribution of the satellite package. It remains to be seen if the illegal earth stations will become legalized through this elaborate process or will remain outside the present law. The situation is further confused by the imminent licensing of pay television services; it is not clear how the CANCOM "package" and pay television might be offered jointly or whether they must be kept separate. Also, the Canadian government is very aware of the development of direct broadcast satellite (DBS) technology—indeed its own research staff is involved in research and design for Canadian satellites of this type (Communications Canada 1980). Future usage of this technology by American communications corporations to distribute services of all kinds throughout North America is a prospect of great concern to Canadian policymakers and communications industries.

Conclusion

Inevitably, discussion of Canadian communication policy in virtually every field involves coming face to face with the geographical proximity of the American giant. In this respect, Canada seems only to have been several decades ahead of other countries in the world that are today experiencing similar problems of cultural and economic sovereignty against well-financed and effectively organized multinational corporations, whether it be in filmmaking, publishing, or television programming. Now, coupled with the instantaneous transmission capabilities of international satellites (especially direct-broadcast satellites), the geographical proximity that Canada has experienced will be no different from that of many other countries of the world.

Of course, Canada has also had internal policy problems in communications. Major ones have been the tensions between urban and rural areas, between Quebec and Ottawa, and between the center for English Canada focused in the densely populated Toronto metropolitan area versus the periphery (including virtually all the other English-speaking provinces of the country). These types of internal stresses seem common to many countries, but in Canada they have been compounded by, and are therefore related to, the problems created by American proximity and domination.

The battle for survival, particularly of the English television-program industry, has demanded a marshalling of economic resources into one center in the hope of building up a sufficient core of expertise, experience, and financial backing to enable Toronto to produce programming on a level competitive with that on the American networks. Unfortunately, this has been done at the expense of the regional television stations in the west and east of the country, and not without considerable protest and bitterness. Indeed much of the public outcry against the attempted policy of the CRTC has been that the periphery, the other provinces, do not want their rights to watch American programming interfered with if all that is going to be offered in substitution is what they see as Toronto programming.

Those who have been concerned with the analysis of Canadian broadcasting policy over the past decade have said from time to time, "Canada provides a great example for the rest of the world—we are a great case study of what *not* to do!" That is said somewhat facetiously but then somewhat more seriously. The nagging question presented by an analysis of the history of Canadian broadcasting policy is whether, in the face of such odds, it would have been possible to do anything different. With regard to data-communications systems, the use of satellite communications, and the interactive information services of the future, Canada still has some opportunities to determine policies appropriate to the country and its people. Those opportunities will be whittled away if there is a continuing absence of social and political will to achieve cooperation and support of all sectors of society—the regional, economic, and ethnic groups that make up contemporary Canada.

References

Aird, Sir John, chr.
1929   *Report of the Royal Commission on Radio Broadcasting*. Ottawa: King's Printer.

Annan, Lord, chr.
1977   *Report of the Committee on the Future of Broadcasting*. Cmnd. 6753 (March). London: Her Majesty's Stationery Office.

Babe, Robert E.
1975   *Cable Television and Telecommunications in Canada: An Economic Analysis*. East Lansing, MI: Michigan State University.

1979   *Canadian Television Broadcasting Structure, Performance and Regulation*. Economic Council of Canada Study. Ottawa: Supply and Services Canada.

Canada Minister of Communications
1973*a*   *Proposals for Communications Policy for Canada: A Position Paper of the Government of Canada*. Ottawa: Information Canada.

1973*b*   *Computer/Communications Policy: A Position Statement by the Government of Canada*. Ottawa: Information Canada.

Clyne, J.V., chr.
1979   *Telecommunications and Canada*. Report of the Consultative Committee on the Implications of Telecommunications for Canadian Sovereignty. Ottawa: Communications Canada, Supply and Services Canada.

Communications Canada
1980   *The Canadian Space Program: Five-Year Plan (80/81–84/85)*. Discussion Paper Serial no. DOC -6-79 DP. Ottawa: Supply and Services Canada.

Crean, S.M.
1976   *Who's Afraid of Canadian Culture?* Don Mills, Ontario: General Publishing.

CRTC (Canadian Radio-television and Telecommunications Commission, formerly Canadian Radio-Television Commission)
1969   *Annual Report 1968-69*. Ottawa: Queen's Printer.

1971   *Canadian Broadcasting: 'A Single System'*. Policy Statement of 16 July. Ottawa.

1974*a*   *Annual Report 1973-74*. Ottawa: Information Canada.

1974*b*   *A Resource for the Active Community*. Ottawa: Information Canada.

1977   *Report of the Committee of Inquiry into the National Broadcasting Service*. Ottawa.

1981   *Annual Report 1980-81*. Ottawa: Supply and Services Canada.

Cundiff, W.E., and Reid, Mado, eds.
1979   *Issues in Canadian/U.S. Transborder Computer Data Flows*. Montreal: Institute for Research on Public Policy.

Davey, Senator Keith, chr.
1970   *Report of the Special Senate Committee on Mass Media*, 3 vols. Ottawa: Information Canada.

Dominion Law Review
1932   "Re Regulation and Control of Radio Communication," vol. 2.

Drury, Honorable C. M., Minister of Industry
1968   *White Paper on a Domestic Satellite Communication System for Canada*. Ottawa: Queen's Printer.

English, H. Edward, ed.
1973   *Telecommunications for Canada: An Interface of Business and Government*. Toronto: Methuen.

Feaver, P. Charles
1976   "The Politics of the Introduction of Television to the Canadian North: A Study of the Conflict between National Policies and Needs of Native People in the North." Master's Research Essay, Institute of Canadian Studies, Carleton University.

Fowler, Robert M., chr.
1957   *Report of the Royal Commission on Broadcasting*. Ottawa: Queen's Printer.

1965   *Report of the Committee on Broadcasting*. Ottawa: Queen's Printer.

Godfrey, David and Parkhill, Douglas, eds.
1980   *Gutenberg Two: The New Electronics and Social Change.*
Toronto: Press Porcepic Ltd.

Hindley, M. Patricia; Martin, Gail M.; and McNulty, Jean
1977   *The Tangled Net: Basic Issues in Canadian Communications.*
Vancouver: J.J. Douglas.

Kent, Tom, chr.
1981   *Report of the Royal Commission on Newspapers.* Ottawa: Supply
and Services Canada.

Kesterton, W.H.
1967   *A History of Journalism in Canada.* Carleton Library Series.
Toronto: McClelland and Stewart.

Litvak, Isaiah, and Maule, Christopher.
1975   *Cultural Sovereignty: The* Time *and* Reader's Digest *Case in
Canada.* New York: Praeger.

Madden, John C.
1979   *Videotex in Canada.* Ottawa: Communications Canada, Supply
and Services Canada.

Massey, Vincent, chr.
1951   *Report of the Royal Commission on the National Development in
the Arts, Letters and Sciences.* Ottawa: King's Printer.

McNulty, Jean
1979   *Other Voices in Broadcasting: The Evolution of New Forms of
Local Programming in Canada.* Research Report funded and
published by Communications Canada. Ottawa: Information
Services.

Parliament of Canada
1932   Canadian Radio Broadcasting Act, c. 51.

1936   Canada Broadcasting Act, c. 24.

1958   Broadcasting Act, c. 22.

1959   " 'Radio (TV) Broadcasting Regulation,' " *Canada Gazette Part II*,
December 9, SOR/59-456.

1968   Broadcasting Act, 1967–68, c. 25.

134

| 1969 | Telesat Canada Act, 1968–69, c. 51. |

| 1975 | Canadian Radio-television and Telecommunications Act, 1974–75, c. 49. |

| 1977 | Canadian Human Rights Act, 1976–77, c. 32. |

Peers, Frank W.
1969   *The Politics of Canadian Broadcasting, 1920-1951.* Toronto: University of Toronto Press.

1979   *The Public Eye: Television and the Politics of Canadian Broadcasting 1952-1968.* Toronto: University of Toronto Press.

Quebec Minister of Communications
1973   *Quebec, Master Craftsman of Its Own Communications Policy.* A statement presented by the minister of communications at the Federal-Provincial Conference of Communications Ministers in Ottawa, November.

Rohmer, Richard, chr.
1972   *Canadian Publishers and Canadian Publishing.* Report of the Ontario Royal Commission on Book Publishing. Toronto: Queen's Printer for Ontario.

Rutherford, Paul
1977   *The Making of the Canadian Media.* Toronto: McGraw-Hill Ryerson.

Science Council of Canada
1979   *A Scenario for the Implementation of Interactive Computer-Communications Systems in the Home.* Position Paper of the Science Council Committee on Communications and Computers. Ottawa: Supply and Services Canada.

Serafini, Shirley, and Andrieu, Michel
1981   *The Information Revolution and Its Implications for Canada.* Ottawa: Communications Canada, Supply and Services Canada.

Statistics Canada
1976   *Census of Canada 1971,* Cat. 92-723, 92-727. Ottawa: Supply and Services Canada.

1979   *Census of Canada 1976,* Cat. 92-821, 92-823. Ottawa: Supply and Services Canada.

135

1981   *Canada Year Book 1980–81*. Ottawa: Supply and Services Canada.

1982   "Interim Population Count," *Census of Canada 1981*. Ottawa: Supply and Services Canada.

Stewart, Walter, ed.
1980   *Canadian Newspapers: The Inside Story*. Edmonton, Alberta: Hurtig Publishers.

Telecommission
1971   *Instant World: A Report on Telecommunications in Canada*. Ottawa: Information Canada.

Telesat Canada
1980   *Annual Report 1979*. Ottawa: Telesat Canada.

Therrien, Real, chr.
1980   *The 1980s: A Decade of Diversity—Broadcasting, Satellites, and Pay-TV*. Report of the Committee on Extension of Service to Northern and Remote Communities. Ottawa: Supply and Services Canada.

Thompson, Gordon B.
1979   *Memo from Mercury: Information Technology Is Different*. Montreal: Institute for Research on Public Policy.

Weir, E. Austin
1965   *The Struggle for National Broadcasting in Canada*. Toronto: McClelland and Stewart.

Woodrow, R. Brian et al.
1980   *Conflict over Communications Policy: A Study of Federal-Provincial Relations and Public Policy*. Montreal: C.D. Howe Institute.

5

Communication Policy in Sweden: An Experiment in State Intervention

Göran Hedebro

Göran Hedebro writes that in few other Western countries has the state involved itself in media politics as in Sweden. The purpose of state intervention is to guarantee a diversified flow of information that will enable an informed citizenry to participate in decision making in society. "The right to communicate" is a Swedish concept that has gained attention in the debate on a new world information order. The basic components of such a concept are that the channels of communication must be accessible to all citizens, who must have the competence to produce and disseminate information through these channels. Sweden is a country with strong libertarian values that have had to be adapted to economic and structural considerations. The ideals of freedom of the press and of the competition of ideas have had to be modified because of a basic desire to preserve a diversified communication structure. A high living standard with a relatively even distribution of wealth; a political climate where negotiations have normally been carried out in an atmosphere of willingness to compromise; and the interconnection between political groups and grass-roots organizations make Sweden a unique society in the Western world. State intervention in the press and broadcasting attempts to preserve the unique characteristics of Swedish society, but the effects of the resulting centralized bureaucratic structure can already be seen in bland programming. In Hedebro's view, this is a tendency to be guarded against.

Like many other developed countries, Sweden has witnessed a great number of changes in the communication field during recent decades. There is now more information being circulated, a tendency that Sweden shares with most other industrialized countries. Radio and television have increased their hours of transmission, and new media have expanded the possibilities of storing and distributing information many times over. Established media like the print media have encountered

137

severe economic difficulties. Monopolization and concentration of the press is a reality in Sweden as it is in many other countries.

At the same time, Sweden is experiencing another trend. Authorities in both the public and the private sectors are intensifying their uses of information as a means of influencing people's views, values, and behavior. In private enterprise, more and more companies have organized information departments to handle their contacts with the mass media and the public. Government authorities also have increased the flow of decrees and messages about the obligations of citizens through special legislation concerning civic information. There is a great risk and a related concern that state and local governments will acquire unreasonable control and influence over the individual citizen. Officially, the government bodies are not allowed to exert such influence, in the sense that they are allowed to execute only what has been decided by democratic institutions like Parliament and local assemblies. But there is a very thin line between passing out neutral information and exercising undue influence. To a greater extent than previously, the state is intervening in the communication sector in Swedish society. Most mass media areas today enjoy some form of state support, and some are more elaborate than others. In few other Western countries has the state involved itself in media politics to the extent it has in Sweden; however, Sweden has not developed a clear overall policy in this field. Officially, the state has intervened in order to guarantee a diversified flow of information, and even if there have been no cases in which the state has directly intervened in the content of what is being disseminated, the activities and involvement of the state have caused great concern about the freedom of expression. The broadcasting media are an exception. They have to follow certain agreements with the state that concern program contents.

The state has also initiated a number of government commissions to study media problems from different angles, especially what the introduction of new media may mean to society. At present, several commissions are at work on the following problems:

- Freedom of expression
- Mass media legislation
- Tendencies toward concentration in the newspaper industry
- Videograms

Taken together, these trends show that communication issues are given greater prominence than ever before, and that above all, the new technologies will make it necessary to arrive at more explicit communication policies than have existed up to now. Sweden in many ways provides an interesting case of how a country with strong libertarian roots in the communication field has had to adapt to a reality that has made those roots too idealistic and impractical because of economic and structural considerations. The ideals of freedom of the press and the

138

competition of ideas have had to bow to economic considerations, including how to keep up a diversified communication structure at all. In the following sections, the organization of areas of Swedish communication is described and discussed. The issue of state support is of particular relevance to each medium described, as is the problem of journalistic practices.

For the foreign reader to better understand the policies described, a few basic facts about Sweden should be kept in mind. According to recently published statistics (World Bank 1978), Sweden maintains its place as one of the top countries according to living standard, measured as GNP per capita. This wealth is fairly evenly distributed among citizens of the country, at least when compared with many other Western countries. The high living standard that most Swedes—certainly not all—enjoy is a result of such factors as great natural resources in a relatively large country (450,000 square kilometers—about the size of California); a neutral stance during two world wars; a long rule by a Social Democratic regime geared to social reforms; a small homogeneous population (around eight million) with no problems of population increase. Another important characteristic that has contributed to a relatively conflict-free social development is the political climate, where negotiations and various political actions have been carried out in an atmosphere of willingness to compromise and cooperate. Over the years, most controversial issues have been solved in this spirit, which has given Sweden a certain reputation, particularly in the labor market, where "the Swedish model" has attracted a lot of attention. Both the labor unions and the employers' associations have accepted policy by compromise. In the 1950s and 1960s leaders from the two major organizations in the labor market toured different countries to explain the meaning and functioning of the Swedish model.

Many observers drew the conclusion that Sweden was becoming a classless society where clashes between different groups in society could be solved by negotiations. But such a conclusion was much too hastily drawn, as witnessed by the large strike in 1969 in the mines in the north of Sweden; the lockout in 1980 involving one million people was the biggest conflict in the Swedish labor market since 1909. Many observers express the opinion that the Swedish model seems to work only if the economy of the country is expanding. When it is not, the distribution of the available "pieces of pie" becomes much more controversial, and conflicts between the working class and the capital owners are characterized by tougher and more confrontational policies than before. Sweden has now reached this stage. The last decade saw many problems in the Swedish economy, and the 1980s do not look more promising. It is not difficult to foresee many conflicts and clashes between different interests in Swedish society, even if the willingness to arrive at solutions by discussion is still there. The question is whether this willingness is enough.

One factor that over the years has helped to create a harmonious political climate is that political groups in Sweden have always had strong connections with popular organizations at the grass-roots level such as religious, temperance, and adult education movements. These popular movements are often not divided by political views, but focus on certain specific topics, and people with different political sympathies work together. This trait is unique to Sweden, and has left its mark on the organization and running of society. A number of Swedes belong to such popular movements and attend meetings regularly.

Most of the popular movements were formed in the first decades of the twentieth century, during a period of struggle for improved material life conditions. Since then, many of the movements have changed, and they are now under criticism for being just as "establishment" as the organizations they once fought. Critics claim that they have turned into defenders of the society they once tried to alter. However one views this criticism, it is evident that these organizations are still very active and influential. They have a lively organizational press, and own 60 percent of the stocks of the single largest media institution in Sweden, Sveriges Radio "(the Swedish Broadcasting Corporation)."

Many of the principles that today mark the way for communication in Sweden have their origins in a clear libertarian tradition with its main objective to stimulate expression of different views on public matters. Information should be characterized by diversity and pluralism.

According to statements in Parliament, the press and other mass media are considered vitally important to maintaining continuous communication between elected political leaders and other citizens as well as between various groups in society. The mass media are to provide citizens with the information they need to decide on different societal matters of vital importance. Through the mass media the elected leaders are to obtain knowledge of the views of individuals and organizations in different political issues. The mass media are independent of state authorities and they shall comment on what is happening in society, reflecting their own views or the interests of organized groups. The mass media are also to serve the important function of scrutinizing activities in various sectors of society. The underlying philosophy is that a free exchange of different opinions is necessary in a democratic society such as Sweden.

An important prerequisite for diversity and pluralism is wide freedom of expression, on which Sweden has one of the oldest laws, dating from 1766. The legislation now in operation dates from 1949, but contains basically the same principles as the 1766 law (*Svensk Författningssamling* 1949; 1977*b*; 1977*c*). The following are the most important principles:

- The freedom to establish a newspaper. Anybody who wishes has the right to start a newspaper.

- No censorship. Any form of prior censorship is forbidden as well as any actions that may prohibit the dissemination and distribution of a newspaper. This is valid for all media in Sweden, except for film, which is subject to prior control.
- Protection of sources. Individuals who provide newspapers and other media with information are guaranteed anonymity. This guarantee is valid even if the information is secret. There can be no investigations into who has provided the information.
- Publicly available documents. All papers that come to public authorities or are written within such institutions are available to the public, even if the person who wants to see them is not personally affected. There are just a few exceptions to this rule, such as some hospital records and military documents.

Freedom of expression applies to print media as well as to radio and television. However, in a special agreement between the state and Sveriges Radio, freedom of expression has a limitation. The reason for this is that radio and television have a monopoly on their transmissions, while in the case of print media anybody has a legal right to start and publish papers (at least in theory). I will return to the special limitations under which radio and television operate.

There are also some exceptions to the general rule that anything may be published. These include the prohibition of slander, which here means to publish something in order to create disrespect for somebody. Such statements are allowed, however, if they are true, or if there is reasonable ground to assume that they are true. The laws also protect the so-called vital interests of the country, so that the publishing of information relating to war or espionage is prohibited. Likewise, the laws protect certain values by the prohibition of statements that threaten or denigrate ethnic groups or religions.

The responsibility for seeing that the laws are not violated lies with the responsible editor of a newspaper or with the radio and television producer, not with the individual journalist.

Generally speaking, Swedish legislation is far-reaching and guarantees a wide freedom of expression. Most violations are judged very leniently, and few major cases are brought to court. The procedure is such that only after publication can anything be tried. In most cases some kind of compromise is reached before the matter is brought to legal procedures.

Unlike the practice in many other Western countries, politicians and other public persons are very careful when accusing newspapers or other media of abusing freedom of expression, even if they know that they may win a legal case. Furthermore, in serious cases, violations are solved in a conciliatory way. For example, when a former minister of justice a few years back was falsely accused of having had affairs with prostitutes, the matter was not brought to court at all. The major morning newspaper that was responsible for the accusation admitted its mistake, and offered compensation. This was accepted by the former minister, who then on his own initiative donated the money to a fund dedicated to improving investigative journalism!

Newspapers*

There is no other country where people buy as many newspapers as they do in Sweden, which has a relatively high number of newspapers compared to the small population of eight million. But this also creates a problem, since if one newspaper increases its circulation, the rise will be offset by a loss in the circulation of other papers. The newspaper market is saturated. Since production costs are increasing, the consequence is that newspapers in Sweden are facing a very troublesome economic situation, perhaps more difficult than in many other countries. Since the end of the Second World War, a number of newspapers have had to close, but the number would have been much higher if the state had not provided the press with subsidies.

Sweden has about 150 newspapers, with a total circulation of around 5 million copies per day. Most papers are small, and only 4 have circulations larger than 50,000. Newspapers in Sweden are generally differentiated according to their market: metropolitan morning papers, evening papers, and provincial papers. The two Stockholm morning papers are circulated throughout the country, whereas most provincial papers are distributed over only limited areas. Nearly all morning papers, and most of those appearing three times a week or more, enjoy monopolies in their place of issue. Morning papers derive two-thirds of their revenue from advertising and one-third from sales, compared to evening papers for which the opposite is true. Evening papers are sold only at newsstands, while morning papers base their economy on subscriptions.

Traditionally, the Swedish press has had close ties with the various political parties, and the vast majority declare a political affiliation. The Swedish press shows a clear bourgeois bias, with nonsocialist papers accounting for about three-fourths of total circulation. Only a little more than one-fifth of this total is affiliated with the Social Democratic Party, which regularly has attracted the vote of around 45 percent of the electorate. The Liberal press on the other hand has about 37 percent of the total circulation, while the Liberal share of the electorate in the 1979 election was only slightly over 10 percent.

The government's press policy was developed in the late 1960s and

*The figures in this section on different media are based on Hultén (1979), if not stated otherwise. I am grateful to the author for permission to draw on the material presented there.

early 1970s. Two main factors lay behind it—the increasing concentration of the press and the constant underrepresentation of the two largest parties.

Many groups in the society saw the increasing monopolization of the press as a threat to the democratic processes in the country. Sweden relies to a great extent on a libertarian democratic model, based on the assumption that the best solution will win if different facts and views are presented to the public, who then make their choices through free elections. In order to arrive at these optimal solutions, the individual must have access to various views and opinions. First of all, views are put through the print media. The increasing concentration of press ownership was thus a threat not only to the press itself, but also to the democratic system, where the role of the newspapers is regarded as providing people with different facts and views. It was also argued that monopolization would mean poorer journalistic performance and greater difficulty for various social groups to make themselves heard through the newspapers. The situation was considered to be particularly serious because of the traditionally strong ties between party and press. Also, some feared that local monopoly might reduce press surveillance of authorities and politicians, particularly in those cases where the monopoly paper was allied to the locally dominant party.

At first the idea of state subsidy was rejected in view of the risk of political control it seemed to imply. However, newspapers eventually received support, and after the establishment of a loan fund and joint distribution rebates, selective support was directed to a number of secondary papers, which are defined as competitors having less than 50 percent coverage of the home market. With this principle, many Social Democrat newspapers qualified for support, as well as other low-coverage papers. As a result, no secondary papers have closed during the 1970s and many have even increased in circulation. The government program of press subsidies expanded rapidly during the 1970s; alleviations include exemption from the value added tax and postal concessions. Rebates to encourage joint distribution have been offered since 1970, and today some 90 percent of all Swedish newspapers are jointly distributed.

The main instrument of government support today is the program of production subsidies introduced in 1971, and largely restricted to low-coverage newspapers. The amount of subsidy is directly related to the volume of newsprint devoted to editorial content (measured in column-millimeters) and to circulation. Newspapers containing more than 50 percent advertising are not eligible. The highest amount granted a metropolitan paper is around US$5 million, and among provincial papers the corresponding figure is US$1.5 million. There are also other forms of support, but these are the principal ones. Government subsidies to the press are financed by a 10 percent tax on all advertising, except newspaper advertising, where the tax rate is 3 percent.

143

Intervention from the state was not met with open arms by the publishing organizations. From their viewpoint, any interference from the state is a serious threat to the independence of the press. It is another matter that state support would not be used to exert direct influence over the content of the papers.

Although publishers had several objections to the idea of state intervention and state support, they also had to face other factors that might possibly pose even worse alternatives. If the increasing monopolization had continued—and all the signs indicated that it would—the newspaper owners might have had to face legislation more directly concerned with content. It was obvious that the state was not going to watch silently while some newspapers created monopolies and thereby strengthened the political parties they represented. (One possibility that obviously was discussed was to have newspapers represent various political opinions and not just one political party.) There was also the risk that newspaper concentration would create undue influence for a few individuals—the owners. This risk, however, was not considered very great, since in Sweden ownership is more scattered than in many other countries. No real newspaper chains exist.

In short, the problem for the publishers was to keep the privileges that accompany the libertarian freedom of the press, while recognizing that the remaining papers would be responsible for a wide exchange of opinion, thus contributing to democracy in society. In this situation, state support was accepted and the press further demonstrated its responsibility by formulating more elaborate codes of ethical conduct—an attempt to avoid the enactment of more stringent legislation.

The Swedish system of press codes has gained an international reputation. The Swedish Press Council, established in 1916, increased considerably in importance through a reorganization in 1969. The task of the council is to decide whether what is printed is in line with good journalistic practice or not. It consists of members from the Swedish Newspaper Publishers' Association, the Swedish Association for Journalists, and other press organizations. The decisions of the council take the form of statements which newspapers that are criticized are obliged to publish. Since 1969 there has also been a press ombudsman who works in conjunction with the board to handle complaints from the public against newspapers and to try to achieve corrections in the press by voluntary means. If the ombudsman is not successful, the matter may be referred to the Press Council for a final decision. The press ombudsman also has the right of initiative, which means that matters may be raised even though a complaint from the public may not have been made.

This reliance by the press on internal rules for their practices is not accepted by all. Some claim that the sanctions are not strong enough to influence press behavior. The proponents, however, say that more stringent legislation would impair press freedom. This is an ongoing discussion.

The expectation has been expressed both in Parliament and by government representatives that in the future newspapers will have to cooperate even more than they have in the past. On the technical side newspapers have been cooperating with each other only marginally. But the incentives for collaborating are very strong; the newspaper industry must increase its productivity through various forms of rationalization in order to be able to make a profit, or even to stay alive economically. A great amount of technical and administrative rationalization has already taken place through the introduction of new, often computerized technology. In Sweden there has been very little conflict when the new techniques and procedures have been put into practice. This is surprising, since many other countries have seen severe conflicts among journalists, publishers, and printers over the new technology. It is also surprising considering that the new techniques will demand a lot of changes in journalistic practices. The relatively harmonious Swedish political climate has reduced such clashes in the labor market to a very low level.

But even if there is cooperation and rationalization, it seems inevitable that readers will have to accept paying considerably more for their newspapers than they do today. The question arises whether people will be prepared to do so at a time when unemployment is increasing, when radio and television offer a much cheaper alternative, and when video cassette recorders are flooding the information market. To a great extent, this will depend on how good the papers are, and this highlights another area where the newspaper industry is facing great problems. There is clear need for new journalistic thinking and ways of working that will provide people with adequate information, and information that fulfills the function of surveillance of the various institutions in society. This is not to say that the Swedish information system is poor. On the contrary, from an international perspective the Swedish press is of relatively high quality, with many competent journalists.

I will return to this problem of standards in journalism in the concluding section, since this question concerns not only newspapers but also radio, television, and other media. Journalistic practices within different media are quite interwoven in Sweden, and journalists often tend to have very similar work experiences.

Publishing

Periodicals

Sweden has a great variety of weekly and monthly magazines and journals, including both commercially published periodicals sold to the general public on subscription or on a single-copy basis, and "house organs" of various organizations and movements, distributed primarily to members. In 1981, at least 2,500 magazines and journals of some importance were being published regularly in Sweden (Hadenius and Weibull 1978). The most important group in economic terms, with roughly half the known total circulation, is the commercial popular press. The organizational press, however, accounts for the most titles, and this group, together with cultural and political journals, has been of particular concern to government policymakers. These are seen as the periodicals that best reflect the idea of having the press function as a meeting place of ideas relevant to the formation of public opinion.

The Popular Press

The popular press in Sweden is roughly the same character as that in other countries, being composed of general-interest commercial weeklies and special-interest magazines dealing with leisure activities, technical/scientific interests, serial cartoons, and so on. The combined circulation of the popular press is quite large. According to a study by Bernow and Osterman (1978), three-fourths of the adult population read at least one weekly magazine regularly. The average Swedish household reads a couple of weekly magazines regularly. A handful of publishers dominates the market, and since circulation has stagnated in recent years, competition for readers is keen. An apparent trend is that broader-interest family magazines appear to be regaining some of their lost ground. Another tendency is toward more specialized periodicals aimed at reader groups with a particular interest in hobbies, sports, and other leisure activities. But one common feature of the popular press in most countries is missing in Sweden: there are no Swedish weekly newsmagazines on the Swedish market. The largest circulation of any single publication of the popular press is around 400,000 copies. Around 80 percent of the revenue comes from subscription and single copies sold. The commercial popular press receives no economic support from the state. On the contrary, it contributes a good share of the money distributed to other branches of the press via the general levy on advertising revenues (10 percent), which was mentioned earlier.

The Organizational Press

Roughly half of the periodicals in this category are published by voluntary "idealistic" organizations (religious, political, temperance groups, etc.). Cooperatives, trade, and commercial associations publish some two hundred titles, and labor and professional unions some one hundred titles. An additional two hundred titles are produced by miscellaneous groups. Most organizational publications work in a difficult economic climate. Without their sponsors' subsidies and/or the aid extended by the state since 1977 many would go under. Some organizational magazines, however, do not experience these problems. They are addressed to special-interest groups that are attractive to advertisers, and are financed through advertising.

The parliamentary decision to extend support to the organizational press was motivated by recognition of the contribution these publications make to the effective functioning of Swedish democracy. Free and self-reliant organizations, Parliament asserted, constitute a guarantee of multifaceted, pluralistic discussion of public affairs. (See *Riksdags-protokoll* 1977 leading to *Svensk Författningssamling* 1977a.) Such publications convey to a broader audience the ideas and ideals to which these organizations subscribe. Financial support from the state consists of a general subsidy plus a subsidy for each copy distributed. Publications containing more than 50 percent advertising do not qualify for support.

Cultural and Political Journals

Approximately 250 periodicals are devoted to the arts, the humanities, or politics, with the aim of stimulating debate. Circulations are generally quite small and such magazines and journals do not readily reach large circles of readers. As early as a decade ago, the state made funds available to guarantee the continuation of many such publications. The small Swedish market could hardly support such a variety of publications otherwise. The overall rise in costs and the recent decision to discontinue postal rate discounts to periodicals has hit publications lacking organizational support particularly hard. State support is not being offered in a standardized form. Publications seeking state funds must apply to the National Council for Cultural Affairs, stating what they hope to achieve with the funds requested. The Council then distributes the funds among the various applicants as it sees fit. In 1981, some 185 cultural periodicals received state support amounting to approximately US$1.5 million.

Books

Although the Swedish language is spoken by only a small proportion of the world's people, a great number of new titles are published every year. In 1980 about 7,500 new titles appeared. The aim is to keep the flow of literature rich and varied. However, just as in the case of the press, economic conditions endanger these aims. The average demand per title is low, and costs are rapidly increasing.

The publishing industry is now highly consolidated, and two companies account for about half of the fiction published annually. Book clubs have also been very successful in recent years. The difficulties of distributing a wide selection of good books through mass marketing channels are one of the topics of discussion. Market forces threaten the flow of just those books that are perhaps the most important from a cultural viewpoint.

Libraries are a very important resource for the circulation of books in Sweden. Public libraries, for decades the responsibility of local communities, are of a high standard and used regularly by many Swedes. A number of different forms of support to literature have been introduced recently on the recommendation of a literary commission, which has now finished its work. Publishing and distribution of books that rest almost exclusively in private hands were the latest cultural sectors to receive state aid.

The basic principle guiding state activities is to stimulate all links of the chain between authors and readers, primarily through selective measures. The oldest form of state support, however, is general in nature: since 1962 authors have been remunerated for loans of their books from libraries, in accordance with a fixed tariff per loan. A little more than half of the appropriation is paid directly to authors and the rest is channeled through the Swedish Authors' Fund and distributed in the form of stipends, grants, and so forth.

Through the National Council for Cultural Affairs, around US$3 million is spent selectively on books published. Although it will no doubt grow in relation to total book sales, state support is marginal. But even marginal support that is selectively geared to precisely those areas of publishing most vulnerable to market conditions can play an important role.

Several publishing companies experienced a severe economic decline during the period 1970–72, while the period 1973–77 was more economically profitable. Because the industry is very dependent on total sales, the amount of profit is more or less related to fluctuations in sales, and a single best-seller often has a decisive influence on the net profit of a whole company. This will probably be true for years to come. Companies will meet rising costs of production by rationalization and concentration on fewer books that may become successes in terms of the number of copies sold. If, as seems likely, the book companies follow this strategy, they will have to adapt even more to the preferences of the public. This will probably mean that specialized cultural books will be fewer than now—the publishing companies will not be able to afford them if they want to stay in business.

Another problem is in the distribution of books. Good bookstores that carry a wide selection cannot be maintained in areas where the population is declining in size. New forms of distribution, with collaboration between retailers and other links in the chain, will be necessary. State support will probably have to be focused differently to take into account the economic realities of the book industry. Instead of being geared to the production and publishing of certain valuable books, it will have to take into account the need to distribute books to the readers. Demand from the public has to be stimulated in order to avoid the great risk that the present distribution system will be replaced by an inferior one, where bookstores containing a wide selection will be rare and found only in urban areas. It seems inevitable that the book industry will face many problems that will be further aggravated in the future by having to compete with the new information technology for the attention of the consumer.

Film

Film as a pastime and as an art form has deep roots in Sweden. Cinemas were built early, and the volume of domestic film production was relatively large prior to the advent of television. By 1963 both cinema attendance and film production had declined to the extent that public support was deemed necessary to stimulate production and distribution. An act of Parliament in 1963 (*Svensk Författningssamling* 1963) created the Swedish Film Institute to administer this support. A twenty-year agreement between the government and the film industry provides the institute with 10 percent of the gross revenue of ticket sales of major cinemas (cinemas with more than five performances a week). The figures in Table 5-1 illustrate the situation within the film industry in 1980.

Table 5-1
Swedish Film Industry Statistics (1980)

Number of cinemas in Sweden	1,200
Cinema attendance	26 million
Ticket sales revenue	c. US$80 million
Number of new foreign films shown	320
Number of new Swedish films shown	20

Sources: Hyltén-Cavallus 1981; *Statistical Abstract* 1981.

Four chains own most of the cinemas and thus dominate the domestic distribution of film. Swedish subsidiaries of U.S. distributors dominate the import of foreign films. A general point of criticism has been that quality films are seldom shown outside the major cities and university towns. Art films have only small audiences and few outlets. There are, however, about 130 film clubs in Sweden, which does improve the situation somewhat. In cooperation with many communities, the Swedish Film Institute sponsors the showing of quality films where they would otherwise be unavailable. During the 1940s about forty films were produced in Sweden every year, and in the 1950s more than thirty. During the past few years the figures have been fairly stable at around twenty films per year (Hyltén-Cavallius 1981; *Statistical Abstract* 1981).

In recent years production costs have risen much faster than the willingness to invest in film production. This has both cut the volume of Swedish film production and given rise to a growing need for state support to supplement the funds from ticket sales. It has also caused the Swedish Film Institute to play an increasingly important role as producer and coproducer. Whereas in the late 1960s the institute produced a couple of films a year, by the early 1980s about half of the feature films were being produced by or in collaboration with the institute (Hyltén-Cavallius 1981; *Statistical Abstract* 1981). The institute has tried to encourage distributors to take a greater part in production and has concluded agreements to that effect with both Swedish television and the major distributors.

Film has faced a more severe crisis than any other medium. The forms of support to production provided for in the 1963 agreement are no longer sufficient. Some people have criticized the institute for being too much under the influence of commercial interests, whereas others contend that it is too dedicated to satisfying the film workers' need to express themselves. Some claim that there is a creativity crisis, others that more money will solve the problems. Around US$5 million from the ticket sales go to support production, and the rest to support other activities, such as importation and distribution of quality films for children and adults, restoration of "antique" films, and maintenance of a film archive. There is still censorship of films, which especially tends to examine critically the existence of "entertainment violence" (Hyltén-Cavallius 1981; *Statistical Abstract* 1981).

Radio and Television

Structure

Sveriges Radio (Swedish Broadcasting Corporation) was founded in 1925 after a long debate about the organization of the company. Sweden chose a model that did not see the distribution of information services as a technical problem only. The Swedish structure was influenced by England, where the BBC is organized as a public service company. From the beginning Sveriges Radio was organized as a joint stock company, in which the shares are owned by private enterprise interests, the press, and popular organizations. Radio and later television broadcasting became the exclusive monopoly of Sveriges Radio. The state charges the National Telecommunications Administration with the sole responsibility for the distribution of programs.

A commitment to providing equal service to all parts of the country has governed the gradual expansion of broadcasting facilities in Sweden. Every citizen, no matter where he or she may reside, should be able to receive all the programming offered—in stereo or color, as the case may be. Considerable amounts of money have been invested so that localities of as few as twenty-five households can receive television channel 2, which transmits on UHF frequencies. Sveriges Radio is totally financed by license fees, and there is no advertising on radio or television. A family who owns a television set and a radio pays around US$100 per year.

Since 1979 Sveriges Radio has had a new organization, but the monopoly situation remains. The organizational structure is explained in Figure 5-1. Sveriges Radio is now the parent company, which fully owns four separate independent subsidiaries. The distribution of ownership is 60 percent by popular movements, 20 percent by the press, and 20 percent by business (Hadenius and Weibull 1978).

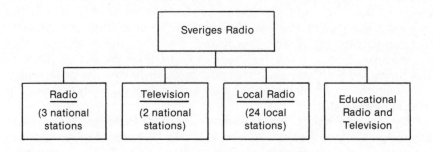

Figure 5-1
Organization of Sveriges Radio

The motive for this new structure, which is now in full operation, was to make radio and television independent from each other in order to increase the pluralism and diversity of opinion offered. Another aim was to enable the media to develop their unique characteristics. Critics of the new structure express the fear that the subsidiary companies will have greater difficulties in meeting external criticism of programs. It is too early to evaluate the benefits and costs of this new system.

Program Content

The state exerts control over the programs in the broadcast media in several ways. The Broadcasting Act requires that the companies carry out their activities based on facts and in an objective and impartial manner, while at the same time taking into account the objectives of freedom of information and freedom of expression. Furthermore, the companies are obliged to assert and uphold the basic values of the democratic society and the principles of equality for all, and the freedom and dignity of the individual.

In separate agreements between the state and the program companies, the requirements for programs are specified even more. Some of these are:

- The programs shall with quality, availability, and diversity of views satisfy the different needs and interests the audience may have.
- The programs shall provide knowledge, disseminate experiences, and provide entertainment.
- The programs shall give information about the events in society today in a suitable form, orient viewers to important cultural and societal matters, and stimulate debate around issues of this kind (Sveriges Radio 1982).

The state further appoints all members of a special Radio Council, which determines whether programs that have already been broadcast correspond to the rules and guidelines set forth in legislation and in the agreements between the program companies and the state (*Svensk Författningssamling* 1978b). The council may examine programs either in response to complaints filed against them or on its own initiative. It thus functions both as an agent of post facto review by the government and as a body to which the public may turn with complaints concerning program content.

The council, hence, acts as a surveillant of the freedom of expression allowed in Sveriges Radio. Between 1972 and 1975, about seven hundred complaints per year were scrutinized by the council. Of these, around 3 percent were found to be against the rules—most of them because the programs were considered to be partial, or both impartial and not based on relevant facts. These decisions have a great influence on journalists and producers working for the companies because they delineate the limits of freedom of expression. The activities of the Radio Council attract wide attention.

Transmission

The distribution network consists of three nationwide FM radio channels with a total output of around four hundred hours, and reaching 100 percent of the population. There are also two nationwide television channels, both with color, that can reach the whole population. Parliament has voted for the establishment of a fourth FM radio channel for local and educational broadcasts. The Swedish system of two channels operating independently of one another is basically the result of a compromise between opinion favoring the introduction of commercial television in the 1960s and that favoring the preservation of a public-service monopoly. The text of the parliamentary decision creating this system stresses that the two channels should be equal parties in a mutually "stimulating contest." (See Proposition 136/1966 in *Riksdag-stryck* 1966 for the arguments presented.) The new broadcasting act preserves this overall scheme, although the idea of contest has been toned down in favor of coordination and specialization in certain areas (*Svensk Författningssamling* 1978a).

Since 1978, regional television news broadcasts have been started on a small scale, and by 1982, about half the country was covered. There is also regional radio broadcasting, and for a short time there has also been "special local radio," where voluntary, religious, labor, and political groups can broadcast on their own terms. These broadcasts are being transmitted on FM frequencies and have a range of about five kilometers. Programs do not have to live up to the standards of objectivity and impartiality of other broadcasts. These kinds of experimental radio broadcasts are now being evaluated, and it seems very likely that they will continue on a permanent basis.

Audience

Surveys (for example, Wigren and Gahlin 1981; Kjellmor 1981) indicate that 75 percent of the Swedish population between the ages of nine and seventy-nine listen to the radio on any given day. The average listening time is a little less than two hours a day, of which one hour is devoted to music and entertainment and twenty minutes to news and information. Television audience ratings show that slightly more than three-quarters of the population watch television every day and that the viewing time averages roughly two hours a day. Of this time, slightly less than thirty minutes are devoted to news and information programs, and about one hour to entertainment and fiction.

Despite the fact that people devote about the same amount of time to radio and to television, the patterns of consumption differ enormously. Listening to radio is a secondary activity, whereas watching television is a primary activity that supersedes other activities. A study conducted in 1974 showed that on the average, Swedes devote half their week-day evening leisure time, between 6 and 10 p.m. (less household chores, child care, etc.), to watching television. Social contact, studies, hobbies, and all other media share the other half (Wikman 1974).

The Broadcasting Act of 1978 (Sveriges Radio 1982) contains a provision that is of interest in this context. Referring to the fact that television viewing already dominates Swedes' leisure activities, Parliament stated that an increase in viewing time is hardly to be desired. Consequently, television received no resources with which to extend its program schedules. This again may be something unique to the Swedish system. Although television is considered important for disseminating information and presenting entertainment, there is a limit to its value. When people devote a lot of time to television viewing, other activities suffer. It is recognized that too much viewing contributes to passivity.

Television is regarded as valuable as long as it contributes to encouraging people to take part in societal life by providing relevant information. But its value decreases rapidly when its consequences are the opposite, and when people instead are separated from society.

153

Problems and Prospects

Sveriges Radio has a very central and influential position in the Swedish media scene, because of its monopoly structure. Consequently, and not surprisingly, the corporation—and now the companies—is constantly under critical focus. Some points of criticism which are regularly expressed are the following:

1. Some observers claim that the broadcasting monopoly has accumulated too much power and influence. This view has been voiced both by those advocating the introduction of commercial television and by those perceiving a lack of pluralism within the noncommercial system.
2. It has been said that Sveriges Radio and its employees have tended to insist too much on *their own* freedom and integrity. Accessibility and the public service ideology have been neglected in the face of increasing internal loyalty.
3. It has been charged that the large share of American and British fiction on television and the amount of commercially produced popular music on the radio do not satisfy the aims of Swedish cultural policy. The production of more expensive types of domestic programs, such as television theater, documentaries, and entertainment (shows, revues, etc.) has declined sharply since 1974. The reason for this is that Sveriges Radio's purchasing power has failed to keep pace with inflation, while salaries, social security, and other salary-based fees have risen sharply (Hultén 1980, 1981).
4. Although Sveriges Radio is not operated on a commercial basis, it tends to use the same criteria as the commercial media when it comes to news selection and presentation, and other forms of programming. This again reflects the fact that journalists working in Sweden have acquired more or less the same professional values in both commercial and noncommercial media.

But there is also another point, perhaps of greater significance. Through its structure, Sveriges Radio to a very large degree reflects values that are being promoted by the established circles of society. There is a built-in tendency to promote the views and positions of those groups in society that have power, and to oppose changes. The rules for the corporation are interpreted to mean that the content of programs has to be true and relevant. However, the interpretation of what is relevant is often that the views shown or presented are those of a majority in society.

I have argued (particularly in the section on newspapers) that Sweden is characterized by a strong bourgeois domination in the sphere of opinion formation. When Sveriges Radio evaluates what is relevant, it starts from these values. Hence, it is by its own rules bound to act as a defender of the status quo in society. The owner groups—popular

154

organizations, press, and business—also represent such established interests. The result has been a certain degree of anxiety among program-makers and a reluctance to be critical of established interests in society. A degree of self-censorship has developed. It is enforced by the Radio Council, which reminds producers of the boundaries they must not cross. This does not mean that there is a total lack of critical programs. Actually, there are many such programs, but compared to the total output, they are in a minority.

New Media

The rapid pace of technological development in the fields of electronics and telecommunications has drastically altered the situation of the mass media. Throughout the world, new media are being introduced and discussed. So also in Sweden, where the interest in communication satellites, broadband and narrow-band technology, videograms, and teletext services is beginning to have an important impact.

Several commissions are examining various aspects of this new technology, and as in other countries, opinions vary widely. Some claim, for example, that data-television services will increase the freedom of expression in society, while others express the fear that only those who have the financial resources and know how to handle technical equipment will benefit from it.

There are a number of social consequences to be examined: How will the introduction of technologies affect society as a whole and people's daily lives, both at home and at work? Will the technologies create more isolation and increase alienation? Are we heading toward a totally technocratic society, and in that case—are we prepared for it?

The most important issue in Sweden at present concerns the question of launching a Nordic satellite to connect all of the Scandinavian countries: Denmark, Finland, Iceland, Norway, and Sweden. The original objective was to broadcast the region's ten radio channels and seven television channels simultaneously via satellite in each of these countries with subtitled translation for television programs. For decades "Nordists" have urged an increase in the exchange of radio and television programs in order to strengthen the traditional cultural ties throughout the region. When satellite technology became a viable possibility, these interests united around the concept of "Nordsat." The Nordic Council of Ministers has studied and discussed Nordsat since 1976 and a final decision is expected in 1982. The respective legislative assemblies of the Nordic countries must then deliberate on the issue and, if they approve, ratify the necessary contracts and agreements. The earliest date at which Nordsat might come into full operation is 1985.

The issue is controversial. According to its proponents, the reasons for use of the satellite are:

1. To increase Nordic viewers' freedom of choice;
2. To satisfy cultural minorities' need of programs in their own language (principally the Sami people, as well as Finnish-speaking residents of Sweden and Swedish-speaking residents of Finland);
3. To strengthen the cultural and linguistic community of the Nordic peoples.

Criticism of Nordsat centers mainly on this last point. Each of the Nordic countries imports between 40 and 50 percent of its television programming. Some particularly popular program categories, such as films and serial dramas, are entirely dominated by English-language imports, and many such imports are shown in all the Nordic countries. Critics claim that the satellite is a poor solution precisely from the viewpoint of Nordic cultural policy, since only very few viewers may be expected to choose to watch the programs produced by their Nordic neighbors on the multitude of channels Nordsat would make available. It would be better, they argue, to invest the money that satellite distribution would require in domestic production. Such investment would reduce the region's dependence on foreign imports, while stimulating domestic production. Inter-Nordic exchange might continue by conventional means and Nordic programs would most likely reach larger audiences. The costs of a fully operating Nordic direct broadcasting satellite cannot be calculated exactly, but the greatest economic burden would be borne by the consumer through direct expenditure, with an additional indirect contribution to production and distribution through taxes. The reception apparatus would remain between US$500 and US$1,000 from the individual viewer. There would also be an increase of around 10 percent in Swedish receiver license fees.

The Nordic investigations are now all completed, and it is up to the politicians to make the final decision. It is difficult to anticipate the outcome, but at least in Sweden there is a political majority—but not a very strong majority—against the satellite. It is reasonable to assume that if Sweden—the largest Nordic country—is against the project, it will be difficult to put into operation. Some also infer that the technical planning has gone so far that it would be too costly *not* to launch the satellite. A possibility would then be to bring the satellite into orbit, but not to use it for the transmission of television programs. Instead, it could be used for other transborder data flows, serving, for example, the private enterprise system in the Nordic countries.

Civic Information

An important communications domain in Sweden is the flow of messages from administrative authorities at different levels to citizens, informing them about their rights and obligations in society. The senders of information may be governmental bodies, Parliament, municipalities, communities, and so on. In many cases such information has news value, and the mass media are interested in publishing it. But in other cases this is not so, and state bodies or other authorities buy advertising space. In all instances the objectives of the state and municipalities are not only to inform citizens about their rights and duties, but to encourage people to think or behave in certain ways. One example is the change to right-hand traffic that Sweden successfully implemented in 1967. A large campaign, financed by tax money, was carried via the media to make the shift as smooth as possible.

This type of communication flow raises the fundamental question of the right of the state to influence and control its citizens. Does the state have the right to protect some people by limiting the behavior of others? How far is it legitimate to use state powers for this purpose, and to what extent is state intervention consistent with the kind of democracy Sweden recognizes as its own? These important questions have so far been carefully avoided by state authorities. In the discussion about civic information, the debate has centered not only around the information that citizens receive, but also on the information they pass out to the authorities on whom they depend. Some argue that civic information should not go only in one direction, but should be—at least to some extent—characterized by flows in both directions. This would be valuable from a democratic viewpoint. At present, the participation by citizens in society is clearly biased, as can be seen from Table 5-2 taken from a governmental commission a few years ago. Critics proclaiming an alternative view argue that apart from informing citizens, civic information should also aim at reducing the communication gaps that the figures in Table 5-2 indicate, by stimulating people to become more active.

The discussion about civic information seems to have stagnated somewhat in recent years. But there are several important issues involved, and many such decisions still to be taken.

Conclusions

In the preceding pages, the main characteristics of the Swedish approach to communication policy have been described and analyzed. The communication system is organized to facilitate the flow of diverse information, an approach that has strong roots in libertarian thinking. The development of such a system in Sweden illustrates well how the state is trying to uphold some of the fundamental ideals of libertarian ideology when economic realities have shown weaknesses in the underlying philosophy.

The elaborate support system and its consequences are the two most distinguishing aspects of the Swedish communication system. Although the state has entered almost all media branches, one cannot say that the state has intervened in order to steer media toward clearly specified objectives. The state interventions have up to now had a clearly

Table 5-2

Citizen Participation in the Swedish Social Process
(percent)

Activity	Social Class			All Classes
	I	II	III	%
Has written letter to the press/article	33	12	5	10
Has given speech or made intervention at meeting	56	30	16	24
Politically organized	30	21	16	18
Organized in trade union	43	44	46	45
Has taken part in a public demonstration	12	12	16	14
Has made contact with decision makers	18	8	40	7
Has formally complained about decisions of the authorities	36	22	11	17
Has the capacity to write to the authorities	86	56	32	45

Source: Commission on Low Incomes, as reported in Abrahamsson 1972.

defensive character. The aims have been to repair or to balance the commercial systems and values that most private media sectors rely on. The state is trying to maintain a diversified and pluralistic media arrangement in a market that would otherwise be dominated by strong capital interests, creating oligopolistic conditions.

The interventions of the state have usually not had an offensive, future-oriented character, but there is little coherent policy. Different arguments are put forward for the various media, so that in the case of the Sveriges Radio a monopoly can be defended, while in the case of the press, monopoly is undesired. There are many examples of such inconsistencies in media policy. One very good illustration of this situation is the great uncertainty surrounding the new media that are already established, as well as the media to come. The current debate on Nordsat is also a bit confusing at times. There is a lack of specified cultural and social objectives against which a potential satellite can be judged.

However, this general criticism should not obscure the fact that the general direction of communication in Sweden is fairly clear. I said earlier in this chapter that the major aim is to provide Swedish citizens with information, which makes it possible for them to take part in society in the broadest sense. A citizen not only has the right to relevant and adequate information, but the media have an obligation to pass out such information in the interests of the democratic process on which Swedish society is based.

Compared to many other countries, the Swedish media system is characterized by diversity of viewpoints, and there is a fairly wide spectrum of viewpoints put forward, even if alternative information takes some effort to find. Radio and television have so far not been totally invaded by the commercial values that most private media elsewhere adhere to. And there is at present no reason to assume that advertising will be introduced in the electronic media, for there is widespread political agreement that advertising should be kept out of them.

The popular movements have played an important role in shaping the media policy of the country. The organizations all include education as one of their major activities and, since they involve most groups in society, have contributed to the shaping of such an "educational philosophy" for the media system as a whole. It is probably true that radio and television, and some of the press, are characterized by a fairly great proportion of information (as opposed to entertainment) and serious material, at least if compared to many other Western countries.

The media system is constantly under critical scrutiny, and there are a number of issues to be examined critically in order to improve media policy. Three such points will be discussed here: state intervention, improved journalism, and the improvement of each citizen's communication skills.

State Intervention

State intervention and the state support system in particular are basic factors in Swedish media life. However, there have been few attempts to *evaluate* the positive and negative effects of the clearly visible hand of the state.

Under the system of press subsidy it is assumed that the mere existence of a second newspaper in a town will lead to a better kind of democracy. Although several newspapers now depend totally on state support for their existence, they are at the same time competing in a commercial market with newspapers that do not receive any support at all. This creates a strange competitive situation, and given that newspapers also compete with other media, raises many questions. If the aim of state subsidies is to improve democracy, there is no evidence that the support of secondary newspapers is the best way. It could be argued that there is a lack of incentive for the secondary paper to become better. If more copies are sold, the economy of the paper does not improve dramatically, since the state support then decreases. And what is there to say that the amount of space devoted to editorial matters has anything to do with improved democracy? Very few people read editorials, and the adequacy of a paper is for most people determined by the other pages in the paper.

In the realm of broadcasting, the state plays a very active role since it determines both the budget (through license fees) and specific requirements it has formulated concerning program content. Here, as with the press, the influence of state intervention is hard to estimate. On the positive side is the fact that Sweden has been able to avoid the most grotesque consequences of a commercial broadcasting system, and the programming arrived at has been of a reasonably good standard compared to other Western countries. But these considerations have to be weighed against the resulting highly centralized, bureaucratic organization and programming that has been guided by the values of "objectivity" and "impartiality" thus reflecting the values of bourgeois groups in society. Through these explicit limitations on freedom of expression, really critical programs have had great difficulties in getting produced. It has been difficult to create programs that at the same time fulfill the goals of being objective *and* stimulating to the viewer or listener.

There is need to evaluate various aspects of the broadcasting system. Unfortunately, very few research projects have dealt with this matter (for example, Nowak 1979; Kjellmor 1979). The Audience Research Department at Sveriges Radio has concentrated on limited problems with only a few, but important exceptions like studies labeled "Communication Gaps." There is a great need for more studies of a similar kind, and for scientific examination of the production of programs and the media organization, to balance the overemphasis on audience studies.

To sum up, the state intervention system, which characterizes the Swedish communication scene, is not the best of all possible constructions. There are negative elements, which have to be systematically and critically scrutinized. So far discussions of problems have focused on technical matters and have only to a small extent gone into problems concerning what kind of freedom of expression Sweden wants to have and what kind of democracy. The media have clear connections with such ideological issues, and these should be brought into focus. Only then will it be possible to start a serious and wide discussion on an overall communication policy.

Improved Journalism

The journalist has an essential role in the ideology of the media. He or she is the one to dig out all the facts and opinions that may be relevant to the reader or listener. Journalists together survey society for us, and by doing this they fulfill the watchdog function of the press. These ideals were once expressed, and are still being kept alive by journalists themselves and even by the media owners. But practice and experience shed great doubts on the idea that these functions are satisfactorily fulfilled by the journalists or the media today.

Journalism practice in Sweden is characterized by a high degree of uniformity between different media forms. Journalists often have the same background, and there are only two university departments dealing directly with journalism. This means that all media use more or less identical criteria for news and news presentation, as well as the choice of program topics. The professional values that have developed have not always been in accordance with the idea that the first loyalty of the journalist should be to the public. Instead journalistic values have been shaped first of all by economic considerations. The press is the oldest medium and it is the press that has been leading the way to the journalism that now prevails.

The press has constantly been facing economic crises, where the goal of making a profit—or at least surviving—has been foremost. This means that there has been a search for ways of cutting costs at all stages in the production and distribution chain. One way of reducing costs has been to keep expenditures low for raw materials, that is the inflow of material that could lead to articles. The private press created its organization with this in mind, and the result is a concentration on similar types of events and a few persons, who continually appear in the public sector. Hence, Swedish papers are filled constantly with items concerning official institutions, authorities, and "well-known people." The whole inflow of raw news is highly standardized and is organized to give a mix of content that has proven saleable to the consumer. There is built-in resistance toward change in the selection and presentation of items just because of these economic factors. This kind of news content is not in opposition to the interests of the media owners. Considering that the press in Sweden is dominated by bourgeois interests—as is the commercial popular press—this kind of content is not a political threat to the groups in power. But seen from the viewpoint of the general public and the aims of Swedish society, the situation is not satisfactory. Critical analysis of the authorities, the private enterprise system, and the description of ordinary people's daily lives, does not live up to the goals the libertarian ideology once formulated.

This kind of criticism is also valid for the monopoly in broadcasting. Although Sveriges Radio does not work with commercial aims, it uses many of the commercial criteria that other media follow. The similarity between the press and the broadcast media is striking in the fields of news, features, and entertainment.

It would be going too far to say that Swedish journalism is in crisis, but from the viewpoint of comprehensive surveillance of society, the situation is serious. The degree of self-censorship among journalists in Sweden ought to be investigated in depth. An immediate way out of the present situation is difficult to see. There seems to be little discussion among journalists themselves about these matters, which is of course a consequence of the fact that journalists often work in isolation from each other. Increased awareness among journalists could possibly lead to a general discussion on the objectives of journalism, and the gaps between ideals and practice.

Communicative Skills

A Swedish communication policy has to be based on ideals that stress the importance of people's right to participate in decision making in society. From such a perspective, it is clearly unsatisfactory that only certain groups have the capacity to complain about decisions, to communicate via the press, to contact authorities, and so on. Although these differences between social groups reflect other forms of socioeconomic differences, there is good reason to invest in decreasing these differences. "The right to communicate" is a Swedish concept that has gained attention in discussions about a new international information order. Even if this concept is not very precise, it is probably useful in a national context like that of Sweden.

To send and receive information is a resource of a special kind. It is a prerequisite for influence in society, and in order for all groups to exert such influence, two conditions have to be fulfilled:

- There have to be channels through which people can exert influence.
- People must be competent to produce and distribute information through these channels.

In Sweden, both these aspects must be improved. On the second point people will have to be given better opportunities in order to use their democratic rights. Already in school there should be more stress on how to handle information—to find it, to understand it, and to use it. These ideas are part of the formulation and implementation of a communication policy based on democratic ideals. Such a policy has to touch upon all parts of the communication chain, from senders to receivers, since these parts are dependent on each other. Although it is easy to argue that the main problems lie on the sending side, the reception of information is also highly important. The problem is both to produce relevant information and to have it widely used. This is the challenge when formulating adequate communication policy.

References

Abrahamsson, Kenneth
1972   *Samhällskommunikation. Om kontakten mellan myndigheter
                     och medborgare* [Societal communication: The contact between
                     the authorities and citizens]. Lund: Studentlitteratur.

Bernow, Roger and Österman, Torsten
1978   *Svensk veckopress 1920-1975* [The Swedish weekly press 1920-
                     1975]. Solna: Forskningsgruppen för Samhälls- och Informa-
                     tionasstudier.

Hadenius, S., and Weibull, L.
1978   *Massmedier* [Mass media]. Stockholm: Bonniers.

Hultén, O.
1979   *Mass Media and State Support in Sweden*. Stockholm: The
                     Swedish Institute.

1980   "Future of Broadcasting—Public Service Broadcasting in the
                     1980's." *Massacommunicatie* 3-4:109-22.

1981   "Why NORDSAT—Why Not?" *Media, Culture and Society*
                     3:315-25.

Hyltén-Cavallius, G., ed.
1981   *Swedish Films 1981*. Stockholm: Swedish Film Institute.

Kjellmor, Staffan
1979   *Arbetsliv och informationsklyftor* [The work world and
                     information gaps]. PUB nr 13/1979. Sveriges Radio.

1981   *Radions publik: Lyssnandet under tre år* [The radio audience:
                     Three years of listening]. PUB nr 23/1981. Sveriges Radio.

Nowak, Lilian
1979   *Informationsklyftorna: en spegling av det ojämlika samhallet*
                     [The information gaps: Mirroring the unequal society]. PUB nr
                     20/1979. Sveriges Radio.

***Riksdagsprotokoll* [The minutes of Parliament]**
1977

***Riksdagstryck* [Parliament publications]**
1966   Proposition 136.

163

Statistical Abstract of Sweden 1981.
1981   Vol. 68. Stockholm: Norstedts.

Svensk Författningssamling [Swedish Public Laws]
1949   Act 105.

1963   Act 173.

1977a   Act 607.

1977b   Act 1016.

1977c   Act 1035.

1978a   Act 476.

1978b   Act 482.

Sveriges Radio
1982   *Basic Provisions for Radio and Television.*

Wigren, Gunnila and Gahlin, Anders
1981   *Publikåret 1980/81* [The audience years 1980/81]. PUB nr
                            25/1981. Sveriges Radio.

Wikman, Anders
1974   *Alternativa kvällsaktiviteter* [Alternative evening activities]. PUB
                            nr 35/1974. Sveriges Radio.

World Bank
1978   *World Development Report.* Washington, D.C.

Further References

Furhoff, L.
1974   *Makten över medierna* [The power over the media]. Lund: Bo
                            Cavefors Forlag.

Furhoff, L.; Jönsson, L.; and Nilsson, L.
1974   *Communication Policies in Sweden.* Paris: UNESCO.

164

Gustafsson, K.E., and Hadenius, S.
1976   *Swedish Press Policy*. Stockholm: The Swedish Institute.

Ortmark, Å.
1979   "Sweden: Freedom's Boundaries." In *Television and Political Life: Studies in Six European Countries*, edited by A. Smith. London: Macmillan.

6

Communication Policy in the Federal Republic of Germany: Democratic Expectations versus Political and Economic Interests

Ed Wittich

Ed Wittich argues that the peculiarities of Germany's split history provided the opportunity for a more conscious development of democratic, federal institutions in the post-1949 era. They gave an aura of relatively coherent planning in the area of communication policy formulation in comparison with the other countries discussed in this volume, or with what would have been the case had Germany's history not taken the dramatic course it did in the war years. The state's deliberate response to Germany's politico-cultural past, as well as the quasi-imposed democratic order inherited from the Allies, influenced the present communication structure. Another important historical influence on the communication structures of the Federal Republic of Germany (FRG) results from the relationship of groups within German society to the state. It is the political parties that hold the allegiance of the German people: the state is traditionally mistrusted. Thus while the need for the state to have some effective powers of regulation is recognized, there is considerable caution about state intervention in the communication process. At the same time there is public concern in the FRG about the powerful coalitions of private interests that have become more and more concentrated since the 1950s.

These two major groups—party-political interests and private business interests—conflict with the basic public democratic interest that underlies much of the policy thrust, and provide a central theme of conflict that runs through discussions about the press, publishing, cinema, broadcasting, and telecommunications in the FRG. The attempted policy resolutions described show that democratic principles as a basis for communication policy formulation provide no guarantees of protection against the power of economic and political interests.

Any attempt to examine the communication policy of a particular society necessarily entails some perception of the social condition of that society.

Like all aspects of culture, the orientation of a society toward communication policy consists of the kinds of responses made in coming to terms with the significant aspects of both the physical and the social environment. This holds true whether the resultant cognizance remains tacit or becomes formulated explicitly.

The sorts of institutions and practices evolved by a society in coming to terms with its communications environment (the import of which rocketed into prominence with Gutenberg's invention, around 1450, of the printing press using movable type), and the major recurring themes and conflicts that result, cannot be understood in isolation from the social and historical circumstances that produced them. In the FRG these institutions and practices represent the cultural prism, as it were, through which the contemporary pressures and demands of the German social milieu, and the sets of political exigencies thus generated, are refracted into the process of political life today.

A number of developments rooted in Germany's cultural past must be clearly understood in order to grasp the thematic content underlying much of the contemporary debate and conflict. The following thumbnail sketch glosses over many a complex and delicate issue, but is intended to briefly inform the reader rather than provide a definitive work on the cultural and social history of Germany.

The "present" that we must understand encompasses a society relatively recently restructured along democratic lines, and still very self-conscious about its democratic status. After World War II (1939–45), a deliberate response was made to Germany's politico-cultural past and the nation was, to a great extent, imposed upon and guided by external forces. The Allied powers directly planned and supervised both the dismantling and the reconstitution of German institutions along the lines of democratic, decentralized powers, as was particularly manifest in the balkanization of the broadcasting medium. The present political structure of the FRG consists of a federal parliamentary democracy based on the new constitution of 1949, which was framed by representatives of the *Länder* (states) in accordance with guidelines set by the Allies. Unconditional sovereignty was not granted until 5 May 1955. The federal parliament consists of two chambers—the Bundestag (Lower House) and the Bundesrat (Federal Council). The composition of the ninth Bundesrat is shown in Table 6-1, where some discrepancy in proportional representation is also apparent.*

The recent establishment of this quasi-imposed democratic order comprises the root dimension against which the themes and conflicts

---

*A useful and readily accessible source for an overview of West German political, social, and economic institutions is *Facts about Germany*, published by the FRG Press and Information Office (1980).

Table 6-1
Composition of the Ninth Bundesrat (1982)

Länder	Number of Representatives	Population (millions)
Baden-Württemberg	5	9.1
Bavaria	5	10.8
(West) Berlin	4	1.9
Bremen	3	0.7
Hamburg	3	1.7
Hessen	4	5.6
Lower Saxony	5	7.2
North Rhine-Westphalia	5	17.0
Rhineland-Palatinate	4	3.6
Saarland	3	1.1
Schleswig-Holstein	4	2.6
Total	45	61.3

Sources: FRG Press and Information Office, Bonn; *Statistisches Jahrbuch* 1980.

that persist from the past communications culture must be reckoned with or fought out.

Prior to this abrupt break from the prewar past, German politico-cultural tradition could be best characterized as having structures of institutions and authorities that were strongly steeped in feudal rule. The decay of this form of social organization was not precipitated until World War I (1914–18), and the monarchy of Bavaria persisted to as late as 1919, when it was finally overthrown by the forces of the democratic movement in the November Revolution.

For our purposes, two major factors to be highlighted in this considerable period of development are:

1. That the German kingdoms only formed a central, national political unity in 1871, when the king of Prussia was declared German emperor. That year also ushered in the era of the powerful Bismarck, who became the new minister-president of Prussia.
2. In the long history of the struggles of the democratic movement of the German people, played out against a background of powerful feudal and semifeudal rule, the political party developed prior to the nation-state. As a consequence, the primary allegiance of groups within the structures of German society has been to the political party rather than to the state, which is traditionally mistrusted or even hated. The social history of the democratic movement in Germany evinces a path clearly marked by brutal and severe suppression at the hands of

the aristocratic-military ruling elite, from well before Martin Luther and the peasant wars up to Hitler and beyond.

The prior development of political parties as primary reference points for groups in the overall loyalty structure may be illustrated from the period of the infancy of the German nation-state. In an attempt to grapple with the threat of a thriving, populist party that championed the cause of the democratic movement—the social-democratic party—Bismarck sought to criminalize and thereby suppress the strong party movement by means of his anti-socialist legislation of 1878. (The party then outlawed has evolved into the present-day SPD [Social Democratic Party], currently the party in power.)

The subsequent events of World War I, as well as the renewed postwar endeavors toward the further democratization of German society, including the Weimar period and the sorry history of usurpation by a strongly centralized, authoritarian form of state supremacy, are familiar enough in modern history to require no further explication here. (For more information, see Streisand 1976; Czajka 1968; and *Lehrbuch der deutschen Geschichte* 1960).

What must be reiterated, however, is the strong legacy left by the salience of party-political relations. This helps to explain both the intensity and the pervasiveness of the politicization of German public life, particularly in the cultural sphere of the communications media. Politics is everywhere. And, in light of the extent of politicization in this sphere, in the FRG as in nearly all of the Western democracies, the range of political debate has been narrowed considerably and, indeed, is in danger of being rendered ineffectual at times by the bipolarism that results from the unfortunate development of a virtual two-party system.

The major and valid themes of debate and conflict that recur in the sphere of communication policy in the FRG today essentially, then, concern problems associated with the power of the state in relation to the control and regulation of the communications process. Here the newly founded democratic expectations center around primary notions such as plurality and balance, and noninfringement of democratic rights to freedom of expression, and freedom of information. Thus, while there is recognition of a need for the state to have some effective powers of regulation, there is at the same time considerable caution about state intervention. This has been a major issue, particularly in the press sector. In the public realm of broadcasting, on the other hand, the incursion of party-political interests into the broadcasting institutions has provided the major issue. A corollary of these major themes has been the overall concern about the effects that the inroads made by specific interest groups, whether private or party-political, will have on the democratic processes of the communications sphere. The national compromise between the logical extremes of partisan polarization on these issues is, in many respects, still being sought.

A further problem, brought to light by the post-1949 experience in the communication policy arena, is of great consequence not only within the FRG, but also to all the democratic societies. That is the problem of how a recently established, democratic, federal system of government (as in the FRG), or any democratic government for that matter, committed to an ideology of fragmentation and decentralization of power, can manage to deal with powerful coalitions of private interests. Those interests are themselves becoming more and more concentrated and centralized (as well as often being party-politically aligned) in the process of the accelerated economic trend toward monopoly and oligopoly business since the 1950s.

This issue has occasioned particular concern within the FRG, not only with regard to the press, but also with regard to the increased possibility of the incursion of powerful private interests into broadcasting, as well as into the single monopoly public authority of posts and telecommunications, as a result of new technological innovations in that field. The direct and vigorous nature of this broad, fundamental issue results from the high priority that cultural power receives as a special category of political power (within Germany), over which various groups and the state compete.

Under the present structure of the FRG as a parliamentary democracy, legislative authority rests primarily with the individual *Länder*. The federal government possesses such authority only to the extent that it is specifically provided for under the constitution. Authority over the cultural sphere and, hence, over the area of communication policy, comes extensively under the legislative jurisdiction of the *Länder*. The federation possesses only a broad "framing authority" to regulate only general, legal relations in this sphere, but not their detail. For example, in accordance with Article 75, section 2 of the Constitution of the FRG (1949), the federation has the right to pass federal "frame" or skeleton laws about the general legal status of the press and of film. However, the few attempts at passing such "frame laws" have by no means always met with success, largely due to fervent opposition from the professional organization of the German press, which presented itself as an effective pressure group at the inception of the very first such attempt in 1952.

The Press

The position of the press in the FRG is articulated in both the Constitution of 1949 and the statutes, under the general concept of freedom of thought, which encompasses freedom of information and freedom of the press.

Every German person has the right to freedom of expression by speech, writing and pictures or any other means, and to freely inform himself from generally accessible sources. These rights may not be interfered with by virtue of work-relations and no one may be disadvantaged as a result of making use of these rights. There shall be no censorship. [Article 5:1].

Thus freedom of the press as well as of reporting by radio and film are guaranteed.

These provisions also cleared the way for those publishers and journalists who had been banned from practicing their trade as a result of their activities during the period 1933 to 1945 to resume their work.

Communication policy concerning the press is, in the FRG, not only revealed clearly through negative response such as legal restraints, as in the case with some of the other countries presented in this volume; it is also strongly in evidence through the positive notion of "public mission" prescribed for the press, which merits special attention in the sphere of legislation enacted.

The host of legal restraints that are common to many countries are set out under Article 5:GG in accordance with general law. For example, the protection of minors (indecent publications); the State Secrets Act which, under Paragraph 353-C of the Legal Code, provides sanctions against members of the press communicating state secrets; protection of personal rights of honor and reputation; and in the Legal Code also is specific reference to "defamation of the dead" as well as to libel and defamation "of one's fellow citizens." German libel laws do not possess the same potency for stifling public discussion as those of countries like Australia and New Zealand, for example, which are strongly steeped in the British legal heritage. The German federal government has sought to extend the "personal protection law" (i.e., libel and defamation codes) on several occasions, failing each time due to opposition of the press, which has principally rejected stipulations about the right to damages for injured parties.

Another key area of legal restraint in which the FRG has been unsuccessful is the attempt to introduce clauses into the emergency powers legislation that would restrict the freedom of the press (1960–68). In a remarkable event that saw the magazine *Der Spiegel* seized and impounded in October–November of 1962 for publishing an allegedly treasonous article, the Penal Code had to be amended to allow a distinction to be drawn between "normal" and "journalistic" state treason.

The center of attention has, however, remained steadfastly focused upon the "public mission" of the press, in keeping with the political importance of cultural power.

In prescribing such a public mission for the press (*die offentliche Aufgabe der Presse*), the postwar emphasis has clearly shown a concern for framing the professional standards with which the press was to be entrusted. To this end, consciously democratic notions such as "public office," "public duty," and "public responsibility" were invoked as guiding principles, with the basic idea that the press should be neither a business nor a private institution but rather a special type of public office. In order to guarantee the capability of the press to fulfill this special role, provision had to be made to protect the press against intervention by both the state and other powerful social groups and interests—that is, the issue of state intervention versus self-regulation in the management of the press. Further, the position of the press also needed to be secured against the potential of advertising interest to exercise a domineering influence on publishers. This would be achieved by strengthening the position of the editors—that is, the issue of "internal democracy," which has also come to be of considerable concern in the public broadcasting institutions over recent years (the "statute movement"). In effect, neither of these aims has been successfully implemented.

The issue of internal democracy dates right back to the period of reconstruction following World War I, when, during the 1920s, the newspaper owners were at the height of their influence throughout Europe (e.g., the giant Hugenberg concern of Weimar Germany and its vigorous campaign against that Republic, with Hugenberg himself eventually being appointed to Hitler's cabinet). Journalists began to question the ethics of the authority of newspaper ownership. Moves were instigated by the professional association of German journalists (Reichsverband der Deutschen Presse) to bring new press laws into effect that would protect press freedom against the direct, private influence of the publishers. This was to be achieved by regulating the relations between the proprietor and the editorial staff, setting out their respective responsibilities. The key point at issue concerned the use of the chief editor to represent merely the proprietor's views and interests. It was argued that the chief editor should be allowed to represent the overall interests of the newspaper as expressed by the entire editorial staff, not only those of the proprietor. The journalists' association therefore added the requirement that the owner sign his or her name to any personal views expressed through the newspaper. The legislation drafted was, however, never enacted.

In the period of reestablishment during the early 1950s, the issue erupted again and has broadened to a clamoring, by staff, for wider participation in executive decisions. The major bugbear preventing the appropriate changes from being effected was the industrial relations law of 1952 (*Betriebsverfassungsgesetz*). This legislation restricted union counsel from participating in management in all lines of business termed "trend businesses." Publishing concerns came within this definition.

In spite of the considerable protests by the two professional organizations of journalists—the German Journalists' Union (Deutsche Journalisten-Union—DJU), and the German Journalists' Association (Deutscher Journalistenverband—DJV)—the 1971 amendment of the law retained the above restriction. The newly elected SPD government intended to rectify the matter in 1973 and again in 1976 but, in the face of a powerful and conservative press, got no further than giving notice to present a new press "frame law" aimed at overcoming some of the considerable variations between the *Länder* laws, and also at regulating the relations between publishers and editorial staff.

During 1978 the DJV reminded Chancellor Schmidt of the earlier promises in this regard and drafted the following points for inclusion in the proposed bill to secure and clarify the question of internal democracy for the press:

1. To forbid the publisher from specifically directing members of the editorial staff. However, the principal authority of the publisher was not in dispute.
2. Participation of representatives of the editorial staff in decisions concerning a change in the principal position of the newspaper or periodical.
3. Regulations for conflict arising out of the instigation of editorial representation.
4. Election of editorial representation by all editors excluding chiefs of staff.
5. The integration of editorial representation and the board of management.
6. Special protection against dismissal for the editorial representatives.
7. Participation by the editorial representatives in the hiring and firing of editors-in-chief.
8. Participation of the editorial representatives in exceptional cases concerning personnel, for which the board of management was not authorized to deal.
9. Participation of the editorial representatives in setting out the editorial budget.
10. Establishment of an information committee that would have rights similar to those set out for the management committee (in accord with paragraphs 106–110 of the *Betriebsverfassungsgesetz*) (*Media Perspektiven* 1, 1978:36).

However, given the strength of the reaction previously shown by the Federal Association of German Newspaper Publishers (Bundesverband Deutscher Zeitungsverleger—BDZV), and the support its most powerful members have traditionally shown for the conservative party (Christian Democratic Union—CDU), such a move is unlikely to be initiated in the near future.

Even more central issues related to the management of the press (state intervention and self-management), have undergone similar setbacks, with no satisfactory compromise solution yet at hand. The federation has no legislative authority over this vital area and the German Press Council has no executive authority. The Press Council was founded in 1956, primarily with a view to avoiding state measures and initiatives. It is composed of five representatives each from the publishers' and the journalists' organizations.

An early opportunity to regulate positively for the "public office/public duty" status of the press was unfortunately lost because of an ill-conceived approach on the part of the federal government in its first attempt to exercise its "frame-laws" powers. It attempted a two-pronged attack, ushering in restrictive legislation to control the critical role of the press on the coattails of the positive regulations.

This process was initiated through the agency of the newly formed Department of Interior in 1952 as a result of the fact that none of the *Länder* (with whom legislative authority in effect rests) had really come to grips with the problem of delineating what positive provisions were needed to guarantee the professional standing of the press in its role as a "special type of public office." This situation has remained, even after the new era of press regulations by the *Länder* around the mid-1960s again failed to make any provision for the establishment of press councils or for any form of publicly constituted social control.

The federal government sought to fill this gap and, at the same time, establish greater national consistency over the regulation of the press. In drafting the 1952 "Leuder bill" the government presented two main objectives:

1. To rigorously delineate the "public mission" of the press, including the normative structuring of the internal relations of the press (i.e., internal democracy).
2. To provide the federation with greater control over the critical role of the press in the event that it exceeded the normal bounds secured under paragraph 93 of the German Legal Code and was, hence, deemed to contravene the spirit of "protection of the image of the German federation and its democratic order" and so forth.

The first objective presented, on the whole, a sensible and, in retrospect, necessary approach to the basic problem of preventing powerful interests from dominating through centralization and concentration of press ownership, and also provided for the detailed regulation of publisher-editor relations. Certain problematic points and some elastic phrasing, however, left room for disquiet about the possibility of extensive government interference. Overall, the positive aspects of this draft also strongly threatened the private interests of the owners or publishers.

The second of the objectives aroused the collective ire of the professional organizations of the private press and was used to mobilize the support of both these groups (publishers and journalists) in opposition to the bill. It was strongly felt that Article 18GG of the Constitution made adequate provision for such instances, as it dealt specifically with the maintenance of the democratic order against "threats."

Opposition by the press, in its main thrust, centered around a clause providing for both federal and state press committees made up of two judges from the respective courts, and of four representatives from the publishers' and from the journalists' organizations. A particularly sore point was that the committee members were to have been named by the appropriate presiding governments. The overall intent of the bill, to enforce self-regulation, was coupled with a considerable potential for governmental interference and influence. The press campaign was vigorously conducted around the latter aspect, and demonstrated clearly the advantage of the power to define and present issues that is enjoyed by the powerful, private interests of the press.

When the bill finally foundered because of the strong opposition of the press, its positive aspects were wiped out along with the rest, without really coming to prominent notice. Journalists regretted the defeat in some respects, since the bill would have provided for the detailed regulation of the publisher-editor relationship in accordance with the goals of the journalists' association (Mahle and Richter 1974:16-21). In spite of the concentration and centralization of ownership within the German press that has proceeded apace since the mid-1950s, no federal government has since attempted to pass such a "frame law." Discussion about such law has only been resumed since 1969.

A look at the concrete developments that have taken place within the press sector of the FRG shows that the press is almost exclusively organized as a private business. Its current structure evinces the following features:

1. A large number of daily newspapers, many of which are, however, regionally and locally situated and editorially dependent upon the large papers for all but local news;
2. An undeniable tendency toward strong concentration of press ownership, though a plateau seems to have been reached in the late 1970s;
3. The virtual lack of development of a strong party press;
4. The lack of strong capital-city dailies and interregional newspapers;
5. A growing dependence on advertising;
6. The growing politicization of the illustrated periodicals;
7. The diversity and range of these magazines (though not as great as the choice available in England, for example).

A variety of news sources are available to the German press. The major agencies, both international and local, are DPA (Deutsche Presse-Agentur), Reuters, UPI (United Press International), AFP (Agence France-Presse), Tass, and ADN (Allgemeiner Deutscher Nachrichten-dienst), which though not normally available to the West German press, is often cited via East German sources. The prime German agency is DPA, which is a corporate body comprising 208 shareholders, none of whom may own more than one percent of the shares—a safeguard against the possibility of any one publishing concern attaining controlling interest.

The rapid concentration of ownership of the press occurred in two distinct periods. The first, around the mid-1950s, was characterized by a series of mergers; the second, around the mid-1960s, was marked by mergers as well as the attrition and collapse of various newspapers.

These two periods of rapid structural change occurred during the following phases of economic transition within the FRG:

1. The first phase of the so-called "German economic miracle" between about 1950 and 1963, when the disposable income of the average German family rose markedly from DM305 per month to DM847 per month.
2. The second phase of that program, which involved the parliamentarily controlled reorganization of capitalism in the FRG from 1964. (This is discussed in relation to industry as a whole by Lenel 1968:22, and Holzer 1971, Ch. 3:2, 74–103.)

The results of the shifts that took place within the press sector over these periods, marking a very strong trend toward centralization and concentration of ownership, are shown in Table 6-2.

Table 6-2
Statistical Data Concerning the Press in the FRG

Year	Independent editorial organizations	Newspaper publishing houses	Newspapers in existence	Circulation (millions)
1954	225	624	1500	13.4
1964	183	573	1495	17.3
1967	158	535	1416	18.0
1976	121	403	1229	19.5
1979	122	400	1240	20.5
1981	124	392	1258	20.4

Source: Compiled from the works of Schütz, W.J., 1976 and 1981.

The data presented in Table 6-2 provide a fairly self-evident account of the structural shifts that have occurred in the German daily press. While there are still 124 independent editorial organizations operating, it has been estimated that up to 50 percent of the personnel in these organizations originated from a mere 16 newspaper publishers (Schütz 1976 and 1981).

Overall, the generally accepted impression appears to be that the tendency toward greater concentration and centralization seems to have stabilized since 1976, if only because there are hardly any goals left to achieve in this regard. And, while the period from 1954 to 1976 was characterized by a steady decline in the number of newspaper publishing houses, independent editorial organizations, and newspapers in existence, along with a steady increase in circulation, only the number of newspaper publishing houses has continued to decline since.

Also, it needs to be pointed out that in spite of the 1979–81 figures for "newspapers in existence," no real founding of new daily newspapers has taken place in the sense of titles not previously on the market.

By 1981, newspaper monopolies existed in almost one-third of the cities and counties of the FRG, with only five nationally distributed dailies in existence, compared with twenty such newspapers in the prewar period. Two of those five belong to the powerful, dominant Axel Springer house. The five are the *Frankfurter Allegemeine Zeitung, Die Welt, Süddeutsche Zeitung, Handelsblatt,* and *Bild Zeitung (die überregionale Presse)*, with *Bild* and *Die Welt* being the Springer newspapers.

The newspaper *Bild*, with around 4.7 million copies sold daily, is the uncontested leader in the circulation stakes for continental Europe. (The English paper the *Sun* is the leader in the whole of Europe.) In the mid-1970s, it was estimated that around 17.7 million Germans read *Bild* regularly. This represented about 42 percent of the total population (Meyn 1974:44). The extent of its domination of the nationally distributed dailies is shown in Table 6-3. Furthermore, the two big Axel Springer

Table 6-3
**Nationally Distributed Dailies (*die uberregionale Presse*):
December Quarter, 1980**

Newspaper	Publisher	Circulation
Bild	Axel Springer Verlag AG, Hamburg/Berlin	4,710,209
Süddeutsche Zeitung	Verlagsgruppe Süddeutscher Verlag/Friedmann Erben, München	330,469
Die Welt	Axel Springer Verlag AG, Hamburg/Berlin	203,681
Handelsblatt	An economic paper not belonging to any of the top ten newspaper publishers.	83,278
Frankfurter Allgemeine Zeitung	Frankfurter Societäts-Drückerei GmbH, Frankfurt	78,061

Source: Diedrich 1981:521–36.

dailies, *Bild* and *Die Welt* each have their own Sunday edition counterparts in *Bild am Sonntag* and *Welt am Sonntag*, each of which boasts extremely high circulation rates: 2.46 million and 0.326 million, respectively.

Another indication of the strength of concentration and centralization is provided by the market share profile of the five largest newspaper publishers, as shown in Table 6-4.

Table 6-4
Newspaper Publishers by Market Share:
December Quarter, 1980

Publisher	Market Share (%)
Axel Springer Verlag AG	28.27
Zeitungsverlags-gesellschaft Brost & Funke	6.00
Verlagsgruppe Stuttgarter Zeitung/Rheinpfalz/ Gruppe württembergische Verleger	5.20
Verlag M. DuMont Schauberg	3.73
Verlagsgruppe Süddeutscher Verlag/Friedmann Erben	2.37
Total	45.57

Source: Diedrich 1981:521–36.

A similar picture is presented by the market structure of periodicals publication, where four large concerns tend to dominate (see Table 6-5). The market position enjoyed by the "big four" has remained relatively unaltered since the mid-1970s.

The situation that these developments have wrought for the press in Germany was aptly summed up by Stuart Hood when he said that:

> the number of gatekeepers—those men and women, who, by discarding or accepting an item of news, by printing or spiking a report, by passing or rejecting an editorial, decide what the public shall read—has decreased appreciably. A smaller selection of news and opinion is therefore being read and consumed by a larger number of people. (Hood 1972:60)

These changes in the market structure within the press sector have resulted from a combination of cost-push and technological factors with which only the larger firms have been able to keep pace, together with the acquisitive drive of the larger publishers. Such factors of power and

Table 6-5
The Market in Periodicals Publishing:
December Quarter, 1980

Publisher	Titles Published (number)	Total Circulation (millions)	Market Share (%)
Bauer	18	17.36	20.53
Burda	9	10.29	12.17
Springer	8	7.14	8.44
Bertelsmann*/ Gruner & Jahr	9	5.64	6.67
Total	44	40.43	47.81

Source: Diedrichs:1981.
*The Bertelsmann concern constitutes by far the largest publishing business in the FRG and reputedly the largest or second largest in the world, including interests in the U.S., France, Spain, and other countries. Bertelsmann AG was first and foremost a book publisher, having also snared 22 percent of the U.S. paperback market, and has diversified into periodicals such as the popular *Der Stern* and *Brigitte*, video cassettes, music, film, and records. The director, Reinhard Mohn, who is the founding Bertelsmann's grandnephew, has in sharp contrast to his rival Axel Springer, sought to steer a neutral political path (*Der Spiegel* 35, 7, 1981).

market survival are inextricably linked to the broader structure of the political economy of the FRG. Furthermore, these factors have led to a closer integration of newspapers (and periodicals) with other powerful, private interests of acquisitive economics—to wit, increasing dependence of all of the mass media on advertising, though more so for the press, since broadcasting sustains a base of guaranteed revenue through licensing fees. This increasing dependence may be measured by the value of advertising attracted by the various publishers, a ratio that also highlights the role of newspapers and periodicals as conveyers of private economic interests to broad sections of the public.

Between 1970 and 1974 some 60 percent of all advertising expenditure went to the newspaper and periodical publishers. This represented an inflow of around DM2,500 million for 1970 and almost DM4,500 million for 1974. In relation to overall income, advertising accounted for an average of 65 percent for newspaper publishers, and 60 percent for the publishers of periodicals over the period 1970–74. The daily press has become more directly dependent upon advertising related to the job and business markets (apart from some local, mixed advertising) following the loss of consumer advertising to periodicals as well as to radio and television. It is precisely this section of the trade—the daily press—that is most closely affected by movements within the economic market.

One of the dangers of this increased dependence between press and advertiser is that the political line of any given newspaper can be either honored or negatively sanctioned at the behest of powerful, private interests. Such a development does not mesh well with the "public office" and "public mission" concepts of the press, as the following example illustrates.

On 30 and 31 January 1972, the top representatives of the West German economy, including such people as the chairman of the board of directors of BASF, Dr. Kurt Hansen, met together with the Hamburg publisher, Heinz Bauer, to discuss the campaign that the Bauer publishing enterprise was to wage against the Social Democratic partner of the coalition government of the day. During this meeting Heinz Bauer recommended that the members present direct their advertising to his publications rather than to the periodical *Der Spiegel*, which was sympathetic to the coalition partner. It was not made known whether firm agreements were made along this line, but as it turned out, *Der Spiegel* and another "sympathetic" periodical, *Der Stern*, incurred considerable losses in advertising revenue during 1972 (Meyn 1974:58).

While this does not in any way constitute firm proof, it nevertheless points out the danger of the extent to which, under the present structure, political pressure and direction may be exercised by the concentration of private interests.

Another example of the way in which the advertising interests can simply cut certain publications out of market competition is afforded by the case of the periodical *Konkret*, which took a critical line on the organization and running of the German economy; huge firms such as BASF, Hoechst, Dunlop, and VW did not advertise in *Konkret*, which ceased publication in the late 1970s (Meyn 1974:58).

In choosing to exercise this kind of critique, *Konkret* breached the "zones of silence" (*die Schweigezonen*) required of the press in its regulatory function for society: that is, the role of the press has become one of shielding the vulnerable areas of the system by depoliticizing the masses and also leveling the threshold between the circulation of goods and the circulation of news and information.

Nowhere are the dangers of such political influence and abuse corrupting the democratic processes of the public medium of the press more apparent than in the position of the Springer press within the FRG.

As indicated earlier, the Axel Springer Verlag AG is without peer in the European newspaper publishing business, in its position of market dominance, and the willingness of its owner to thrust his political ideology at the readership. Within the FRG, Springer owns the largest national daily (*Bild Zeitung*), the largest evening newspaper *Hamburger Abendblatt*), the two largest Sunday papers (*Bild am Sonntag* and *Welt am Sonntag*), the biggest weekend paper (*Das Neue Blatt*), and the largest-selling television and radio journal (*HörZu*), with a weekly circulation of 3.94 million copies in 1981. This accounts for 28.27 percent of the market for dailies (*Bild* alone has 23.24%), 83.6 percent of Sunday papers, 51 percent of the market for radio and television journals, and 8.44 percent of the periodical market (Diedrichs 1981; Schütz 1981).

The Springer press empire, like that of Rupert Murdock of Australia, is a multinational concern having significant business interests in Latin America, particularly in Chile, where, it is rumored, the Springer press played a not-insignificant part in the events surrounding the military overthrow of the elected Allende government in September 1973. Such activities fit easily within the basic political line Springer's press has consistently advocated in the politics of the FRG—that of right-wing demagogy and a clamor for a return to the old German order (Müller 1968:291).

Axel Springer's basic philosophy for his newspapers, articulated around 1959, is based on the idea that the postwar German essentially did not wish to think about anything (Müller 1968). This is reflected in the conscious efforts of his newspapers to present sensationalized "human interest" stories related very much to sex. Crime as well as an emotionally charged headline style of news presentation is also part of the formula. According to his critics, the overall strategy has resulted in a kind of quiescent depoliticization of his vast readership.

While such a policy tends, on the face of it, to give credence to Springer's espoused view that the press has no right to strive for political power, closer examination reveals a markedly different practice. The politics of right-wing demagogy scream out of those emotive and sensationalist headline-style presentations. In this way the Springer newspapers have consistently fired up hatred and animosity against active groups such as the student movement, hippies, minorities, the political left, and politicians deemed to be of that ilk.

A famous example of this type of political abuse arose in 1972 when the Springer newspaper *Die Welt* headlined a statement misrepresenting the words of the then-chancellor, Willy Brandt, to read: "I don't care about the nation." Chancellor Brandt had in fact stated: "For me [the term] 'nation' is meaningless if it is only a nice word used on public holidays" (Meyn 1974:31–32). While it is all very well to claim that there is a council of appeal for such cases of breach of the truth (also established in 1972), the public damage is not undone by the brief lines of apology buried somewhere in the body of the newspaper at a later date.

Within the organization of his newspapers, Springer's personal line is ensured by loyal editors. The issue of "internal democracy" dares not rear its head there, as experience has shown. During 1977, the well-known social critic, Günther Wallraff penetrated the newspaper *Bild Zeitung* by working as a journalist in Hannover. He soon found many of his stories tampered with or omitted entirely by the chief editor if they did not concur with Springer's outlook. Wallraff's ensuing book, detailing these practices, has become the subject of legal proceedings by the

Springer concern against Wallraff. Their outcome in 1982 established that Wallraff had himself been somewhat overcommitted to a specific orientation against *Bild* and hence some of his claims had to be retracted, though the legal (and otherwise) battle between Wallraff and *Bild* continues to rage (Wallraff 1977; *Der Stern* 1982:316).

Springer's considerable power extends over not only the publication of news, but also the distribution side of the market. An example of this type of influence is afforded by the occasion of the television journals conflict. In this case, Springer put direct pressure on the distributors not to handle a competitor's television guide (*TV-Fernseh-Woche*) because its publication of East German programs conflicted with his political views. This led him to form a league of television journals around his own *HörZu*, insisting that as long as details of West German programs were not given in the East, the West should do likewise.

In sum, the dangers posed by the dominance of such strong, private interests in the sphere of a public medium like the press are considerable for the democratic process as a whole and, as part and parcel of this, for the "public mission" of the press:

> The concentration of such power in the hands of one man raises large questions of principle and demonstrates how, under financial and technical pressures, the press may lose that element of pluralism which is its main virtue as compared with radio and television, and how a uniformity of views may be imposed without even those minimal controls which are exercised over broadcasting by councils, advisory committees and boards of governors. (Hood 1972:50)

General concern intensified about the undesirability of these types of developments in concentration and centralization, and resulted in the appointment in 1967 of a commission of inquiry into the state of the press in the FRG. The Günther Commission (officially known as the Kommission zur Untersuchung der Gefährdung der wirtschaftlichen Existenz von Presseunternehmen und der Folgen der Konzentration für die Meinungsfreiheit in der Bundesrepublik Deutschland) was to investigate the effects that these changes could have on the freedom of communication. Within months of its appointment, two recommendations for immediate action were made:

1. An almost total acceptance of the publishers' recommendations for tax relief;
2. Cheaper credit for the press.

In its final report (1968), however, the commission included some further recommendations:

3. That the market proportions of any one publisher be limited;
4. That local competition be advanced to establish market balances;
5. That the smaller publishers be supported.

These latter recommendations were decried as unconstitutional by the publishers' association (the BDZV) and a few commission members as well. The association then wanted across-the-board financial relief for all publishers, regardless of size, and definitely did not want any purposeful policies for shaping and controlling the structure of the press in the FRG.

In the end, the federal government went only so far as to take up the commission's recommendations for an annual report on the structure of the press and to require property and stock reports from the publishers by law. Also, rules of competition and a board of newspaper technology and business were established. Credit and tax relief for small publishers had already been granted from the outset (1967), as was the case with the decision to make only half the normal rate of the value added tax applicable to newspapers.

What can be said about the effect of German press policy in the face of the developments described here? As has happened in virtually all other developed countries experiencing the steady diminution of newspapers and independent editorial entities, admonishment without the real teeth of regulatory powers has proved a useless device. The German Press Council, which many would argue ought to be granted regulative power, has no executive authority and no authority to impose sanctions.

Monopoly control systems have similarly met with failure in many societies. In the FRG, the establishment of the Cartell Bureau (Kartellamt) has failed to prevent even a single further merger from taking place. The idea behind its inception was that any mergers between two newspaper interests that would bring their combined annual turnover to a level of DM25 million had to be reported, with the aim that the Kartellamt would prevent the mergers from taking place. However, faced with the dilemma of permitting the merger or letting one of the newspapers collapse, the Kartellamt has also been powerless to achieve this objective (c.f. Smith 1978:Ch. 12).

Subsidy by means of nonpolitical grants of cash seems to be one way around the problem. Yet, given the cultural milieu in which it needs to be instituted, this option faces considerable hazards. For example, the 1975 newspaper industry plan to set up a Press Foundation for this purpose was not put into effect.

On a more positive note, a significant victory for the workings of the new democracy against powerful coalitions of private interests was won during the late 1950s, when the efforts of the BDZV to ban advertising from public broadcasting and to participate in a private broadcasting system were defeated. The 1957 BDZV lawsuit to have advertising banned from public broadcasting was defeated on the grounds that it was both illegal and uncompetitive. The move to gain rights to participate in broadcasting, particularly television, was thwarted by the judgment of the Federal Constitutional Court in February 1961. This historic "television judgment" will be discussed in more detail under the section on broadcasting.

Publishing

The book-publishing industry of the FRG has continued to exhibit the pattern of strength and growth so prevalent throughout the 1970s. In fact, 1980, a record year for the number of titles published, showed an increase of 8.2 percent over 1979. Of the approximately 67,000 titles published in 1980, 12,604 were new titles, and about one-tenth were translations of works from other languages, most notably English and French (Börsenverein des deutschen Buchhandels 1981:7). The annual Frankfurt Book Fair (Frankfurter Buchmesse) further attests to the strength of the book publishing sector. Over 5,400 exhibitors, 4,000 of them foreign, took part in 1980, its thirty-third year.

The FRG ranks as the third largest book-producing country in the world behind the United States and the Soviet Union which, according to UN statistics, each publish about 85,000 titles annually (Börsenverein des deutschen Buchhandels 1981:7). Figures released by the Association of German Book-Publishers (Börsenverein des deutschen Buchhandels) show that there is not even a hint of diminishing numbers of publishers, nor of a concentration of the market around a few best-seller titles. In 1981, there were 1,835 book publishers in the FRG, with a further 3,276 distributors listed with the Börsenverein des deutschen Buchhandels (1981:53).

In 1980, fiction titles accounted for 18.5 percent of all publications. This represented a slight decline from previous years, 20 percent in 1979 and 22.9 percent in 1978. Publications in the fields of economics and the social sciences followed with 7.7 percent, down from 9.9 percent in 1979. Religion and theology placed third with 5.7 percent, up from 5 percent in 1979, and perhaps providing an interesting point of cultural comparison with some of the other leading Western nations. Technical books and law texts were the next substantial groups, with 5.4 percent and 5.3 percent, respectively. The natural sciences accounted for 4.6 percent of the market, and calendars and almanacs ranked at the bottom, with only 0.2 percent of the market. The market share of paperbacks fell slightly to 11.6 percent as compared with 12 percent in 1979, 12.4 percent in 1978, and the high of 13 percent in 1977. The number of actual paperback titles published have, however, continued to climb, increasing by 350 titles over the 1979 output to reach 7,793 in 1980 (Börsenverein des deutschen Buchhandels 1981:13–21).

Special mention ought also to be made here of the growing concentration of the Bertelsmann group which, through its various publishing houses, offers a range of some 5,000 different titles (including fiction, scientific literature, cartographical, and other publications). These, together with the Bertelsmann foreign publishing affiliations such as Bantam Books and the Zurich-based "Krimi-Verlag" net this group an annual turnover of approximately DM465 million from book publication alone (*Der Spiegel* 35, 7, 1981). This compares with an average turnover of DM2 million to DM10 million for 31.3 percent of German book publishers, with a further 20 percent of publishers attaining an average turnover of about DM29 million (Börsenverein des deutschen Buchhandels 1981:61).

Despite a modest but steady upward trend in the price of books, over half of the titles published during 1980 were still available at prices below DM15, which compares very favorably with book prices in other leading book-publishing countries. The price structure of the book-publishing industry is shown in Table 6-6.

Table 6-6
Price Structure of Books Published, 1980

Selling Price (DM)	Percent of All Books Sold
Below 5	22.5
5–10	19.1
10–15	9.9
15–25	16.7
25–50	12.1

Source: Börsenverein des Deutschen Buchhandels, 1981:39–41,

On the retailing side, the profile of the book-publishing industry looks extremely healthy, with roughly 6,000 booksellers, not counting the approximately 3,000 door-to-door and mail-order outlets (Börsenverein des deutschen Buchhandels 1981:54–58).

Within the publishing trade there is a special association of esteemed authors known as the PEN Center of the FRG (PEN-Zentrum Bundesrepublik Deutschland), which in 1972 came under the leadership of Heinrich Böll. This organization took upon itself a more active political role during the 1970s, as a noticeable change back toward the old right became more and more apparent in major institutions throughout the decade. From about 1971, the PEN Center became increasingly more outspoken against the implications of the steady concentration of press ownership as well as against the guidelines drawn up by both the federation and the *Länder* on the "question of constitutional enemies of the civil service" (1972) which had strong antidemocratic connotations (*Berufsverbote* 1972).

While no direct form of censorship over publishing exists as such, the supreme authority that the *Länder* possess over cultural decisions does allow for a type of censorship over distribution and accessibility. For example, the Bavarian minister for culture (*Kultusminister*), Hans Maier, decided in 1978 to censor and ban all books by German "critical authors" (those he interpreted as being critical of German society) from use as school texts in Bavaria. His party also raised in parliament the question of the existence of "leftist" bookshops in Munich. Moreover, during 1978 three printers deemed to have published material sympathetic to the Baader-Meinhof terrorist group were imprisoned. In addition, there have been similar, though less serious actions in the sphere of broadcasting and films (*Blatt* 117, 1978:18).

Film and Cinema

The reestablishment of the German film industry after 1949 faced considerable hurdles from the outset. One of these was provided by Germany's own strong, prewar film culture and the other by the ubiquitous and persisting problem of readily available, relatively much cheaper foreign imports (particularly American films).

When the practice of the Allied powers' licensing of film production was swept away in 1949, the door was opened for the backlog of old Ufa films (the dominant Universum Film AG established in Germany in 1917) to enter the market once again, as it had been and continued to be for the comparatively cheap American imports that are generally dubbed in Germany prior to commercial release. This spelled disaster for any possibility of local film production strongly reemerging, and a variety of both federal and *Land* government film-assistance schemes began to come into effect.

Federal assistance measures have ranged from the awarding of prizes for feature films, cultural films, and scripts, to assisting young directors in the production of their first film (e.g., the Munich-based Kuratorium Junger Deutscher Film, est. 1965), all of which failed miserably in financial terms, resulting in the individual *Länder* taking over the trust fund for film assistance in 1969.

However, new federal legislation in 1971 saw the establishment of a public institution for the advancement of German film, the *Filmförderungsanstalt* in Berlin, with authority for supervision residing with the Ministry of Economics. This time there was also some expression of intent to raise the overall quality of film production rather than a mere view to market profitability. The measures to be undertaken were subsidizing German-foreign coproductions; advising the federal government on film policy; cultivating cooperation between television and the film industry; and establishing greater efficiency in the distribution of local film. Funding was to be derived from a levy (DM0.10, which was increased to DM0.15 in 1978) on each seat sold for all commercial screenings in the FRG, and reallocated to film producers in the form of subsidies on the basis of the commercial success of films already produced.

The upshot of this 1971 *Filmförderungsgesetz* has been that the producers of commercial sex-films have managed to appropriate funds initially intended to foster artistic development. Part of this is because the status of the FSK (Voluntary Self-Regulation of the Film Industry—Freiwillige Selbstkontrolle der Filmwirtschaft) has been left in an ambiguous position by Article 5 of the Constitution, which deals with freedom from censorship. The rest of the blame must be placed squarely on the criterion governing assistance—that of rewarding commercial success.

This situation finally led to a parliamentary proposal for amendments to the *Filmförderungsgesetz* in 1978. Submissions to the proposal were lodged by both the film lobby and the association of film journalists. The former group represented those economic interests of the film industry that saw their future primarily, perhaps exclusively, in the production of the money-making sex films and therefore wanted even the few sentences pertaining to quality in the present regulations eliminated altogether in the amendments. The association of film journalists, on the other hand, strongly urged the inclusion of clauses that would provide specific impetus toward achieving a "national quality" for German film. The parliamentary process finally worked through to the point of presenting a fourth amendment to the *Filmförderungsgesetz* that was passed in the Bundestag on 11 May 1979, but rejected by the Bundesrat in June, with recommendations for considerable modification.

However, it appears that the new-found quality of German film, which broke through to both domestic and international recognition at the end of the 1970s is threatened by the political machinations of the federal Christian Democratic Union-Christian Social Union (CDU-CSU) opposition. As they have done with broadcasting institutions, the CDU-CSU is attempting to halt the liberal development of films and to shackle this area of cultural development with political controls to make films conform to its values.

The work of the directors belonging to the new film-making resurgence in the FRG throughout the 1970s and maturing significantly in the latter years of the decade is the phenomenon know as "*der junge deutsche Film.*" The best-known of these directors on an international basis are Bohm, Brandner, Fassbinder, Geissendorfer, Hauff, Herzog, Kluge, and Schlonndorf. The recognition of their achievements has been realized via international distribution, including *Die Blechtrommel* (*The Tin Drum*) and *Maria Braun* by United Artists and *Nosferatu* by Twentieth Century-Fox, as well as by screenings at film festivals throughout the world.

188

In spite of this, however, the CDU-CSU opposition continues to denounce and defame both the films and their makers as radical-left antinationalists. According to the logic of the two "Christian" parties, these films and filmmakers are not only undesirable, but also unworthy. As in publishing, the Bavarian ruling party, the CSU, is zealously pursuing its political values in the cultural sphere. On the federal level, the generally more moderate CDU is the senior party in the opposition coalition, which, nominally at least, is seen in jest as a kind of self-proclaimed "holy alliance," but it should be noted that Franz Josef Strauss, the CSU leader, led the CDU-CSU alliance in the 1980 federal elections.

The CSU cultural priorities for Bavaria are reflected in the actions of the Munich city council, which turned away a film festival staged by thirty prominent directors in 1979 due to the lack of suitable venues. The directors then moved the festival to Hamburg amid proclamations of approval by the ruling party that these "undesirables" had departed (*Der Spiegel* 33, 25, 1979:178–83).

The political debate surrounding the proposed fourth amendment to the *Filmförderungsgesetz* is thus set in context.

Apart from one thorny point arising out of the Berlin FFA proposal to set up a three-member grants board for low-budget productions, the real political significance has centered around two other paragraphs that relate directly to funding of film projects. (The proposed grants board was specifically aimed at nurturing a new, third generation of young directors because those in the current swag of *Jungfilmer* are either in their forties or fast approaching them.) The main bone of contention is entirely political-ideological, since it is essentially the federal opposition rather than bodies within the film industry that objects to the proposed legislation. The paragraphs in dispute concern the provision of funding for film projects even where no final copy of the script has been submitted. Approval is to be by a simple two-thirds majority of the Projektkommission der Filmförderungsanstalt. The CDU-CSU wants to have these provisions revised or vetoed with the express intent of formulating regulations that will force German film production to conform more closely to its own political values. This has become clear from one of its internal party documents headed "Arbeitskreis Film der CDU/CSU," which disparagingly lamented the possibility that further critical-type films such as *Deutschland im Herbst* might be financed thus. This film portrayed the dangers of the renewed shift to the right in the FRG (see the discussion under "Publishing"), particularly in relation to the new, wide-ranging state and police powers passed to combat terrorism (*Der Spiegel* 35, 25, 1979).

Within the industry itself, ongoing debate has continued to center around the possibilities for establishing a more liberal funding system than both the commercially oriented Berlin model (Berlin contributes DM13 million annually to film production) and, as the filmmakers see it, the politically managed Bavarian model (Munich contributes over DM15 million annually). There has also been the growing realization of the need to supplement the three sources of production funds by a *Länder*-based *Filmförderung* in an attempt to avoid the sort of political muzzling of film that the federal opposition is advocating. The three production sources at the federal level are the *Filmförderungsanstalt* with an annual budget of DM25 million, the television institutions contributing DM79 million over a five-year period, and *Bundesmitteln* making up around DM8 million annually.

The question of cooperation between television and the film industry with regard to coproduction is a very interesting development in itself. Such coproduction was initially viewed as the only realistic way of salvaging the German film industry from its economic malaise, a view that has since been vindicated by the general acknowledgment that this step has, indeed, been the factor that has saved German film from imminent extinction over the past two decades. The relative importance of coproduction may be gauged from the fact that between 1960 and 1980, coproduction work has generated a turnover of DM5,700 million for the German film industry (*Filmstatistisches Taschenbuch 1981*, cited in *Media Perspektiven* 11, 1981:772–81).

It was felt that because television has spirited away a staggering percentage of cinema patrons, thereby forcing many cinemas to close, the television institutions (ARD and ZDF) ought to take some responsibility for helping the flagging film industry out of its crisis.

Since the introduction of television, the drastic decline of the cinema as the major source of entertainment in the FRG may be readily gauged from the sharp drop in the number of cinema seats sold since the 1950s. For example, in 1959, 671 million seats were sold; by the mid-1970s the figure was down to 115 million. To this drastic loss of patrons and, hence, revenue, one must further add the ever-increasing cost of film production in order to appreciate the situation fully. However, in the latter 1970s, the figures started to show a moderate upswing as the German film began to reassert itself as a successful national entity. Thus we see, for example, that in 1977, there was an increase of 7.9 percent over the previous year in the number of seats sold; this increased by a further 9.8 percent in 1978 (135.5 million seats sold) and was up again by 4.8 percent in 1979, with a further slight increase of 1.3 percent in 1980 (143.8 million seats sold) (*Media Perspektiven* 11, 1981:780).

By comparison, the number of television sets registered in the FRG over the same period rose from 2.1 million in 1959 to 18.3 million in 1973, with a 1981 near-saturation rate of over 98 percent of German households possessing at least one set. This represents a guaranteed annual revenue (from licensing fees) of well over DM1,500 million.

The distinct financial advantage enjoyed by the television institutions in relation to the situation for filmmakers needs to be explicitly stated. The former receive a guaranteed monthly revenue from licensing fees (DM13 per set or DM156 annually) which makes up the handsome revenue cited above. The filmmakers, on the other hand, need to rely on the meager DM0.15 levy per seat sold in the nation's cinemas.

It was because of this situation that German television was convinced to come to the aid of the film industry in some limited way. The ARD, ZDF, and the Union of German Film and Television Producers (der Verband Deutscher Film and Fernsehproduzenten) together agreed in 1970 to buy the transmission rights to one hundred German feature films. A rider that the films could only be transmitted five years after their first release to the public cinemas was added.

The assistance offered by television has led to a marked improvement over the situation that existed under the old *Filmförderungsgesetz* of 1967, which had been biased in favor of the established film industry. It tended, as a result, to isolate the young filmmakers and force them into nonbeneficial coproductions with the television institutions which, via contract agreements, blocked the path to public cinema release for these films.

This unsatisfactory situation has since been altered. In their 1978 proposal to amend the *Filmförderungsgesetz*, the film lobby and the association of film journalists specifically recommended that there be more cooperation between television and the film industry. Indeed, it was requested that the broadcasting institutions pledge wider supportive measures for film and television coproductions and also that the conditions of contracts governing this sphere of activity be liberalized.

Further, in September 1981, representatives of both the German film and television industries issued a notice of appeal to the ministers president of the *Länder*, requesting that the proposed increase in licensing fees (by DM2.24 from 1 January 1984) be brought forward to 1 January 1983 and raised by DM3 to DM4 in order that their continued support of the German film industry, indeed of German film culture, may be more soundly guaranteed (*Media Perspektiven* 9, 1981:667).

With this point, we arrive at one major aspect of the economic problems confronting German film that is also shared by television production, namely the problem experienced in trying to compete against the relatively cheaper, readily available and eminently distributable, technically accomplished goods imported from that movie giant, the United States or, in the case of color television programs, Japan. The havoc that this plays with the development of local productions needs no further comment, since the FRG is by no means alone in suffering from this particular problem. It is made manifest by the virtual domination of the German cinema screen by American and other foreign-produced films (though the extent of this moderated in the late 1970s), as well as by the substantial quota of foreign programs on German television. However, it is necessary to point out that relative to other countries, German television screens a good deal of locally produced material. Prime-time viewing, especially, is largely filled by German productions. See Table 6-7.

Table 6-7
New and First-Release Films Exhibited in the FRG, 1977-80

Year	1977	1978	1979	1980
Total number of films	340	314	304	336
German productions	58	60	67	51
German/foreign coproductions	14	7	12	12

Source: Filmstatistisches Taschenbuch 1981, cited in *Media Perspektiven* 11, 1981:780.

Broadcasting

The collective Allied stamp of the Potsdam days is strongly reflected in the constitutional basis for the organization of broadcasting in the FRG. The control over this cultural sphere has been very consciously separated from the state's executive.

Division of the areas of competence between the federation and the individual *Land* governments, as previously discussed, evidences no specific reference to broadcasting under relevant sections of federal Basic Law: Articles 70-75. Broadcasting is thus the prerogative of the *Länder*, with the only reference to it in the Constitution being in Article 5:1. However, it took a constitutional court ruling in 1961 to establish this unequivocally (Judgment of the Federal Constitutional Court, 2 February 1961; see, for example, *Rundfunk und Fernsehen*, no. 2, 1961).

The federally departmentalized or regional structure of broadcasting directly reflects the practices established during the Allied occupation when four stations (two run by the Americans, one by the French, and one by the British) operated in their respective zones of occupation. The French and the British organized their stations in accordance with their native systems, which were centralized, and this, particularly the British model, bequeathed a significant legacy to the organization of broadcasting in the FRG. The British founded the massive NWDR (Nordwestdeutscher Rundfunk) in Hamburg to cater to the whole British zone together with their sector in Berlin, where they also established a studio. This was later to be split into three separate broadcasting institutions: NDR (Norddeutscher Rundfunk) in Hamburg, WDR (Westdeutscher Rundfunk) in Cologne, and the Berlin studio became part of SFB (Sender Freies Berlin).

This legacy left a system that could hardly be described as balanced in terms of the requirements of the FRG as a whole: for example, the position of the tiny Radio Bremen (RB) right alongside the giant Hamburg station NDR has generated problems of financial inequality among the member stations of the present regional system.

The other major endowment of this period was the constitution provided for each of the stations. The constitutions were generally incorporated into *Land* legislation to ensure that the stations would be corporations of public law. Constitutional control is therefore in the hands of representatives of the public and definitely not the province of government or any one single interest.

Control over public broadcasting today is thus exercised by the public institutions—the *Gemeinnützige Anstalten des öffentlichen Rechts.*

Additional clout for the case of public control over all broadcasting was provided by the all-embracing formulation of the British NWDR's constitution, which extended to future technical innovations such as television as well (Williams 1976:Ch. 1). The British zone's NWDR, apart from being one of the wealthiest stations, had also, by some quirk of fate been left with the only intact equipment in the country after the war, including television equipment. It was therefore the only station in the running to commence experimental work in television, striking up an early agreement with the Deutsche Bundespost (German Post Office), its sole potential rival at the time, to be allowed to do so.

The significance of these developments was that once the *Land* authorities had assumed legal responsibility over broadcasting, they were in a prime position to repulse any advance into this area by the federal government.

After the transfer of control from the Allied powers to the German federation, the autonomy of the *Länder* over broadcasting was firmly entrenched. Those stations that served only a single *Land* were constituted by enactment of *Land* law alone, while stations serving wider regions were constituted by inter-*Land* agreements. Thus, for example, in 1954 when North Rhine-Westphalia opted out of NWDR to set up its own station in Cologne (WDR), the remaining three *Länder* of the former British zone concluded an agreement to found NDR.

In this way, nine regional broadcasting stations were established. They joined forces in 1950 to form the Arbeitsgemeinschaft der offentlich-rechtlichen Rundfunkanstalten der Bundesrepublik Deutschland, known universally as ARD since 1955. This represented clear endorsement of the federalist ideal. The upshot of these developments was the inception of a federation of public broadcasting institutions (sometimes translated as "broadcasting corporations" in other literature) that still serves the FRG today. The structure of this federation (the ARD) is as follows: six of the nine regional stations broadcast within their respective *Land* only: WDR (Westdeutscher Rundfunk) Cologne, North Rhine-Westphalia; BR (Bayerischer Rundfunk) Munich, Bavaria; HR (Hessicher Rundfunk) Frankfurt, Hessen; RB (Radio Bremen) Bremen; SFB (Sender Freies Berlin) Berlin; and SR (Saarländischer Rundfunk) Saarbrücken, Saarland. One of the nine serves only part of a *Land*—SDR (Süddeutscher Rundfunk) Stuttgart, which serves the northern part of Baden-Württemberg. Another, SWF (Südwestfunk) in Baden-Baden, serves the southern part of this *Land* plus the whole of the neighboring Rhineland-Palatinate. Finally, NDR Hamburg serves the three northern

Länder of Hamburg, Lower Saxony, and Schleswig-Holstein. NDR has, as a result, proved the most problematic to run because of political disagreements, which will be discussed later.

The same spirit of cooperation that accompanied the founding of ARD was carried into the founding in 1963 of the second television service ZDF (Zweiter Deutscher Funk), which was made possible by an inter-*Land* agreement involving all eleven *Länder*. Throughout the 1950s, however, the federal government mounted repeated challenges to this type of central association of pluralism. Impetus for a more centrally regulated guiding authority (i.e., federation) was provided by the granting of full sovereignty (May 1955), when the loss of Allied supervision over matters such as wavelength agreements, shortwave and longwave broadcasting, and the like needed to be taken up.

In these matters, the three competing groups, the *Länder*, the ARD, and the federation agreed on at least two basic points—the need to join forces over the question of wavelength allocations, and the need to establish a broadcasting station to represent the FRG internationally.

The case for central legislation on these matters was won by the federation, securing it the right under federal law to establish two such stations—DW (Deutsche Welle) which broadcasts worldwide on the shortwave band, and DLF (Deutschlandfunk) which transmits on the longwave band to the rest of Europe, and is particularly aimed at the German Democratic Republic (East Germany). These were created by law in November 1960 and, as they represent no danger of infringement on the other stations, DW and DLF were later also admitted as members to the ARD.

An area where real conflict over authority did arise between the federation and the *Länder* was in the Adenauer government's attempted involvement in setting up a second television channel in 1960. The federal government was firmly rebuked by the *Länder* and the Constitutional Court.

A combination of improper political motivation (a forthcoming election for Adenauer in 1961), an uncomfortable nexus of government and powerful private interests that smacked a little too much of the immediate Nazi-era past (a consortium of industrialists and newspaper publishers that moved to launch a privately owned station, Freies Fernsehen GmbH, in December 1958 had initially received strong support from the government), and, most important, a deadlock with the ARD over various counterproposals spelled disaster for Adenauer's final push for a joint federal-*Land* funded regulated channel (Deutschland Fernsehen GmbH).

The *Länder*, instead of being coerced into such an arrangement by Adenauer's tactic of simply launching the necessary capital, challenged the federal government's actions in the Federal Constitutional Court, alleging the attempt to set up and regulate such a channel was, in fact, unconstitutional. The historic ruling of that court in February 1961 unequivocally confirmed the constitutional status of broadcasting as a sphere well outside the control of the state and, hence, beyond the reach of the federal government. Two things were made emphatically clear by the judgment that was handed down:

1. That public broadcasting cannot under any circumstances be subsumed under the general heading of post and telecommunications since it is a user of such installations and not an integral part of them;
2. That any area of legislation that transcends regional boundaries does not automatically fall under the jurisdiction of the federal government. For broadcasting, particularly, is a cultural activity and therefore remains the prerogative of the *Länder* (Judgment of the Federal Constitutional Court, 2 February 1961).

With these principles clearly established, it was left to the two remaining groups—the ARD and the *Länder*—to stake their claims over the founding of a second television channel.

Adopting the principle of "a bird in the hand," the *Länder*, having secured their rights from the federation, ventured forth alone to hammer out a joint proposal for a second channel that was to be independent of the already existing structures—a channel that would also be in a position to offer a contrast to the existing program of the ARD's "First German Television." To this end an appropriate inter-*Land* agreement between all the *Länder* was struck up in June 1961, with ZDF opening for transmission in 1963.

While ZDF is a public corporation with a similar administrative structure to those of the broadcasting institutions, its special position of serving the whole of the FRG meant that additional provisions had to be included. This involved a pledge of a rather tall order concerning the task of providing a comprehensive picture of the total German reality as well as promoting the formation of independent opinion. By seeking to fulfill this task it was felt that the establishment of ZDF would eliminate both the kinds of problems of coordination inherent in the first German channel, with its nine independent entities, and the loss of variety in programming. In practice, however, the system's potential has been undermined by the inherent financial weakness of ZDF, by fictitious competition between the two channels, and, further, by the inability of the political parties to keep their fingers out of this pie of a nationwide broadcasting channel, as will be discussed later.

Overall, then, the present-day organization of broadcasting in the FRG consists of nine regional stations (both radio and television), two central radio stations (DW and DLF), one central television station (ZDF), and one American radio station broadcasting out of Berlin in the German language. (The Allied NATO powers stationed in Germany, notably Britain and the United States, also have their own armed forces networks with stations broadcasting in their respective tongues, e.g., the British Forces Broadcasting Service in the north of Germany.)

The regional stations of the ARD all broadcast several radio programs, often in conjunction with one another. The nine broadcasting institutions that make up the ARD are not strictly regional insofar as most areas in the FRG can receive upwards of three VHF (very high frequency) programs. The development of the VHF band itself results directly from the slender postwar allocation of medium wavelengths to the FRG. As previously stated, the regional stations also share the first German television channel, DFS (Deutsches Fernsehen). They also share a third, primarily educational, channel, which is on air for only part of the day, joining the first national program at 8 p.m.

DFS, the channel initiated by the ARD in 1954 and shared by the nine member stations, can hardly be said to represent a composite of regional services. Its inter-*Land* agreement obliges stations to contribute to a common program operating through a standing program conference of intendants chaired by the DFS program director. (This arrangement implies no intention to infringe on the right to broadcast individual programs, though costs toward the national program still have to be met. Few cases of opting out of the national program actually occur.) The conference plans the DFS program on the basis of suggestions from individual authorities who offer material to meet their commitment of contributions (which are obligatory). The ratio of contributions is calculated in a way that reflects the structure of financial equalization within the ARD (i.e., equality between donor and recipient stations in the reallocation of licensing fee revenue to stations servicing smaller, less populous regions). In accordance with this, the share in national programming for television (DGS) is as follows:

WDR	— 25%	SFB	— 8%
NDR	— 20%	SDR	— 8%
BR	— 17%	RB	— 3%
HR	— 8%	SR	— 3%
SWF	— 8%		

Given this form of organization, one would expect the choice of programs to be rich and varied. However, there is far less variation in practice because of the high degree of sharing of individual items and, in many cases, of part programs as well (i.e., the stations run a minimum of two full programs and one additional part program).

Because ZDF was set up to provide an alternate program to that of DFS, ZDF is precluded from joining the ARD by its constitution. However, the desired contrast has not really eventuated, as the two channels have tended to vie for the same audiences. Still, they do provide the opportunity for some choice in viewing. They would not all cover the wedding of Britain's Prince Charles, for example, as almost all the Australian channels did.

Of the three key features of the organization of broadcasting in the FRG—federal departmentalization, public holding, and the principle of social control—the last is probably its most distinguishing and significant feature. Social control is legally anchored in the structure of broadcasting and is exercised through the creation of special supervisory boards which, for nearly all of the broadcasting institutions, comprise a three-tier system of control consisting of a broadcasting council (*Rundfunkrat*), and administrative council (*Verwaltungsrat*), and the all-important office (and personage) of the intendant (*Intendant*, sometimes translated as "director general" or "superintendent"). The two stations to which this does not apply are SFB and the American station in Berlin.

The broadcasting institutions are self-administered and are not subject to state supervision with regard to programming. Their economic independence is secured by direct financing through licensing fees and in part by revenue from advertising.

While there are essentially the three above-mentioned organs of control, there are two basic constitutional models in operation. The difference between the two lies in the balance of power that exists between the three organs of control, as well as their link with the public.

The broadcasting council is the highest organ of control, for it is the one deemed to represent the public or community interest in the field of broadcasting—in effect, social control over it (as does the respective television council in the case of ZDF). The task of the broadcasting council is to supervise the whole operation of the station. It supervises compliance to programming guidelines, advises the intendant on programming, determines the institution's budget, and usually has the right to elect the intendant. This is the case at NDR and WDR, for example, whereas at SWF the intendant is elected by both the broadcasting and the executive council. In most cases the broadcasting council also has statutory authority; for example, the statutes of SFB and SDR are enacted by their respective *Land* legislatures, whereas the statute authority at BR and SWF lies with both the broadcasting and the executive or administrative councils (Mahle and Richter 1974:61–71).

The administrative, or executive council, by comparison, fulfills no representative function. Its sole task is to supervise the administration of broadcasting, effectively supervising the intendant's management of the station. However, at both NDR and WDR the administrative council possesses the further authority to participate in the election of the intendant and to exercise control over adherence to the program guidelines.

As a monocratic executive organ, the intendant plays a vital role within the supervisory organs of the broadcasting institutions (the special problems of this key role will be discussed below). Briefly, the essential task of the intendant is to represent the station externally and to run its business in accordance with the decisions of the broadcasting and administrative councils.

Stations NDR and WDR both have a fourth organ of control, the programming advisory committee, or programming co-council (*Programmbeirat*), whose authority is limited to advising the intendant on program development. It does not share equal status with the other organs of control.

The two main models around which this whole system of control by the supervisory boards (organs of control) is constituted are generally known as the pluralistic or estate model and the parliamentary model. The former is found in most of the broadcasting institutions, while the latter is confined to NDR and WDR, although their programming advisory committees are also constituted on the pluralistic model. Specific, major problems in relation to this parliamentary model arose with respect to NDR during 1979–80. These shall be discussed after an outline of the two models has been presented.

Most simply stated, the basic difference between the two models is that in the pluralistic model, the "relevant social groups," that is, those groups deemed to determine the quality and character of society at large, make up the membership of the broadcasting council—representatives of a plurality of such social groups sit together with political party delegates on the broadcasting council. In the parliamentary model, on the other hand, the *Landtag* or *Land* parliament ultimately determines the membership of the broadcasting council.

The independence and impartiality of the broadcasting institutions are guaranteed in the laws governing the composition and functioning of the supervisory bodies, particularly of the broadcasting council.

How such representation of "all relevant social forces" is to be effected is outlined under Article 5 of the Basic Law, with some variation occurring in practice in accordance with *Land* law. A list of "socially relevant groups" that contribute a representative to the broadcasting council might include the following: the *Land* governments, the universities, the three major religious denominations, representatives of educational circles and of youth organizations, representatives of employees and business interests, and five or so deputies who are elected by the *Landtag* according to the *Proporz* or proportional spoils (along party lines) system. The *Land* government has the power to modify these basic guidelines. The period of office for members of the broadcasting council is six years, with one-third of the members leaving every two years in a rotational system. Reelection is, however, permitted.

While the representatives are chosen from a carefully balanced set of "socially relevant groups" in order that a wide range of public tastes and interests may be taken into account, a prime concern of the broadcasting council must always be the quality of the actual broadcasting service. As a result, members tend to be drawn from similar social strata since they are all expected to be leaders in their given areas of activity (which presupposes a certain level of education, income, social status, etc.). This is a definite weakness in the pluralistic model since it places certain economic and minority groups at a disadvantage. Furthermore, the relatively fixed nature of the catalogue of "socially relevant groups" makes it difficult for elements of social change to gain recognition. An eminent authority in communications studies in the FRG, Professor Langenbucher, has summed up this overall problem of public interest access and control by stating that

> The choices of socially relevant groups should not be, at least not exclusively, made according to their social importance (power, size, etc.) but according to the criterion as to how far the respective groups' chances of access to public communication are endangered. This communications sociological selections criterion may be generally formulated thus: the access chances of groups to the broadcasting council should be inversely proportional to its chances of access to public communications. (Langenbucher and Mahle 1973:322–30)

Closer examination of the second basic model, the parliamentary one, reveals that by the addition of the fourth organ of control, the programming advisory committee, the absolute separation of programming and administration has been abolished.

In this model, the broadcasting council is elected by the *Landtag* on the *Proporz* principle. Members serve for a period of five years and may be reelected. Of the twenty-one elected members, not more than four may belong to the *Landtag* and the Bundestag (federal parliament), as is also the case for their deputies. However, since the two other supervisory boards emanate from the broadcasting council, they cannot be said effectively to offer an inherent counterbalance to the influence of the state legislature, as may be seen from Figure 6-1.

Here, the only reference to "socially relevant groups" comes in relation to the program advisory committee where the standing rules provide for nineteen groups representing seven societal divisions (e.g., church, youth, education, etc.) to suggest three candidates each for membership. The broadcasting council then selects from these and has the right to appoint a member of its own choice in the event that a group does not offer a recommendation. These members serve for a period of six years and may also be reelected.

Under the parliamentary model, the administrative council clearly emerges as the most powerful organ of control. It elects the intendant and supervises the station's adherence to program guidelines and, in individual cases, can also give the intendant instructions (this is not permitted in the pluralistic model). It is also less subordinate to the broadcasting council than is the program advisory committee.

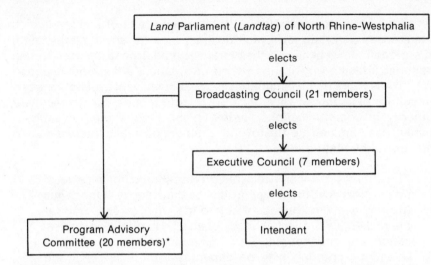

Source: Meyn 1974: Ch. 5.
*Of these 20 members, 19 are elected by the broadcasting council and one is nominated by the *Land* government.

Figure 6-1
Diagram of the Structure of the Supervisory Boards of WDR

Summing up the two basic constitutional models, Williams stated that

> The unsatisfactory element in the parliamentary model is not so much the fact that the *Landtag* performs the first basic selection of representatives; the weaknesses reside rather in the division of competence between the controlling bodies. The method by which representatives are selected for the three bodies is in itself satisfactory; what is questionable is the government's unwillingness to assign decisive power to the representatives of society, investing it instead in the body most likely to represent itself [the government]. (Williams 1976:111)

Recent events strongly underscore the critical nature of the problems inherent in the parliamentary model if pushed to their extreme by senior politicians choosing to ignore that broadcasting is indeed a public prerogative. These events also need to be seen in the context of a fairly long-term process of party-political incursion into both types of supervisory boards, particularly the parliamentary model. This sort of political incursion was stepped up around the late 1950s, with the *Proporz* principle of appointments becoming firmly entrenched between the middle and latter part of the 1960s.

Overall, the interests represented under the umbrella of pluralist social control have come to be more strongly dominated and regulated by representatives of the state, of the political parties, and of bureaucratic associations. This may be readily gauged by looking at the composition of the 282 members of the supervisory boards of the nine regional broadcasting institutions that make up ARD. Of this total number, 114 (over 40 percent) are directly government and party-political related representatives, with some directly elected by *Land* parliaments, others recommended by *Land* parliaments, and a small number (7) nominated by the *Land* government. Of the remaining 138 members, who represent the various "socially relevant groups," only 14 represent the various labor organizations (Deutscher Gewerkschaftsbund) which, as a mass association, represent a very sizable social interest group. Hence a very sizable section of society, the wage earners, are grossly underrepresented on the supervisory boards, signifying at least one clear aspect of the weighted interests of participation in this "public" sphere (c.f., for example, Holzer 1977 and Müller-Doohm 1972).

The real problem, however, does not lie so much in the composition of the numbers of the supposed interests elected, as in the far more serious and insidious developments of party-political manipulation of all positions on the supervisory boards. For if the so-called public representatives are nothing more than mouthpieces for the political parties, then no amount of legislation, no electoral safeguards, no intent of policy whatever can guarantee the freedom of broadcasting. The matter boils down to this: if the members of the supervisory boards fail to carry through their constitutional duty, the system simply cannot work.

Evidence of contraventions of broadcasting laws are not altogether rare, and have previously been made public. On the whole these document the way in which the work of the stations is blocked and also the way senior appointments, as well as posts in the programming areas of news and politics, are shared out on a political basis, indicating the extent of the party-political erosion of the public safeguards. It has been lamented by notable commentators on the German broadcasting scene that it is scandalous when an office of the significance of the intendant is filled on the basis of acceptability or nonacceptability of the person to the two main parties, the CDU-CSU and the SPD, rather than on experience and personal merit (Williams 1976:Ch. 8).

The developments described here have brought the position of intendant even further into the limelight. As the public authority of broadcasting has come to be more and more threatened, the intendants have found themselves caught between the twin pressures of party-political incursions from above and the push to counterbalance them from the journalists and production staff below.

An overview of developments taking place within the FRG indicates that the incursion of party-political interests into broadcasting accelerated during the period of the coalition government of 1966-69 (CDU-

SPD) when both parties sought to clearly establish their independent images. In response to this and the many political directives from government that ensued during the rise of the student movement and the more widespread youth movement, with their accompanying change in personal politics toward the politics of liberation, the broadcasters themselves (journalists and production workers) began to clamor for wider participation in editorial control.

The argument put forward by the journalists and production staff was that this would, in the main, help to preserve the constitutional basis of the public position of broadcasting. Politicians (seeking to gain ground in the institutions themselves) and some of the intendants were quick to argue that this was a move to secure the self-interest of journalistic and production staff and, hence, to erode the position of the intendants. As a result of vigorous politicking, the real issue—the Constitutional basis of publicly controlled broadcasting—became lost in the welter of accusations that the "statute movement," as it came to be known, was essentially about instigating codetermination of programming. What the journalists and production staff were, in fact, beginning to say was that broadcasting freedom is most relevant at the point where the actual program is produced rather than at the point where it is decided whether or not it be shown. They therefore felt that their role embodied the very requirements of the *Staatsvertrag* (state contract) of which the intendant is the symbolic head.

This, in essence, is what the issue of "internal democracy" (*innere Freiheit*) as embodied in the "statute movement" (*Statutenbewegung*) has been all about. It derives its name from the attempt to establish a set of producers' charters or codes that first commenced at NDR around 1970 and, as indicated, was generated by the supervisory powers' ignoring the principles of their respective stations' constitutions, resulting in insidious pressures being brought to bear on the broadcasters to conform to party-political patterns. The point at issue was, and still is, that there is nothing explicit in the constitutions to protect the broadcasters when the system is subverted. Only their own strength of character and commitment can hold them.

The broadcasters at NDR actually endorsed the constitutional status of the station and pledged to join the intendant in establishing a number of principles to guarantee the fulfillment of that station's constitutional obligations. There was not a hint of any attempt to overthrow either the constitution or the intendant. Rather, the aim was, and still is, to resist the various illicit pressures on the station that curtail the freedom of the broadcasting institutions by producing a form of internal censorship that goes directly against the basic rights of broadcasting.

The key point about this sort of internal pressure is that the political parties are able to pursue their objectives within the bounds of the broadcasting constitution most of the time. Because of this, the broadcasters have countered with the statute movement to seek guarantees from the individual institutions that their personal roles as upholders of the constitutional contract of public responsibility and social control would not be jeopardized.

While the statute movement has made some limited gains (e.g., winning recognized status as "program workers" at NDR and the right to speak as part of other representative bodies at the remaining stations), its significance undoubtedly lies in the fact that it has generated renewed and serious debate around the whole concept of public broadcasting and social control. This is particularly so in the area of program responsibility. Intendants, for their part, have also had to think more constructively about their relationship to their fellow workers. The political parties, similarly, have also been forced to reexamine the whole idea of broadcasting and their legitimate role in it (c.f. Williams 1976:Ch. 8 and Smith 1978:Ch. 6).

Developments throughout 1979–80, however, have shown that the party-political side of this reexamination has taken a more negative and divisive rather than a positive and unifying direction. The waves created by moves to exercise a more direct political control over NDR at one stage threatened the basis of the existence of the whole of the ARD.

Other politically inspired conflicts have seriously beset one or the other of the broadcasting institutes from time to time, but they have not really had the far-reaching implications of the NDR split. Examples of some of the other conflicts would be the 1980 upheavals at Radio Bremen over the bid to remove an "intolerable" (*untragbar*) intendant, and an event of some years past that heralded a real victory for the democratic functioning of social control over broadcasting. This victory was won by public action undertaken in Bavaria against that state's bid for party-political takeover of its public broadcasting institution, BR. The resultant plebiscite held in July 1973 rejected overwhelmingly the attempt of the ruling CSU to usurp the public monopoly position of broadcasting, which is seen as a safeguard against the possibility of any one single group or interest gaining control of broadcasting. The further aim of the CSU was also to admit privately run television into the system.

In its 1971 ruling, the Federal Administrative Court (Bundesverwaltungsgericht) in Berlin expressed strong skepticism about the likelihood of independence of any broadcasting body that depended substantially upon advertising for its income. The court felt extreme concern not only in the case of commercial enterprises where public participation would need to be meticulously guaranteed, but also in the existing stations, where the boundaries between commercial activity and public administration are, in some cases, barely distinguishable (e.g., ZDF is dependent upon advertising for almost 50 percent of its income).

Broadcasting in the FRG is, on the whole, funded basically through the levy of licensing fees, the 1981 annual rate being DM35.60 per set for radio and DM156 for television. (A portion of these fees is paid each month.) Advertising, on the other hand, is generally considered a secondary but nonetheless important source of revenue. Their relative weight is demonstrated by figures available for 1977 (prior to the 1978 licensing fee increase), for example, which show that revenue derived from licensing fees approached the DM3,000 million while advertising for television alone amounted to the considerable sum of DM869.7 million (ARD: 528.2 million and ZDF: 341.5 million), with a further DM185.6 million of advertising revenue flowing into the radio broadcasting coffers (*Media Perspektiven* 2, 1978:132).

Advertising is permitted on German television under stringent legal limitations. It is restricted to a solid block of twenty minutes per channel and must be screened prior to 8 p.m., with no advertising on Sundays or public holidays. These regulations over advertising, like the public monopoly situation itself, really set German television in particular, and German broadcasting in general, apart from the other countries represented in this collection.

Throughout the 1960s it appeared, particularly to the newspaper publishers, that the percentage share of advertising attracted by broadcasting, especially by the then relatively new medium of television, was rising steadily. This caused the press interests, the Federal Association of German Newspaper Publishers (BDZV), already thwarted in its attempts to enter the field of broadcasting by the 1961 "television judgment," to file an official complaint with the federal government.

The essence of the BDZV's complaint amounted to a charge that a situation of unfair competition existed between the private press and the public broadcasting institutions by virtue of the fact that the latter's financial position was practically guaranteed through the level of licensing fees whereas the press relied almost solely upon advertising. The BDZV thus went on to make the strong claim that if the current rate of advertising attracted to broadcasting were allowed to continue unchecked, the decline of the free press in the FRG would be well at hand.

The federal government's response was to appoint the now wellknown Michel Commission of 1964 which, in a report presented in 1967, strongly rejected the contentions placed before it by the BDZV. The findings of the Michel Commission are still regarded as a valid expression of the government's position with regard to competition between the press and the electronic media. As the commission stated, with respect to press and television:

> There is no such thing as a two-sided competition for advertising that is restricted to the daily press and television. We must consider the competition of the remaining media also, on this market.
>
> It is impossible to establish just how the advertising revenue of newspapers and periodicals would have developed without

television advertising. What is clear, however, is that the newspapers and periodicals certainly could not have attracted the bulk of the advertising that has gone into television. Certainly television, as a very successful medium, attracts advertising, but the phase of development of this new medium has given the impression of gaining ground on the advertising market-stakes of the other media, while the investigations of this commission have failed to substantiate this assumption.

Of utmost importance in this matter has been the commission's later, firm opposition to any publisher-operated television, on the grounds that it presented very real dangers of creating multimedia monopolies (*Bericht der Bundesregierung* . . . 1974).

That such a situation has been prevented from developing in the sphere of mass communications in the FRG not only shows the good social sense governing this area of policy at least, but also sets Germany apart from most of the countries discussed in this book, particularly Australia, which experiences the worst instances of cross-ownership in the "free world."

The BDZV has also become particularly active and anxious not to be locked out of the new technological developments such as videotext and the Bundespost's additional *"Bildschirmtext"* which they and their political supporters (and supported), CDU-CSU, argue tends to diminish the traditional, clear-cut separation between broadcasting and the press. The broadcasting institute advisers of all eleven *Länder*, however, declared that whatever category the new media may belong to, they do not belong to the category of "press."

There has been some discussion of cooperation between the newspapers and television in presenting news-text, and it is this that the BDZV fears will, in the long run, erode the circulation and, hence, the viability of the German newspapers. According to one publisher, a mere drop of 10 to 15 percent in circulation would be sufficient to threaten the existence of quite a number of the German dailies (*Der Spiegel* 33, 36, 1979:49–55). These developments will be discussed more closely under the section dealing with telecommunications.

The long-time BDZV desire to gain admission for its own, private television transmission has been achieved via the back door, as it were. They joined the international project, the Luxembourg television satellite (to be launched in 1985), which will transmit programs over a wide area of Germany, France, the Netherlands and, of course, also the tiny principality of Luxembourg, utilizing the German, French, and Flemish languages. This satellite is to be a joint venture in terms of finance as well as programming. The partners include Luxembourg (51%); French, Belgian, and American banks and finance groups; the BDZV; and a Netherlands finance consortium (*Der Spiegel* 35, 10, 1981:109–12).

Interestingly enough, the BDZV elected to join the Luxembourg project as a united association rather than to allow individual publishers to participate on their own. The concern here was that it had been apparent for some time that Radio Luxembourg's address in the FRG was the Axel Springer publishing concern's headquarters.

As it is, Springer already holds the largest share (25%) of the BDZV interest in the Luxembourg venture and greeted the proposed satellite project as "a breakthrough for free television in Germany," declaring in the same breath that this medium may be used to ensure that the SPD-FDP loses its parliamentary majority by "counterbalancing" what he considers to be the politically one-sided content of what he likes to term "public monopoly broadcasting" (*Der Spiegel* 35, 10, 1981:109–12).

Telecommunications

Telecommunications, as opposed to the forms of mass communications discussed so far, come entirely under the authority of the federation. The 1928 Telecommunications Installations Act has remained unaltered, leaving the federal government as the only entity having the right to set up and operate telecommunications installations within the FRG. All nonmilitary telecommunications are the sole responsibility of the federal minister for posts and telecommunications, with Article 14 of the Postal Administration Law stipulating that department's responsibility over the right of access to installations and the rate of charges applicable. The Deutsche Bundespost is in priniciple obliged to admit everyone as a user or to connect everyone as a customer to the relevant local network (c.f. Articles 7 and 8 of the Act).

The Deutsche Bundespost constitutes a public monopoly having sovereignty not only over control of existing systems but also over new developments within the rapidly expanding sphere of telecommunications. It is around this sphere that the major policy issues have been centered.

A brief overview of existing forms of telecommunications shows that rapid advances are taking place in virtually all areas, and particularly in relation to the booming field of data communications. Here the introduction of new media comprise the prime policy issues.

The picture with regard to the more traditional, existing forms of telecommunications is one of constant progress. The switched network of telephony (dial-up), for example, which had been described as "lagging considerably behind other highly industrialized countries" (though general postal services were superior) with only 54 percent of households having telephones, has shown remarkable growth (*Der Spiegel* 33, 37, 1979:39–57). At a glance, the situation at the end of 1980 showed that while there had been only 29 telephones per 100 inhabitants in 1973 there were now 46 telephones per 100 inhabitants (*Deutsche Bundespost Geschäftsbericht* 1980:51-55).

Mobile radio services covering land, sea-going, and airborne vehicles have similarly kept pace with growing demand, while the distribution network of radio and television broadcasting (unidirectional) to the public has continued to expand apace.

One area of rapid technological development that has raised a number of important policy issues is the introduction of community antenna television (CATV) systems (*Gemeinschaftsnützungsysteme*). This has led to the possibility of creating a wider scale intellation of return-channel television in the FRG. This project poses fundamental questions about the legal-constitutional basis for the public broadcasting system, as well as questions about the sovereignty of the Bundespost over telecommunications installations. These questions have, again, focused on the division of areas of competence between the federation and the *Länder*.

A commission of inquiry (KtK, or Kommission für den Ausbau der technischen Kommunikationssystems) set up to examine the problems posed by these new telecommunications developments indicated in its July 1976 report that the chief problem was that the new technology for CATVs would greatly increase the capacity of the transmission network and, hence, the number of programs available. As a result, the commission stated, certain aspects of the all-important question of "areas of competence" would have to be resolved.

For the federation it was a problem of whether or not cable-limited broadcasting distribution in local and regional networks would be amenable to different forms of organization in spite of the Bundespost's sovereignty over switched telecommunications networks: that is, the problem of public infrastructure and private use (FRG Ministry of Posts and Telecommunications Report 1976). For the *Länder*, on the other hand, it raised the problem of needing to work out whether, and under what conditions, other organizers of broadcasting programs should or could be permitted to operate in addition to the public broadcasting institutions as presently constituted. A further problem was that the electronic transmission of texts and the possible facsimile transmission of printed matter rendered the boundaries between the press and broadcasting unclear.

Toward the end of 1977 the committee of experts involved in the initial KtK inquiry presented a follow-up study of the experimental CATV operations. They suggested that the distinctions, made in the former report, between *Videotext* and *Bildschirmtext*, which were not entirely satisfactory for clearly marking off the areas of mass communications from those of individual communications on the switched network, be supplemented by the new telecommunications form of *Kabeltext*. This form allows for an enormous and rapid text-carrying capacity in one single television channel operating on 5 MHz. Thus it would become possible to differentiate a number of subsystems from *Kabeltext*: the unidirectional cable-text (*Einfache Kabeltext*), the return-channel cable-text (*Kabeltext Abruf*), and the private-use cable-text (*Individual Kabeltext*). This would provide clear demarcations against the possibility of overlap between mass communications and individual communications, and would also help to establish what may be considered public broadcasting and what may not, on these new telecommunications installations (*Media Perspektiven* 8, 1977:488–93).

Unfortunately, however, this distinction is still hotly disputed when the occasion arises since it represents an enormous clash of financial and political interests between public broadcasting and powerful private interests such as the newspaper publishers, and also raises the question of the sovereignty of the Deutsche Bundespost. A clash of interests along these lines has already been discussed in relation to broadcasting and the satellite television issue.

On the question of cable television, it had initially been decided to wait for the publication of results from overseas experiments rather than to commit a lot of resources to an area in which the FRG saw itself lagging behind other developed countries. The awaited reports did not, however, eventuate. Hence it was decided to go ahead with further experimental projects (*Breitbandkabelprojekte*) in the *Länder* of Bavaria, North Rhine-Westphalia, and Rhineland-Palatinate. A snag was struck with regard to the financial agreement for the running of these projects as the Bundespost was forced to warn the respective ministers president that it would not supply its part of the financial obligations for the cable projects until they themselves fulfilled their part of the agreement. It was estimated that the initial cost of equipping a network of twenty thousand households would be about DM30 million, and that with the addition of extra channels or a return channel, the cost would rise to about DM40 million (*Bundespost '81* 1981).

The other key area of policy concern in this sphere centers around the new or extended telecommunications networks in which microelectronics again plays a prominent role: the development of information processing technology.

Overall, the developments that have been dubbed the "new media" (*Neue Medien*) consist of cable and satellite broadcasting, videotext, and also *Bildschirmtext*. The latter development (*Bildschirmtext*) is, however, only to be categorized as a "new medium" where it offers journalistic information of general relevance. Where its service is restricted to providing specific information for the individual (*Information für den einzelnen*) or to dialogue with the computer (*Dialog mit dem Rechner*), this is not the case.

With regard to developments in the sphere of data communication in particular, it may be said that the breakthrough to software-programmed microprocessors made possible the greater decentralization of data processing, consequently heralding a shift of "intelligence" to the workplace.

The word-processing industry alone, along with allied developments, has mushroomed over the decade of the 1970s. The number of telex terminals in the FRG grew from 103,000 in 1974 to 117,000 in 1975, and to 139,000 in 1980. Telefax terminals (*Fernkopierer*) increased from 1,900 in 1979 to 4,300 in 1980. Teletex, a type of electronic mail, was developed in 1979 and displayed at the International Trades Fair in Hannover in 1980. It was inaugurated on an experimental basis in 1981. The Bundespost expects 40,000 teletex terminals to be in operation by 1985, and possibly 130,000 by about 1990 (*Deutsche Bundespost 1980 Geschäftsbericht* 1980:123–26, 140–48; *Bundespost 81* 1981:47–50).

Data communication available via dialed and point-to-point connections (*Dateldienste*) has in fact been the boom area of telecommunications development in the FRG (Table 6-8).

Table 6-8
Data Stations (Terminals) Connected to the Bundespost Network

Year	1967	1969	1970	1972	1975	1977	1979	1980
No.	300	1,000	4,000	11,000	38,000	56,000	87,000	108,000

Source: *Deutsche Bundespost 1980 Geschäftsbericht*:49–50 and *Bundespost '81*:140–59.

Rationalization is also constantly occurring within this sphere of operations by the Bundespost: to wit the changes in the Datex network to create the Datex-L and Datex-P services.

The European Telecommunications Administration via its EURO-DATA 79 study, has in fact predicted that by the end of 1986 there will be around 235,000 data stations on the Bundespost network with about as many again on private, internal networks (*Deutsche Bundespost 1980 Geschäftsbericht* 1980:50).

There appears to have been an overall, relative shift away from medium and large computers toward small computers over the middle to late 1970s. This reflects the decentralization of data processing in that smaller computers are increasingly being operated in conjunction with larger systems.

Sociopolitical considerations, both national and international, have also had considerable bearing on the policy debate surrounding these areas of development. Concentration here shall center around the national aspects since the international concerns over matters such as "transborder data flow" and the INTELSAT agreements are readily enough available in English elsewhere (OECD 1981). However, EUTEL-SAT resolutions to develop further satellite capacities for the rapid transmission of data throughout Europe should be noted since the Deutsche Bundespost is a participant in EUTELSAT.

Returning to the issues as they relate to the FRG per se, it seems that all parties concerned have attempted to rigorously assess the emerging situation with an eye to whether or not the new developments in the sphere of data transmission (*die Nützung des Fernsprechnetzes zur Datenübertragung*) could, in effect, serve to facilitate a leveling out of the present structure of privileged access to information. Or would they, on the other hand, perhaps generate even further disadvantage?

On the positive side, these developments can, for example, be used for dialogue in educational and health services. On the negative side, there exist the real and serious problems associated with the safekeeping of data, and the danger that the privacy of citizens will be subject to electronic assault by the telecommunications techniques and gadgetry readily available to corporate interests and agencies of the state.

That the FRG was the first nation to introduce legislation to safe-guard the privacy of its citizens against data abuse attests, in part, to the strength of the arguments waged on its behalf. The federal data-protection law (*Bundesdatenschutzgesetz*) was passed in 1977, with a portion of it coming into effect in January 1978, and the remainder in 1979. This groundbreaking legislation, though a welcome step in the right direction, is not without its shortcomings according to its critics. Many see it as a relatively toothless piece of legislation in that it fails to provide any real guarantees against the abuse of data privacy. It is thus regarded more as an expression of intent, of goodwill on the part of the federation, rather than as securing the rights of the individual against both corporate and bureaucratic incursion. Moreover, its critics argue that while the *Bundesdatenschutzgesetz* in principle allows people to find out just what data is stored on their files, the practicalities of this are exceedingly difficult: a fee of around DM30 must be paid for the privilege; the individual must know where to go, how to go about it, which channels need to be gone through; and, finally, there is the time-honored practice of being given the bureaucratic runaround to contend with once you actually get past the initial hurdles (Bundesminister des Inneren 1977). Nevertheless, it somehow seems considerably better to have such legis-lation than not to have it.

The Media Concepts of the Major Political Parties

This area in one sense provides the ideal stamping ground for the major political parties to exonerate and reaffirm platitudes and principles concerning the need for protection of democratic rights and freedom of access to a plurality of information and so forth, whether this is reflected in their political practice or not. Their ordering of priorities fairly indicates the power of interests that each of them traditionally rep-resents.

Until the latter part of the 1960s, the political parties had not accorded high priority to the area of media and new communications developments; the SPD passed the first binding media concept for a political party in 1971, with the others following suit in 1973 (FDP) and 1974 (CDU-CSU).

The Media Concept of the Social Democratic Party (SPD)

The key points of the party's concept, elaborated upon in 1973 and again in 1978 (*Media Perspektiven* 1, 1978), concern journalistic independence in line with some of the earlier discussion on "internal democracy" and monopoly control of the press, which, together with ancillary measures in this respect, are intended to control and restrict economic concentration in the press as a means to preserve a diversity of opinion. The difference between policy intent and the power of existing practices has already been noted.

The party has generated little discussion about broadcasting, since it feels that the federalistic, publicly controlled organization of broadcasting has proven itself on merit. Concern has therefore tended to center around ways to oppose further attempts to put broadcasting into private ownership as well as to further commercialization, particularly through the new developments in the telecommunications technology. Concern applies particularly to the two most recent developments— CATVs and satellite transmission (national and international)—where the party fears the growing danger of an even greater imbalance between economic and political power interests will dominate the social requirements for information availability. The goal of their policy concept in this regard has been stated as:

> All conceptions and models of communications policy need to be viewed from the perspective of whether or not they further the freedom of information and thought of the citizens and also whether they serve to strengthen the "free"—democratic structures of our common existence. (*Media Perspketiven* 1, 1978:25–32).

The SPD thus conceives that cable television must always remain within the province of the public sector.

The Media Concept of the Christian Democratic Union and the Christian Social Union (CDU-CSU)

These two parties have issued a joint statement in keeping with their coalition interests. This document, unlike that of the SPD, tends to leave recommendations well to the background, preferring broad platitudes expressing "hope" for extensive self-regulation of the media systems, recommending the protection of the "positively valued status quo" of the press sector, and examining possibilities for other forms of organization of the broadcasting system, including the admission of private broad-

211

casters. Much of this section of the paper is used to attack what they refer to as the "monopoly situation" of the public broadcasting institutions, and particularly, that these not be expanded to cover the new technical systems (cable television, etc.). Their 1978-updated media statement strongly criticizes the SPD government for not yet having come to any firm decision on the recommendations put forward in the KtK Report (CDU-CSU 1976).

The Media Concept of the Free Democratic Party (FDP)

This party, as junior partner holding the balance of power in the current government, has issued the most rigorous and, in places, the most radical document of all the parties, detailing recommendations for specific regulations rather than expressing mere sentiments (FDP 1977; *Wiesbadener Leitlinien* 1973).

Almost half of their lengthy recommendations concern the problem of "internal democracy" for both press and broadcasting. Much of the SPD's concern about the freedom of mass communication also considers the wider aspects of the rights of citizens in the communications process so that they shall not be regarded merely as passive recipients:

> . . . The media policy discussions that have taken place in recent years have begun to have an influence on the relations between the participants in the mass communications process. This is shown from the following points:
>
> 1. Concern about the guarantee of independence for all those actively involved in the media;
>
> 2. Concern about securing a diversity of outlook and opinion in the media, being able to transmit these—in areas where this has been lost;
>
> 3. Concern about the preservation of the economic independence of the private-enterprise press;
>
> 4. Concern about securing the public, social-control structure of our broadcasting institutes and the strengthening of their independence against extraneous influences (*Weisbadener Leitlinien* 1973:5–32; FDP 1977:33–36).

Conclusions

The peculiarities of Germany's split history, providing the opportunity for a more conscious establishment of democratic, federal institutions in the post-1949 era, have perhaps given a greater aura of relatively coherent planning and measures to the area of communication policy formulation than might otherwise have been the case. The wealth of documentation concerning the total measures by the state and other social groups and institutions to regulate and direct the process of social communications demonstrates this far more than can be said of the other countries presented here.

The central themes of conflict in the process of policy formation have emerged along dimensions set by the immense political importance that is attached to cultural power in Germany. The attempted policy resolutions and the subversion of legally constituted policy, at times, have shown that communication policy formulation, like the principles and ideals of democratic government, is itself no guarantee against the increasing centralization of powerful, private business and political interests.

References

Bericht der Bundesregierung über die Lage von Presse und Rundfunk in der Bundesrepublik Deutschland (1974)
1974   Bonn: Dr. Hans Heger Verlag.

Berufsverbote, Conference of Ministers-president
28 January 1972   Bonn.

Blatt
117, 23 March 1978   xxxxxx

Börsenverein des deutschen Buchhandels E.V.
1981   *Buch und Buchhandel in Zahlen 1981*. Frankfurt a.M.

Bundesminister des Inneren
April 1977   *"Betrifft: Bundesdatenschutzgesetz."* Bonn: Referat Öffentlichkeitsarbeit.

Bundesministerium für das Post- und Fernmeldewesen
1980   *Deutsche Bundespost 1980 Geschäftsbericht*. Frankfurt a.M.

Bundespost '81
1981   Frankfurt a.M.: Bund-Werbung GmbH. und Deutsche Bundespost.

CDU-CSU
22 March 1976   "Zum Thema: Freiheitliche Medienpolitik" erarbeitet von der CDU/CSU—Medienkommission, verabschiedet von den Präsidien und Vorständen der CDU und CSU. Bonn.

Czajka, D.
1968   *Pressefreiheit und "öffentliche Aufgabe" der Presse.* Köln: W. Kohlhammer Verlag.

Diedrich, H.
1981   "Daten zur Konzentration der Tagespresse und der Publikumszeitschriften in der Bundesrepublik Deutschland im IV. Quartal 1980." *Media Perspektiven* 7.

FDP
1977   "Stichworte zur Innen-, Rechts-, und Medienpolitik," FDP im 8. Deutschen Bundestag.

FRG, Ministry of Posts and Telecommunications
1976   *The Commission for the Development of the Telecommunications System's Telecommunications Report.* Bonn.

FRG, Press and Information Office
1980   *Facts about Germany.* Bonn.

Günther Commission Report
1968   *Kommission zur Untersuchung der Gefährdung der wirtschaftlichen Existenz von Presseunternehmen und der Folgen der Konzentration für die Meinungsfreiheit in der Bundesrepublik Deutschland.* Bonn.

Holzer, H.
1971   *Gescheiterte Aufklärung.* München: R. Piper & Co. Verlag.

1977   "Medienpolitik der SPD." In *Der SPD Staat,* edited by F. Grube and G. Richter, Section III, Chapter 6. München: R. Piper & Co. Verlag.

Hood, S.
1972   *The Mass Media.* London: Macmillan.

Langenbucher, W. and Mahle, W.A.
1973   "Umkehrproporz und kommunikative Relevanz." *Publizistik* 4.

214

Lehrbuch der deutschen Geschichte (Beiträge) 12 vols.
1960   Berlin.

Lenel, H.O.
1968   *Ursachen der Konzentration unter besonderer Berücksichtigung
                        der deutschen Verhältnisse.* Tübingen.

Mahle, W.A. and Richter, R.
1974   *Communication Policies in the Federal Republic of Germany.*
                        Paris: UNESCO Press.

Media Perspektiven
1, 1978   "CDU/CSU medienpolitisches Grundsatzpapier: Forderungen
                        der Union für die Pilotprojekte Kabelfernsehen, 31.1.1978."

1, 1978   "DJV zur gesetzlichen Regelung der inneren Pressefreiheit."

1, 1978   "Leitlinien zur Zukunftsentwicklung der electronischen Medien"
                        . . . SPD Parteivorstand verabschiedet 30.1.78.

2, 1978   "Netto-Umsätze der Rundfunkwerbung."

9, 1981   "Gefährdung der Bundesdeutschen Film- und Fernsehproduk-
                        tion durch Rundfunk-Finanzkrise."

11, 1981   "Partnerschaft Film/Fernsehen."

Meyn, H.
1974   *Massenmedien in der Bundesrepublik Deutschland.* Berlin:
                        Colloquium Verlag.

Müller, H.D.
1968   *Der Springer-Konzern.* München: R. Piper & Co. Verlag.

Müller-Doohm, S.
1972   *Medienindustrie und Demokratie.* Frankfurt a.M.

OECD
1981   *Guidelines: On the Protection of Privacy and Transborder Flows
                        of Personal Data.* Paris.

Rundfunk und Fernsehen
no. 2, 1961   "Fernseh Urteil."

Schütz, W.J.
1976   "Publizistische Konzentration der Tagespresse." *Media Perspek-tiven* 8.

1981   "Deutsche Tagespresse 1981." *Media Perspektiven* 9.

Smith, A.
1978   *The Politics of Information*. London: Macmillan.

Der Spiegel
33, 25, 1979   "Deutscher Film—ein neuer Optimismus."

33, 36, 1979   "Fernsehen: Botschaft huckepack."

33, 37, 1979   "Telephon: Milliarden sinnlos verpulvert."

35, 7, 1981   "Spiegel-Report über Bertelsmann."

35, 10, 1981   "Fernsehen: Gold im All."

Statistisches Jahrbuch 1980 für die Bundesrepublik Deutschland
1980   Köln: W. Kohlhammer Verlag.

Der Stern
9 March 1982   "Wallraffs neuste 'Bild' Störung."

Streisand, J.
1976   *Deutsche Geschichte von den Anfängen bis zur Gegenwart.* Köln: Pahl-Rugenstein Verlag.

Wallraff, G.
1977   *Der Aufmacher: Günther Wallraff, der Mann der bei Bild Hans Essler war*, Hamburg: Rowohlt Verlag.

Wiesbadener Leitlinien
1973   Bonn.

Williams, A.
1976   *Broadcasting and Democracy in West Germany*. London: Bradford University Press.

7

Communication Policy in Australia: Pragmatic Planning and Ad Hoc Decision Making

Geoff Evans

Geoff Evans also takes up the theme developed throughout the book in a number of different ways: the difficulty in identifying explicit authoritative communication policies. He examines, in some detail, the procedures of policy formation and the role and influence of different groups in society, and concludes that ad hoc decision making is the inevitable consequence of a lack of comprehensive policy. The results of Australian ad hocery are different from those in the United Kingdom, where there is a traditional and stable cultural base. In Australia the values have generally been imported, and there is a resultant mix of government-supported and commercial systems. The preference by conservative governments for commercial institutions, together with the vocal support of an influential minority for the Australian Broadcasting Commission (ABC) has led to liberal-minded rhetoric in broadcasting policy which conflicts with the political sympathies of the present government. Thus there has been vigorous debate and pragmatic solutions to the many problems and new initiatives that have arisen in Australian communications in the 1970s. Each political party has overturned the decisions of the other, but both have had little understanding of the complexity of the issues they have been dealing with and have expended very little effort on appropriate solutions. The present government is now facing a number of important decisions on the future of the ABC, cable television, networking, a domestic satellite, and telecommunications. Developments are proceeding on all fronts in the established ad hoc fashion with very little attempt to examine overall implications.

The author would like to acknowledge the assistance given in the writing of this chapter by Dr. Ina Bertrand (cinema), Sally White (the press), Trevor Barr (publishing); and general comments by Mark Armstrong, Dr. Peter White, and Professor Henry Mayer.

It is not possible to identify a communication policy in Australia, in the sense of a comprehensive, explicit, authoritative statement about the whole of the communications field or even about parts of it. Instead, one must make a close examination of events as they have unfolded, to isolate strands of widely accepted belief running through them or the dominantly held positions that largely determine those events. Such examination reveals a policy in the sense of a dominance of basic propositions, within broad limits. Within those confines, a spectrum of positions is held, and the development of policy proceeds as a continuous, evolutionary, political process. Change occurs when new ideas move into the mainstream of acceptance, and by political success within that stream. Decisions tend to gel into fixed features, and when reaction occurs it usually results in erosion or partial change of the decision rather than direct negation. The net effect, looked at over a period of time, is change in the strands of policy that do run through development—but usually incremental rather than drastic change. The system is conservative rather than revolutionary. Australia seems to be characterized by a low respect for planning and comprehensive social philosophy. There has often been a lack of theoretical analysis and information in many areas, especially in communications.

In practice, in communications, an elite or informal college of policymakers exists, drawn from political parties, the bureaucracy, commercial interests, activist groups and individuals, the media, and academics. Developments occur by interaction in many ways and at many levels within this elite, and by reaction of the elite with the wider public. The latter functions in something of an arbitral role insofar as issues arising in the field cause the formation of discernible public opinion. The importance of this role is in direct proportion to the degree to which issues rouse the wider public to take note of them. Thus, an important element in the process concerns the formation of public opinion. By the same token, much decision making, or lack of it, within the elite does not attract public attention although it may have profound significance. This is especially true of technological matters. In such cases, the wider public has effectively no say—outcomes are determined by the elite.

Perhaps the most important function of the wider public is in determining who is in power in important areas of the elite. Most importantly, the public determines the political party in power. Party power confers ministerial and cabinet power of decision making. It determines appointments to parts of the bureaucracy, a general persuasive influence over all of the bureaucracy, and much of the framework for interaction within the whole elite. But the party in power does not determine the membership of other areas of the elite, notably the media, the activist groups, and the commercial interest groups (although the tone it sets may have some influence upon these memberships).

These elites qualify governmental power significantly, so that it is somewhat less than it may formally appear to be. In addition, legal restraints and limitations arising out of political connection open the way for diffuseness of power. Increasingly these roles, quite apart from government, appear to be more important. Opposition to government is also provided by political parties out of power, but they are by no means the sole or necessarily the most effective source.

The action of the wider public in electing a government is itself partly a result of manipulation and influence by various elites. But in Australia, as probably elsewhere, actions and policy in communications do not make or break governments. Thus the opportunity for a government's influence on communication policy is not determined significantly by its policy in that field—it is incidental to its being elected for other reasons.

From time to time there have been calls for an authoritative statement of communication policy. Sometimes these have been made for no discernible motive of self-interest, by hopeful people apparently lacking understanding of the way the political system works, but more often the motive is to establish officially and consolidate a position that is to the advantage of the applicant. There have been policy statements by various elements within the elite, but such statements, in general, serve multiple functions. At best, they may be a fair statement of belief and intent, but they contain almost invariably a political tactical content, and are designed to advance the position of the interest concerned. They are usually not a complete statement of policy, but contain only those views that are likely to be received favorably. At worst they are propaganda. Some policy statements, especially those of political parties, tend to be so general as to be almost worthless as guides to intentions. In an arena of controversy and competing interests, it is axiomatic that the more specific the statement the more clearly offensive it will be to those affected adversely, and the more interests must be identified. This is the main reason why it is highly unlikely that any government in Australia will ever issue an official policy statement that is detailed enough to be very useful. Nor will it ever preside successfully over any attempt to get agreement between competing interests to do so.

Ad hoc decision making is the inevitable consequence of lack of comprehensive policy. Over recent years there has been much attack of ad hoc decisions in communications. Almost invariably the complainants are saying that the decision is one that they see as affecting them adversely. The opposite of ad hocery—presumably decision making according to a policy, after lengthy consultation and planning—is better if one's interests are to be affected adversely, because an opportunity is given to moderate, delay, or obstruct the decision. Ad hoc decisions, and complaints about them, are normal in a policymaking system such as Australia's and are unlikely to disappear.

There has been very little academic analysis of communication policy in Australia, although that situation is changing fast. When such a body of work builds up, it too will become an element in the policymaking process. Furthermore, while there have been many official inquiries into aspects of broadcasting in Australia, there has been only one into the whole of broadcasting—the Joint Parliamentary Committee on Broadcasting, in 1942, long before the introduction of television and other developments. In the communications field, there was the very commendable *Telecom 2000* report of 1975, which followed a comprehensive examination of Australia's telecommunications requirements up to the year 2000. However, although it dealt imaginatively with broad general aspects of communications, it did not consider social policy relating to broadcasting, the press, or other media. No inquiry, therefore, has ever been given terms of reference that would lead it to recommend an overall policy, because the interrelationships between parts of the communications system have never been considered together.

In examining the development of policy, and the processes of its formation, it is possible to record only events or outcomes, and formal processes. It is considerably more interesting, however, and more conducive to a true understanding, to examine the processes and motivations that lead up to events. The difficulty is that this approach calls for sources that are often highly subjective and interpretive. There cannot be a final definitive interpretation in an area such as this, and others may place a different construction on events. Nevertheless, the interpretive approach has therefore been adopted where possible, in the belief that it contributes to a better understanding.

In the first part of this chapter, a brief history of the formative processes in the development of Australian communications is given to identify present-day policies. In the second part, critical analysis of some of those policies and methods of policy formation is undertaken, together with a discussion of present trends.

Development of Systems and Policy

Australia is a federation of sovereign states, in which certain powers were given to the Australian, or Commonwealth, Parliament at federation in 1901. Residual powers rest with the states. Both state and federal governments have power in different areas of the communications field. Conflict is not a feature, because federal legislation takes precedence over state, where there is a specific reference of power to the Australian Parliament in the Constitution. In the past, conflict has occurred in defining the limits of that power. Most importantly, wireless telegraphy and telecommunications belong generally in the federal area. Although there have been some challenges to federal power since 1901, decisions given by the courts have been such that today federal power in these areas is accepted, and there is no tension between commonwealth and states concerning it. State law does intrude in general matters such as defamation. In the areas of the press, films, and publishing, state powers are important. The commonwealth has no power to regulate the press or publishing generally, but the states have, insofar as they are sovereign states, and there is nothing specifically preventing them. The states have the important power of censorship. State-commonwealth political relationships have an influence on development of all policy areas in Australia.

The geography of Australia has particularly influenced the development of communication policy. The country is almost exactly the size of the continental United States, but has a population of only 15 million people, who are heavily concentrated along the southeastern seaboard, with a second and much smaller concentration on the extreme southwestern coast. The population is highly urbanized, with two cities, Melbourne and Sydney, having nearly three million people each, and three more cities approaching one million. All of these are state capitals. Australia has only a few sizable provincial cities, but a larger number of country towns ranging up to twenty or thirty thousand people. There is a natural demarcation between "the city" and the rural or country areas. The cities themselves are widely separated, and the rural population is sparse. Where communications costs are a function of distance, or of area covered, they tend to be high on a per capita basis.

The Press

Press ownership in Australia is highly concentrated. Three major groups, the Herald and Weekly Times, News Ltd., and John Fairfax Pty. Ltd. hold a controlling interest in all of the seventeen capital-city daily newspapers published in Australia. A fourth group, Publishing and Broadcasting Ltd., is no longer involved in metropolitan dailies, but is heavily involved in country and suburban papers, magazines, television, and radio. On balance, the Australian press is essentially conservative, and no major paper consistently supports a nonconservative political view. From time to time, however, some papers have deviated from this line in favor of the Labor Party and the press is not always uncritical of the conservative parties. Over recent years there has been more coverage of more significant but less popularly newsworthy events, aided particularly by the emergence of higher quality newspapers directed at a more specialized readership, especially the *Australian Financial Review* (a daily since 1963) and the weekly *National Times*.

None of this improvement in the press has arisen from any overt policy. It seems to have been more a result of the increasing the size and sophistication of the market. There now exist sections of the market large enough to support such newspapers, or at least make it worthwhile for newspaper companies to stake out their share of the market against the day when they do become profitable.

Policy relating to the press in Australia reflects widely held community ideas regarding the press and the policy of the press itself, rather than government policy. From almost the earliest days of the Australian colonies, the British constitutional position on the press was adopted in Australia. Combined with a strong laissez-faire strand of belief, this has meant that there has never been an official press policy, or even much political discussion about one.

Nevertheless, there are ways in which government policy does affect the press, in relation to both content and the business of selling papers and advertising space. Apart from this influence, there is some self-regulation of the press, both as to content and as a business. All formal regulation is by the states, since the federal government has no power in this area. Newspapers must be registered, and are required to display the name and address of the publisher and printer on each copy. This requirement is designed not to provide any barrier to entry to the industry, but to facilitate legal action in defamation or obscene publication cases.

Defamation laws are the major influence on content. It has been claimed that Australia's laws on defamation are archaic and complex. There is certainly complexity, in that they arise from multiple jurisdictions. They are very useful to those who wish to stop discussion of any matter, because of the ability to take out a "stop writ" after which the matter becomes sub judice. There are long delays in cases coming to court. The Australian Law Reform Commission in 1980 proposed extensive changes that would remove much existing abuse, and its proposals have been well received. However, one of the groups potentially most affected by change would be the politicians, and it is not likely that there will be fast movement away from the system that is well understood, for fear of losing advantage in the process.

On censorship, the Australian media have observed a system of D notices. The D stands for defense; the system is a purely voluntary agreement whereby newspapers agree not to refer to certain items deemed by the government to be essential to security. A committee to administer the system has been established by agreement between the federal government and the media proprietors. Requests for imposition of a D notice come from government departments, and information on the items to which notices relate is not made public. Nevertheless, a partial list of items is in common currency among the informed public, and there is much criticism of the system as being an outmoded relic of the cold war era.

In July 1976 the country's newspaper proprietors joined with the Australian Journalists' Association (AJA) to form a Press Council (one major group, the Fairfax group, did not join). The council consists of six members nominated by metropolitan and regional press organizations, three elected by the Australian Journalists' Association, and three others appointed by the chair, and said to represent the public.

The history of the idea is interesting. Some—a very few—people involved in the press had advocated a press council for a number of years. In mid-1975 the minister for the media in the then Labor government pressed the idea, and released a discussion paper on press regulation. The paper included a suggested model for a press council, and a set of options on measures presumably aimed at achieving press improvement. Unwisely, and for no real purpose since they could hardly be achieved and were not being considered by the government, the paper included some options that are anathema to the press, such as a system of licenses. The press reaction was vigorous and hostile and the proposal for a press council was killed. Three months later, in November 1975, the press proprietors decided to set up a press council, but it had a very different composition from that proposed by the minister, which was for a twenty-one-member council, with ten from the industry and ten from organizations such as the trade unions, teachers, law bodies, and civil liberties groups. The proprietors' action was no doubt motivated by the wish to preempt any further official suggestion.

So far, the Press Council has considered a number of complaints against specific items printed by member publications. The council has no legal powers of sanction for breaches of its standards, and must rely simply on member newspapers to publish its decisions. One of the three major groups, News Ltd., withdrew from the council in 1980. With two out of the three giants now nonmembers, its future must be open to serious question.

In October 1980, the Government of Victoria, Australia's second-largest state, announced an inquiry into the state's press. The purpose was to investigate the extent of concentration of ownership and control and to restrict concentration of ownership and control. The inquiry found that there was a high concentration of ownership and control, which seemed to be increasing. It saw no evidence of any deleterious effect of concentration.

An independent authority was recommended to scrutinize transactions in shares and prevent takeovers if deemed contrary to the public interest, although any forced dismemberment of existing concentrations was ruled out.

The inquiry took no account of cross-ownership with other media, and no action has been taken by the government on the report. However, the inquiry was significant because it was the first such one in Australia.

On the noneditorial side, regulation comes from a federal body known as the Prices Justification Tribunal, which under certain conditions may inquire into cover prices of newspapers, and possibly has some deterrent value against precipitate price increases.

Self-regulation in noneditorial matters arises through distribution arrangements and the Media Council of Australia. The latter is an association of almost all commercial media proprietors in Australia. Its function is to regulate the buying and selling of advertising in those media. It accredits advertising agencies and undertakes certain other services. The Federal Trade Practices Commission has investigated the accreditation system and declared that any detriment to competition involved was outweighed by its benefit to the public.

Distribution of newspapers is subject to a zoning system, whereby newsagents are given exclusive rights to sell papers within a particular area. Newsagents are required to sell at or below a maximum price, to remain open for specified hours, and sometimes to provide a home-delivery service. The system is administered by committees of circulation managers from the newspaper companies.

All of these practices have been developed by the proprietors for commercial reasons. Any change will most probably arise only from general legislation applying to all commercial activity, such as trade practices legislation.

A Freedom of Information Bill has now been passed in Australia. It is widely regarded as weak, and its significance to the press will probably not be great.

There has been no official policy on sources of news from overseas, although the Labor Party does have a platform plank that states that a Labor government will "establish an independent and Australian Wire News Service which is capable of supplying news and news film to the ABC, newspapers, and other media outlets which may choose to use it" (Australian Labor Party 1972).

Technological and economic developments occurring in Australia could affect the press. Distribution costs are said to be rising faster than other costs and there is a tendency for suburban newspapers to have increasing importance. Electronic means of transmitting information to the home are in the experimental phase. Each of these could alter the industry profoundly, but it is unlikely that either will be influenced much by other than commercial considerations, because of the strength of the laissez-faire tradition of the press and the ability of the media to perpetuate and foster that tradition. The situation is unlike broadcasting, where the laissez-faire tradition was never as strong, because of the necessity for licenses, and state involvement. In the broadcasting area, the tradition is under strong and increasingly successful attack; however, the necessary interest groups and sources of countervailing power and advocacy do not exist in the press area. While they do not, it is unlikely that governments will act in isolation.

One long-standing exception is a strong element in the Australian Labor Party, particularly at the local-branch level, which believes that that party should redress press bias by starting its own mass media press. At the 1972 policymaking conference of that party, however, the proposal was modified to support a new newspaper, owned and operated by those who work on it. This implies some sort of cooperative or journalist-controlled newspaper, but the idea has never been thought through or

224

planned beyond the stage of a policy plank. A discussion paper released by the party in 1978 as a result of a "self-examination" committee of inquiry put the onus of showing viability of the proposal firmly on those who advocate it. The paper expressed considerable doubt about the proposal, and suggested that a considerable part of the unfavorable treatment that the Labor Party receives is due to its own procedures.

Elements within that party have also advocated that an Australian Newspaper Commission (along the lines of the Australian Broadcasting Commission) should publish a mass media newspaper. Others have been more skeptical, pointing out the considerable political difficulties the ABC experiences through operating by government funding in a commercial world. The most likely way such a newspaper could eventuate would lie in some future blurring of the distinction between electronic and printed transmission, as well as participation by the ABC. Needless to say, no official policy has been formulated on this proposal, and any such development would be resolved in the usual way, between those who advocate it, those whose interests might be adversely affected, and the government.

Publishing

After many years in the doldrums, the indigenous book-publishing industry has blossomed since the 1960s. The same is true of magazines; more than thirty thousand periodicals of all types are produced in Australia, ranging from those published regularly and distributed nationally, to small specialized journals. Women's and so-called family magazines, in particular, have had a tremendous boost in the 1970s, with some half-dozen new titles challenging the few long-established ones. Most men's magazines are published by one of the big media groups. There is little foreign ownership, one prominent exception being the English-based Thomsom organization. Some mass magazines are now sold through supermarkets and other such retail outlets, thus breaking the distribution arrangements still applying generally to the press and most periodicals.

Between 1970 and 1978 the estimated value of retail book sales increased by an average of 4.2 percent per annum in real terms, while real consumption expenditure increased by an average 3.8 percent per annum. The total population increase in the same period was 1.4 percent. Paperbacks display enormous sales in Australia, averaging between 71 and 76 percent of total books sold for the period 1970–78. Between 1970 and 1978 an average of 25 percent of all books purchased were written by Australian authors. Total fiction and nonfiction purchases were roughly equal, though Australian authors have a higher share of nonfiction sales in the categories of biography, history, cookbooks, and children's stories (Australia Council 1978).

With respect to imported books, the Australian book market is a closed system whereby the local branch of a British or American publisher, or an appointed distributor, has exclusive distribution rights throughout Australia for the foreign company's titles. Another form of exclusive trading practice, the Traditional Market Agreement, was broken in 1976. Under this system, U.K. and U.S. publishers refused to accept copyright license for a book from a foreign author or publisher unless they were assured of exclusive rights for publication and distribution of the book in a group of about seventy English-speaking countries, virtually all of the present and former members of the British Commonwealth. Under this agreement, British publishers were able to withhold the paperback edition of a book in Australia until years after release of the original hardback edition. Likewise, Australians were denied the ability to buy an American edition of a publication, even when the British edition was out of print. In response to a civil suit filed with the U.S. Justice Department against twenty-one major American publishers, the British Publishers Association abandoned the Traditional Market Agreement in November 1976, and signed a "consent decree" with the American companies. This prohibits restrictive trade by group arrangements and allows Australian publishers to negotiate distribution of books originating from the United States.

None of these developments have owed much to deliberate government policy, although it does intrude in some areas. Removal of postal concessions in 1973 was one such important step, undertaken by the Labor government despite that party's policy, as expressed in its present platform, of providing "special assistance towards the publication, printing and distribution of newspapers, books, magazines and other printed material . . . fully produced in Australia" (Australian Labor Party 1979).

On the other hand, there is some assistance to commercial publishing. Since June 1960, a bounty has been paid on the production of most books printed within Australia. The bounty scheme, administered by the Customs Department, makes direct payment to Australian printers at the rate of 33⅓ percent of the printer's net invoice. This form of protectionism, especially against Hong Kong printers, amounted to a $A9.5 million subsidy in the year 1977–78. Authors and publishers are rewarded under a Public Lending Right Scheme for books borrowed from public lending libraries. Authors and publishers are paid annually for the estimated number of eligible books held by libraries, currently at a rate of 50 cents for the author and 12½ cents per annum per copy for the publisher. The Literature Board offers writing fellowships and subsidizes publishers of specialized books and magazines, especially in fiction and poetry, by means of special-purpose publishing grants.

The federal government also runs the Australian Government Publishing Service which is primarily responsible for the printing and distribution of government publications. In the year 1976–77 it published 2,921 publications, with a market value of $A13.5 million.

Australia has no specific policy on preventing foreign ownership of publishing (or the press). However, there seems to be general agreement that in the event of a major takeover, ad hoc intervention would probably occur.

Cinema

Constitutional power relating to films in Australia lies with the states, except insofar as the commonwealth has power over imports, and censorship in time of war. The commonwealth has also put money into the development of film and this has been very important in recent years.

Policy development has been erratic, and inconsistent. Up to about 1920, the Australian film industry was healthy, and Australian films were popular with audiences. As a result of overseas competition, the film industry declined in the 1920s, and disappeared altogether by the 1940s and 1950s. In the late 1960s and 1970s the industry was revived by government action. Until then, the policy had been a laissez-faire one, and the only significant area of involvement was in censorship.

In the early part of the century, the popularity of film became a cause of concern to moralist lobbies, who urged governments to accept responsibility for content to ensure moral protection. The argument was complicated by an inability to decide whether the medium was entertainment, art, or a means of communication. The moralists won the argument and by 1914 two state governments had set up censorship systems, using criteria borrowed from American sources. By the end of the First World War, the commonwealth had set up a single censorship system for all imported films. Over the next several decades, the states gradually appointed the commonwealth to act on their behalf; but in recent years two states have reclaimed certain powers and now exercise censorship controls. This return to state control was a reaction to the easier standards and permissiveness of the 1970s. The only conclusion that can be drawn about policy development in censorship is that it seems to wax and wane with community attitudes.

The decline of the Australian production industry led, very slowly, to a reaction. The matter was raised by a 1934 report of the Royal Commission on Taxation (because of its connection with that subject in the argument over local and imported programs). It came into prominence again with the 1953 Royal Commission on Television (1954), through its connection with Australian content. In 1963 a Senate committee inquired into the encouragement of local production for television, whereupon many demands for action to revive the Australian industry were made (Senate Select Committee . . . 1963). Gradually, there was an awakening of public feeling. Apart from the creation in 1946 of a Commonwealth

Film Unit, which produced mainly documentaries, very little had been done by governments to stimulate the film industry. This changed dramatically in the early 1970s—a National Film and Television School was set up, a Film Development Corporation was created to provide loan capital, and an Experimental Film Fund was established. By 1975 an Australian Film Corporation had been created, both to fund films, and through Film Australia (which developed from the 1946 unit), to make films.

For the first time, there was a single authority to coordinate the funding and other film roles of the commonwealth; but as a complication of divided control, new state developments have now occurred. In 1972 the film production resources of the South Australian government and the educational functions of the film library in that state were combined in a new body, the South Australian Film Corporation. This body continued to perform the recognized educational and propaganda functions that state governments had exercised all along, but it was also empowered to encourage and to participate in the growth of a commercial film industry in South Australia. Other states soon saw the possibilities opened up by this move, and similar bodies were established in Victoria, New South Wales, Tasmania, and Queensland. Each is slightly different in its administration and aims, and none has been in existence long enough yet for a clear indication of the policy of each to be available. But the potential for rivalry between the commonwealth's Australian Film Commission and the various state bodies is obvious, and given the history of commonwealth-state jealousy in Australia, it is not a threat that can be ignored.

Nevertheless, the film production area is the one where Australia comes nearest to having a policy. The Australian Film Commission has a policy of the widest possible support for the Australian film industry on cultural, economic, and artistic grounds. There is no reason why the state bodies could not contribute to this policy too, though it remains to be seen whether they can sink their rivalries sufficiently to do so.

But production is only one part of the picture. Australia has no guarantee of freedom of speech, and even if it did, film would not automatically be included within such a right. Moralist lobbies continue to press for controls to limit the permissive society, and libertarian lobbies press for individual freedom of speech and artistic expression. Meanwhile, the trade lobbies press for continued financial support for the local industry or for an absence of restraint of trade. The educational interests and the libraries press for money to develop collections and services, and community groups like film cooperatives and the Australian Film Institute call for government assistance. The government's policy in deciding how to act on or allocate funds for these confusing and often conflicting demands is generally one of political expediency.

An example of this ad hoc decision making was the announcement in 1981 of a 150 percent tax write-off for money invested in film production to offset the financial difficulties suffered by that industry in the late 1970s. The result was a rush of money into the industry from previously uninvolved sources, often for tax avoidance reasons. Prices for talent and services rose steeply. In response, the conditions for deductability have now been tightened somewhat, but the production of many films has been started. As a consequence of this inflow of investor money, the role of government film commissions has diminished.

Radio and Television Broadcasting

Development of radio broadcasting as a service to the public began in Australia in 1923, perhaps for no better reason than that the medium was available and broadcasting was commencing elsewhere. A Wireless Telegraphy Act had been passed in 1905, to regulate the use of the then newly invented technology. Under that act, licenses for all communications purposes were given by what is known as the "sealed set" system: licenses were granted by the postmaster-general to approved companies, and listeners were required to pay a subscription, which depended on the number of stations to which their set was tuned. The set itself was to be sealed, so that other stations could not be listened to. The intention was to fund the service through subscriptions. At first, no direct advertising was allowed, but when the revenue was insufficient, sponsorship was permitted. The sealed set idea was conceived by one of the leading set manufacturers. From the very beginning, a recurring phenomenon of pressure and commercial suggestion, leading to government action, was established. So began the commercial system.

Under the plan, four stations, all in capital cities, began, but the system was not a success, partly because it was possible to tamper with sets and partly because listener response was slow. The public, the set manufacturers, and the companies licensed to broadcast all pressured for a better system. In 1924 a new plan providing for two classes of station was introduced: Class A stations were to derive revenue from receiver license fees paid by listeners, and Class B stations would be financed by advertising. By 1929 there were 12 Class B and 8 Class A stations, serving 300,000 listeners. Licenses were given by the postmaster-general without any form of public hearing, and control was in the hands of his department. The system was entirely privately owned.

Pressure to extend broadcasting to rural and other areas of low population density, to which private companies were not attracted because of the low revenue base, led to changes. In 1927, the Royal Commission on Wireless was held, and following this, the Conservative government of the day sought a merger of the Class A stations, with the more populous areas subsidizing the less populous. This proposal was not acceptable to the companies. The solution, in 1929, was for the government to buy out the Class A stations, and call for tenders to supply programs. In the event, a new company, the Australian Broadcasting

Company (ABC), was created, and it undertook to meet the needs of the various interests seeking specialized programming. No change was made to the Class B stations.

However, the idea that broadcasting should be a national service, or at least have a strong national component, gained increasing acceptance. In 1932, the influence of British models on Australian life was much stronger than it is today and the birth of the ABC probably owes more to the BBC having been founded some six years earlier than to any well-worked-out intellectual commitment to the concept of public service broadcasting. There was, however, some feeling against the already strong advertising influence in commercial broadcasting, and an increasing desire to provide a place for quality and received, as opposed to mass, culture in broadcasting. But perhaps the strongest motivation was the need to get services into remote areas, and the established tradition in Australia of the state taking responsibility for services that are partly social services, and to which private capital is not attracted—a pragmatic, down-market antipodean socialism, the only kind ever really practiced in Australia.

The broadcasting company's license expired in 1932, and the Australian Broadcasting Commission was set up by an Act of Parliament in that year. The bill was passed under a Conservative government, but it followed closely a bill prepared by the Labor government that had been defeated at the end of the previous year. There was a large measure of bipartisan support for the concept, although in 1927 an earlier Conservative government had opposed the idea of a commission, and had tried instead the private company merger compromise referred to above.

The circumstances and timing of the origin of the ABC are important. Unlike the BBC, the ABC was never in a monopoly position, and never had the opportunity to impose an ethos on broadcasting. Secondly, it accepted from the beginning a duty to do the service and minority broadcasting that the commercial sector in Australia was both unwilling and uncompelled to do. The BBC inheritance took the form of a concept of quality broadcasting and received culture. It was a modification of the position set for the BBC by Lord Reith. The net effect of these formative influences was to create an ABC that was seen as sound and reliable, but somewhat stuffy, and never popular in the eyes of the mass audience. But it was central to many areas of Australian life, and cherished by its constituency. But by following the BBC model, which had arisen in a country where there was no choice, the ABC was largely setting itself aside from Australian popular culture. Its station became the voice of formality, received culture, and "educated southern English" in stark contrast to the more indigenous sound of the commercials. ABC listeners tended to find the commercials offensive. Thus the ABC perpetuated a division in Australian culture and came down on the side of a minority. But the 1932 establishing Act, it should be noted, enjoined the ABC to do "adequate and comprehensive programming," and the organization has from time to time asserted its duty to cover the whole spectrum of programming. However, its attitude and performance in popular programming has always been ambivalent. The subject was, and still is, a source of endless debate both inside and outside the ABC.

As a consequence of its history and lack of role definition, the ABC is in a curious position politically. It has acquired an almost traditional position in Australian life. It has a faithful following composed of people with many shades of political opinion who all believe in some version of the ABC idea. But it is still subject to much debate on its role, is defensive, and is unwilling to assert itself.

Simultaneously with the establishment of the ABC, the commercial radio sector grew rapidly. By the early 1930s, it was well entrenched, and most of the stations that exist in the capital cities today had been set up. By the end of the decade, further expansion in country areas had brought the numbers very close to their present-day level. National (ABC) station growth was more steady. (In 1932 there were 12 national and 43 commercial stations; in 1940, 26 and 100 respectively; and in 1960, 57 and 108).

The dual system of ABC and commercial sectors was thus established and would be carried over later (1956) into television. It remained basically unchanged until the emergence in the 1970s of the tiny third sector, public broadcasting. The ABC's role, while officially described as comprehensive, was not that in practice. The commercial stations' role, dictated by the market place rather than by any design or regulation, developed into overtly majority broadcasting, although it did do a certain amount of local or community broadcasting, especially in rural areas.

By the 1930s there was considerable disquiet about the power of commercial broadcasting, especially about the potential for stations to aggregate into jointly owned chains, and about the demonstrated trend of the press to own large parts of the radio system. This concern was greatest on the political left, but was not absent from some conservative elements, who saw in the emergent situation a media bloc that could exert tremendous power. For instance, Archdale Parkhill, a minister in the Lyons (Conservative) government, speaking in Parliament in December 1935 said, "We have growing up in this country a monopoly of newspapers and broadcasting which, in combination, constitute a danger that this Parliament cannot view with equanimity, and steps should be taken to deal with it" (Parkhill 1935).

In October 1935, as a result of opposition by the postmaster-general of the day to more licenses going to existing licensees, and after considerable public controversy, a statutory rule limiting commercial station ownership was gazetted. This rule limited ownership or effective control to one metropolitan station in any state, two metropolitan stations overall, three stations in any one state, or five in the whole country. However, representations were made to the government that the new regulations were "burdensome and inequitable" and only five weeks later, the rule was changed to allow one metropolitan station in any state, four metropolitan stations overall, four in any state or eight in the whole country. The regulations were silent on cross-ownership with newspapers. There has never, at any time, been any restriction on newspaper ownership of either radio or television stations. The fears of the government of the day were not great enough to withstand the representations, much less proscribe press ownership, and there was certainly no suggestion of divestiture (Parliamentary Joint Committee on Wireless Broadcasting 1942).

By the early 1940s there was little multiple ownership of stations outside the newspaper interests, but nearly half the stations on air at that time were controlled by newspaper owners. The initial motivation for this was to gain a stake in the new medium because of the fear of radio superseding newspapers. Although never as clearly articulated then as it has been in retrospect, the restriction on ownership, belated and imperfect as it was, constituted, with the dual system, a policy of diversity.

During those early years (until 1948) program standards existed as regulations made under the Wireless Telegraphy Act (1905) and therefore under the direct control of the minister of the day, as distinct from statutory officials with defined responsibilities and independence. There was also a code of rules drawn up and enforced by the Federation of Australian Commercial Broadcasters. Neither official regulations nor codes of rules covered the ABC, which jealously guarded its own standards. There was no attempt to coordinate the outputs of the two systems, and not much real attempt to ensure that either system actually catered to a wide range of tastes. Regulation was benign, and more directed toward censorship of material considered offensive by community standards, as interpreted, than to anything positive. The overall result was a substantially laissez-faire system dictated by perceived market requirements. There was little real attempt by government to influence events either operationally or structurally. Policy relating to program content was almost entirely reactive. When more deliberate attempts were made in the 1960s and 1970s to obtain higher standards through regulation, this tradition was to prove so entrenched as to be virtually impossible to combat.

During this formative period there also evolved a further policy that was to have important effects in later years. Economic protectionism, or strict limitation of the numbers of stations in any one area, was strongly adhered to. Because of the conservative technical policy adopted by the Postmaster-General's Department in allotting frequencies, the available channels were occupied quickly in Australia. It therefore became widely accepted that there could be very little further expansion of the radio system in Australia after about 1940. However, had there been sufficient pressure for expansion, a different technical policy, involving more sharing of channels and other measures widely adopted elsewhere, could have been adopted.

The real reason for the restriction was economic. Mr. Vivian Brooker, the president of the Federation of Australian Commercial Broadcasters, told the Joint Parliamentary Committee on Wireless Broadcasting of 1942:

> The question is continually being raised that shortage of wave-length or frequencies preclude other services being given to the listener, or that some individuals or organisations desirous of providing broadcasting services cannot be accommodated in the frequency spectrum allocated to radio broadcasting. That is only partly true, and does not completely sum up the situation. From a technical point of view there is room for many more broadcasting stations in Australia, all of which, techni-cally, would be capable of rendering a reliable and highly satisfactory service. The technical aspect is, however, not the only point to be considered in the matter; finance is probably the most important consideration of all.

Brooker went on to predict increases in station numbers as popula-tion increased. He said that "the plea of today that there is a shortage of wavelengths will be regarded as one of the strange stories of the past." He was prophetic: that time arrived in the mid-1970s.

From the beginning, the Australian commercial radio structure contrasted strongly with the American, even allowing for differences in population. For instance, by the 1970s there were still only six commer-cial stations in Sydney, a city of nearly three million people. It was not until 1974 that it was found possible officially to vary the technical policy. By then the radio industry, with the exception of a few country stations, was a very profitable business indeed, and the justification for that degree of protection has long disappeared.

It is seldom argued in Australia that the policy of protectionism was incorrect at the time it was applied, and up to about the early 1950s. The argument is that it outlived its usefulness, because by that time there is no doubt that many markets could have supported more radio stations. The position was to become more critical in the late 1960s and 1970s with the build-up in demand for other noncommercial types of broadcasting, which was also frustrated. Furthermore, the policy had imbued the whole industry, its attendant bureaucracy and political interests, with a sense of complacency about radio broadcasting. Until quite recently, almost all radio sets sold in Australia had the call signs of each station in Australia marked on the dial.

A further strong arm of Australian policy was evident in attempts to foster Australian production. This policy began with the 1932 Australian

Broadcasting Commission Act that set up the ABC, and enjoined the ABC to endeavor to establish bands and orchestras, and to encourage local talent. In 1942, the new Broadcasting Act provided that 2½ percent of music time on both ABC and commercial radio be devoted to Australian works.

By the late 1940s there was a good deal of dissatisfaction with departmental responsibility in broadcasting. The Labor government of the period also wished to see tighter regulation of commercial broadcasting. In 1948 it therefore set up the Australian Broadcasting Control Board (ABCB) with regulatory, planning, and some semi-judicial powers. The ABCB was to hold hearings for new license applications and make recommendations thereon to the relevant federal minister—who remained the postmaster-general. But because the process of deciding the areas for which license applications would be called, and the decision to do so, remained with the postmaster-general, the scope for direct lobbying and political decision making remained as great as ever. The absence of any mechanism whereby a potential applicant could force consideration of his claim strengthened the position of the existing licensees, who were reluctant, for economic reasons, to see any great expansion. As an industry body they were in a powerful position to give advice, which was essentially conservative and protectionist, to the government. This advice played a critical role in delaying the expansion of radio broadcasting. In particular it was very influential in delaying the introduction of frequency modulation (FM) broadcasting until the 1970s. The power to award licenses was also retained by the minister. These conditions were set by the Labor government in power in 1948; in 1949 that government was succeeded by a Conservative government, which retained the 1948 Broadcasting Act unchanged.

With the creation of the ABCB, increased attention was given to program regulation. In 1956, with the coming of television, program standards were required to be formulated under the amendments to the Act of that year (Broadcasting and Television Act). The minister, in explaining the 1956 bill, dealt at length with the social power of television and stated that self-regulation would not be sufficient to secure programs of a suitable standard to satisfy the public. In supporting written standards, he said that "the Government believes that the basic objective of achieving proper standards of quality in television programmes can be realised in this way" (House of Representatives 1956: 1538). The minister was attempting to allay the considerable public concern about the possible effects of television.

The strongly established ethos of commercial broadcasting was too strong for the ABCB to have much effect. It suffered from having virtually no sanctions it could impose, and legal questioning of the validity of its power to make and enforce standards. Appointments to the ABCB were mainly from the ranks of commercial broadcasters themselves, or from within the ABCB's own bureaucracy. The latter, in the beginning, came mainly from the Postmaster-General's Department, and brought with them the values and associations that had grown up over nearly thirty years. The board was located in Melbourne, and was largely cut off from staff interchange with the sources of dynamism in the public service, which was based in Canberra. For all these reasons it never developed the constituency of public support that would have been necessary for it to have much successful impact on Australian broadcasting. It was an obscure body whose public image was negative. It never gave any public leadership in broadcasting matters and was frequently made to look ridiculous in censorship incidents, in which it was widely regarded as being behind public taste and tolerance.

Television began in Australia in 1956, after the Royal Commission on Television in 1953. Although some evidence was given that a different type of structure from radio was desirable, the royal commission considered that its terms of reference dictated adoption of the same dual system of national and commercial stations as in radio (Royal Commission on Television 1954). However, because of an ad hoc decision, the policy of protectionism was varied in a way many consider to have had important consequences. In the country areas, each provincial market was given one station only, which certainly made economic sense. But in the four eastern state capital cities, the Conservative government of the day decided to allot a third license, in addition to the two allotted in each city in the initial stage of development.

The ABCB (1958), on one of the few occasions when it did express opposition to the government of the day, contended strongly that there was room for only two stations in the two smaller capitals, Adelaide and Brisbane. It was overruled. It has been reported fairly reliably that the government was motivated by a desire to see all available channels allotted under its own rule rather than leave a channel vacant for the Opposition Labor Party to allot in government.

For many years the third commercial stations in the capital cities operated at a loss. Although all stations are now profitable, or potentially so, there is much evidence that they are so only within a financial regimen of strictly limited spending on local production and considerable importing of much cheaper overseas products. Given the continual demand on Australian television to try to provide an indigenous Australian look with a revenue base provided by only 14 million people, the allocation of so many channels is regarded widely as a serious blunder. Any substantial increase in spending to achieve quality, and/or quantity, could threaten the system's viability. The stations have successfully used this argument to resist demands, and there is enough substance in it to carry their case. From time to time it has been suggested that it would be better if the advertising revenue, which is not infinitely extensible, were spread over fewer stations, on the grounds that they could then maintain viability and spend more on better, and more local, programming. Attempts at rationalization, however, run up against the ratchet effect—

that it is easier to establish something than to remove it, especially, it seems, in broadcasting. Business interests, bureaucratic and political acceptance, and audience expectations tend to become entrenched.

By the mid-1960s, television coverage of Australia was virtually complete. In pursuit of the policy of diversity of ownership first applied to radio, ownership was limited by the Broadcasting and Television Act (1956) to not more than two stations anywhere in the whole country. With ministerial encouragement, the ABCB applied the local ownership policy zealously. To get a license it was necessary for the applicant to establish to the board his or her potential viability and local character. Beyond that, the board's selection processes were shrouded in mystery. No selection criteria were ever published, nor any explanation ever given of why one applicant was preferred over another. Newspaper links were not a bar, they were an advantage. The board accepted the argument that because of inexperience with television in Australia, media experience residing in newspaper companies was an advantage. Strong press links, extending to outright control in a number of cases, were established. One result of this has been the absence of a consistently strong print media school of television criticism in Australia. At worst, the popular press and magazines have been used as a vehicle to promote individual channels and shows, and expressions of social concern about television have been muted. It is only in more recent times, with the emergence of a better quality press in Australia, and the increased interest in broadcasting as a political issue, that better coverage of television has been given. Such coverage is more on the political and financial side of television than on program criticism.

The ABC has only one television channel throughout the nation. Since this channel is outnumbered three to one in well over half the market, television has a distinctly commercial flavor. As in radio, the ABC suffers from a lack of clarity in goals. It is, under the 1932 Act, obliged to be "adequate and comprehensive," with one channel. This is an impossibility, with the result that in part it competes for the mass audience and in part it is a minority programming channel. In fiercely competitive markets, this approach does not make for cohesive programming; it tends to minimize the audience and weaken political support for the ABC.

Thus, by the late 1960s, the principal elements of Australian broadcasting policy were well established. These consisted of attempted diversity by means of the dual system of ABC and commercial broadcasting, and the ownership policy in the commercial system; economic protectionism by limiting severely the number of stations in radio (but the application of this principle to television was inconsistent); formal regulation by quasi-judicial application of standards; imposition of levels of Australian content; and a conservative technical policy of channel allocation.

Some of these policies are now threatened; later developments are dealt with below in the discussion of present-day policy formation.

Telecommunications

Telecommunications and postal services were begun before federation by each Australian state, along the lines of the British Post Office. The first official postmaster was appointed in the colony of New South Wales in 1809. The first telegraph service began in 1854 in Victoria, and by 1858, Sydney, Melbourne, and Adelaide were linked by telegraph. The telephone was introduced in 1878.

Upon federation in 1901, the new commonwealth government was given control of postal, telegraphic, and telephonic services. Departments responsible for these services in the states were transferred to the commonwealth. A Commonwealth Department of State was created, under the postmaster-general, a member of the federal government. National planning, research and development, financial management, and policy advice to the minister were centralized, but a good deal of operational management was left to regional offices.

Under the Post and Telegraph Act (1901), the Post Office was given exclusive right to the carriage of "letters" as defined, but for other articles it competed with private carriers. It was also given a statutory monopoly right to transmit public telecommunications traffic within Australia. There was never any serious suggestion that private enterprise should provide these services nationwide, although there have often been proposals that private interests should be able to provide particular services, rather than be served by the monopoly. Generally, the Post Office has been successful in resisting such encroachments. One of its arguments has always been that it was forced to apply a large measure of cross-subsidization in its nationwide operations, and therefore it could not afford to lose the more lucrative or lower-cost portions, which were generally involved in private proposals. One of the consistent political pressures that it has operated under has been to provide good services to country areas. Because of vast distances and low population these are high cost. This long-established custom of the state providing services to rural areas, established in the area of telecommunications, was one of the most powerful precedents when it came to setting up the Australian Broadcasting Commission in 1932.

Under the Wireless Telegraphy Act (1905), the postmaster-general was responsible for planning the orderly development of all radio services. The Postmaster-General's Department allotted bands of frequencies to the ABCB for use in broadcasting. For nonbroadcasting uses, the Post Office both allocated and derived revenue from spectrum usage. It was frequently asserted that this placed it in a favored position.

All telecommunications between Australia and the rest of the world are under the ownership and control of a separate body, the Overseas Telecommunications Commission (OTC), which was created as a result of the Commonwealth Telecommunications Conference in London in 1945. By authority of the Overseas Telecommunications Act of 1946, the commission took over communications that were then provided by a private company, Amalgamated Wireless (Australia) Ltd. Communication is by submarine telephone cables, high-frequency radio, and communications satellite. OTC holds a 2.78 percent share of INTELSAT.

The Post Office role was largely unchanged from 1901 to 1975. It was a very large enterprise that was neither solely a social service nor a business undertaking. It was not the object of a great deal of controversy or debate, but what there was centered around this conflict. In 1973, the incoming Labor government set up the Commission of Inquiry into the Australian Post Office. It is not altogether clear what prompted the inquiry, but the motivation probably lay in the general reforming zeal of the new government, together with the fact of the British Post Office having become a more business-oriented body some years earlier, and in the advocacy by some government advisers of a "user pays" philosophy. The commission reported in 1974 and said, among other things, that the Post Office should offer comprehensive services on the basis of a tariff structure that would provide for the reasonable costs of services to be recouped from customers; ensure that the community contributed in proportion to the use each member made of the services; and provide a reasonable return on revenue (Commission of Inquiry . . . 1975). The report was accepted. In other words, the Post Office was to swing toward a "user pays" business footing. In retrospect, it seems a curious thing for a Labor government to have done, given that party's history of a more pooled, community-based philosophy. It may have been motivated by the conviction, then very strong in that party, that country areas had been unduly cossetted for too long, and should be made to pay their way.

The commission also recommended the splitting of the Post Office into two bodies, one dealing with postal services, and the other with telecommunications. In 1975, Australia Post, and Telecom Australia were set up as separate statutory corporations. The office of postmaster-general has now gone. Planning of spectrum usage, and policy, is now under a minister for postal and telecommunications, although in practice, both new bodies are closely consulted in such matters.

The Australian telecommunications network is highly developed. In 1977 Telecom reported at government request on the possibility of a domestic satellite. It rejected the idea in favor of further development of the existing system, which it said was the most economical way to proceed, provided no very large increase in capacity was needed, such as massive television networking transmission.

No sooner had this decision been taken, however, than a further proposition for a satellite arose which was taken seriously by the government. The impetus came from Publishing and Broadcasting Ltd., one of the major television and print media groups, which produced a report in 1977 claiming to show the advantages of a satellite, and advocating a system of television networking completely at variance with the established policy of local control. The report advocated new commercial stations in each provincial market, to create a uniform system of three commercial channels and one ABC channel over the whole of Australia. It also extolled the virtues of a satellite for providing communications and data transmission to remote areas. There is no doubt that the suggestion was for commercial motives, some of which related to the fact that the company in question is investing heavily in sports promotion and telecasting, for which live transmission is necessary. The other two capital-city station groups were cool to the idea, and the provincial stations were hostile, because of the possibility of devastating competition. There is no doubt that the proposed structure would destroy the provincial television industry as it is presently constituted.

In response, the government appointed a task force drawn from government departments and instrumentalities to investigate the proposal. The task force was chaired by the chairman of the Overseas Telecommunications Commission. In its report in 1978, the task force recommended a satellite under a new special authority (Commonwealth Government Task Force 1978). The recommendation for a new authority has been vigorously contested by Telecom Australia. The proposal for the satellite was strongly opposed by telecommunications trade unions, mainly due to fear of loss of jobs, and by provincial television stations, who see the threat to their industry. The report then went before a further working party drawn from the bureaucracy. This process culminated in a government announcement of approval in principle of an Australian satellite. Currently, design work and estimates of user demand are under way, and tenders have been submitted.

The precise use of the satellite is unresolved. It appears that the ABC and other government instrumentalities will be major users. A private company, but so far with the government as sole shareholder, has been formed to operate the satellite. Questions of pricing and the ownership of ground stations are unresolved. It is likely that more than one operational satellite will be launched.

As a policy development issue, the satellite proposal has followed the usual course of ad hoc decision making. It was prompted by sectional interests, and opposed by other sectional interests. Each side has carried out a vigorous campaign of public lobbying and special pleading. There has been much misinformation and lack of information. In considering the issue, some fundamental questions going to the heart of established policy, such as Telecom's monopoly on services, and ownership and control policy in television, are being confronted. It could lead to fundamental change, and some people have pointed out that it provides an opportunity to reconsider the whole system. It is more likely, however, that a compromise will be devised between existing interests.

In mid-1980 the government announced an inquiry into Telecom to see to what extent the private sector could participate in its services. A business telecommunications lobby has been formed to press for participation rather like that now developing in the U.S. There is no doubt that the present government is opposed to a government monopoly on such services, but it is unclear what the outcome will be. Despite the introduction of a largely "user pays" policy in 1975, a large measure of cross-subsidization remains, and this will be a major issue.

Australia is a member of all relevant regional and international telecommunications organizations. It has taken part in radio spectrum planning internationally since the very early days of radio. It has tended to support international resolutions aimed at increasing the flow of news and openness of telecommunications sytems, but has not been especially active in implementation. It has accepted the UNESCO mass media resolution (UNESCO 1978:54–55). Australia's involvement has been greatest in electronic communications; the strong tradition of private ownership of the print media has meant that action in the latter areas has been left to private interests.

Present-Day Policy and Policy Formation Procedures

By far the greatest activity in policy formation lies at present in broadcasting. Otherwise, there is considerable concentration on telecommunications, especially the satellite question, as described previously, and there is also impending or new legislation due and/or discussion in areas of general applicability, such as freedom of information, trade practices, and copyright.

But in broadcasting, all the ingredients for policy development are present—new technology to be employed, powerful business interests, interest groups of various sorts, and media attention. This activity, and the changes that have occurred, were largely associated with or set in motion by the Labor government of 1972–75. The concurrence is by no means exact, however. The significant watershed date is probably 1970, when after long years of futile agitation, it was finally admitted that Australia was ridiculously out of date in not having FM broadcasting. In that year, the Conservative government instructed the ABCB to hold a public inquiry into the subject. Under the Conservative government that took office in late 1975, activity in broadcasting has continued, and there have been a number of important developments.

To describe and analyze present-day policies and identify trends, it is convenient to first deal with methods of policy formation. Formal policy formulation follows the Westminster model, with political parties arriving at broad policy by their various processes, and a neutral public service executing it (disregarding for the moment the increasing importance of the official inquiry as a vehicle through which the interests at any time assert themselves, and as a very important source of policy formulation). In practice, as is now widely recognized, this description is fanciful. It presupposes a sound understanding of the area and its trends by the parties, and in particular their spokespersons for the area. It assumes a neutral public service making no policy choices, with a one-way policy flow to it. It ignores the impact of administration on policy, and the origination of policy by incremental change in the bureaucracy. It ignores the industry, pressure groups, and the press, except insofar as these may influence the original development of party policy. It assumes that parties themselves are of one mind, and that party policy, once determined, is faithfully followed by all members. It assumes quaintly that industry bodies, pressure groups, and the press have no contact with bureaucrats. It ignores the influence and interaction of personalities.

None of these presuppositions and assumptions can be made, and in the area of Australian communication policy, all elements—the parties, individuals in them, bureaucrats, the press, industry bodies and individuals, pressure groups, and even academics—have played important, and at times decisive, roles. This is not to say that party policy is unimportant, especially in setting the wider atmosphere in which the procedures are smoked out, for it is impossible to separate policy determination from the wider background of political events. However, other influences to be discussed are an integral part of policy development.

In Australia, one of the most stable, prominent, and powerful elements in policy development is the industry itself, especially the commercial sector. Because of the prominent part it plays in people's lives, its strong dominance of the very organs of public debate, and its long and stable history, the commercial industry carries much weight. Its command of the channels by which politicians reach their public is not the least of its powers. The media themselves are a significant element of policymaking, through their disseminating role. They are essentially conservative, because the set of views society holds of itself is the same set under which the media system has evolved. It therefore tends to be in the interest of the media to preserve those values.

At the industry level in broadcasting, influence operates through the Federation of Australian Commercial Television Stations (FACTS) and the Federation of Australian Radio Broadcasters (FARB) for the commercial sector. The new public sector is represented by the Public Broadcasting Association of Australia (PBAA). In recent years FACTS and FARB have stepped up their public and private lobbying activity considerably. With the numerous inquiries, they have become more prominent as witnesses and representatives of the industry and have begun issuing policy statements of various kinds. They have the advantages of money and substance in representing an economically and socially important industry. They suffer from the disadvantage of having, on some issues, divided and opposing interests within their ranks, for example, program-originating, stations versus others, in television.

But despite their strengths, industry spokespersons suffer from grave weaknesses. The rise of academic, public, and general intellectual interest in broadcasting has created a more aware and critical elite, and industry spokespersons have difficulty in intellectualizing credibly their close involvement with obviously entrenched interests. For these reasons, they tend to be eclipsed intellectually by others in the bureaucracy, the press, and academia.

The PBAA has the disadvantage of representing a tiny service of almost no political weight and low public prominence. It does have the advantage of being intellectually more in tune with important parts of the bureaucracy and with many of those working for change.

In addition to representation through industry bodies, there is considerable direct lobbying of government by individuals in the industry. Because of the greater business orientation of conservative parties, links have been more easily established with conservative than with Labor politicians.

It is the practice (indeed, it is required by the Broadcasting and Television Act of 1956) for government authorities to consult the above industry bodies extensively. There is also much informal, social contact. These links are of tremendous importance because such relationships make for a blurring of the line between professional and personal spheres. Development of such relationships is one of the most important roles of lobby groups. At its worst, it has led to close identification of the regulatory or official body with the people it is supposed to regulate, and alienation from the public, who are supposed to be represented.

Industry trade unions are the other important industry group of long standing. They have played a prominent part in molding policy, but they suffer from the same disadvantage as the industry itself—their industrial aims are confused with broader aims—and unions have not been as successful as industry groups in cultivating good relationships with people in official bodies.

Before 1970, there were few pressure groups in Australian broadcasting, apart from industry bodies and trade unions. But in the early 1970s, because of a measure of dissatisfaction with services, and partly stimulated by the prominence given media affairs during the time of the Labor government, a host of such groups arose. They still remain today. They have been concerned with greater access to broadcasting, with children's television, with local content, with various interests in public broadcasting, with defense of the ABC, and even with structural matters to do with broadcasting. Various governmental and parliamentary inquiries have given these bodies an opportunity for input, and for publicity. Their spokespersons are becoming increasingly skilled in furthering their cases, and their prominence has begun a debate about the degree to which they represent, or speak for, the general public.

Inextricably associated with increasing pressure group and industry body activity has been increased press interest. It has been both a function and a cause of such activity. Because of some specialization in the press, and greater in-depth coverage, better-educated journalists of the newer school have become more prominent. This has led to much better coverage of media matters, mainly by a handful of journalists. They have become very knowledgeable about the issues, interests, and personalities involved, and have developed good sources. With the exception of a very few ABC programs, and some on public radio, reporting on media issues has been largely confined to the so-called quality press. It has been and continues to be an important element in the policy formulation procedure. The objective of securing a favorable press, by whatever means commanded, is integrated into the strategies of all players in the game. The means include the leak, or deliberate and timely unauthorized release of confidential information, which has played no small part in several significant events.

Academic interest in communications affairs is also increasing. The subject is now taught widely at higher education institutions, and even schools, in Australia. A growing body of analysis is emerging, and there is a healthy tendency on the part of some academics to venture into the topical market places of ideas with submissions and other contemporary work, a tendency traditionally eschewed by Australian academia. While somewhat removed from the more immediate impact of journalism, and hence of longer-term value, such work, and the people engaged in it, are becoming increasingly important in policy formulations.

Policy formulation by the major political parties has also improved in the last decade. In 1970, despite the fact that it set in motion the first of the many inquiries of the last decade, the Conservative government had probably simply not thought about many issues. It was concerned with what it saw as orderly development of the existing system, for example, the introduction of color television. In the absence of pressure, it saw no reason for change. Its bureaucratic advice was coming from the ABCB, and the old Postmaster-General's Department, neither being bodies noted for anticipating problems or for deep analysis. Other than that, the main source of advice to governments was from personal contacts with people prominent in the commercial world. There was no will for change.

The Labor Party, which came to power at the end of 1972, was not much more enlightened, despite an appearance of grappling with media problems. It had appointed a shadow minister for media in the late 1960s, and announced its intention to create a Department of the Media. The dominant thinking in the party, however, seemed to involve a commitment to higher levels of Australian content on television and very little else. It professed itself most dissatisfied with the level of monopoly, or oligopoly, in broadcasting, and with press ownership, without going deeply into just how this operated to the public disadvantage, or planning what could be done about it. There was zeal to correct what it saw as abuses and neglect after twenty-three years of Conservative government, but no great depth of thinking as to how to proceed.

The result was the creation of a Department of the Media which, although strongly regarded by the industry as an unwarranted threat, was largely aimless and ineffective. One of the problems was lack of

243

definition of its role, so that a substantial part of its effort consisted of territorial bureaucratic battles with the ABCB. Most senior appointments were from outside the public service, and these people were inexperienced in the nuances of interdepartmental politics, which limited their effectiveness. The department did attempt to raise Australian content in television by a new rule devised in conjunction with the board, but the net effect was not significant.

Some new commercial radio stations were initiated early in the Labor reign, but it was not until late in its term, in 1974–75, that much tangible change in broadcasting was made—with the introduction of FM radio, the beginning of public and ethnic broadcasting, and some innovative additions to the ABC. On none of these matters did the impetus come from the Department of the Media, which was equivocal about all of them.

The introduction of new radio channels, and the willingness to use them (the Labor government allocated seventeen new public stations, several commercial, six ABC, and two new ethnic stations) seriously dented the policy of protection. The introduction of new kinds of broadcasting stations extended the concept of diversity. The link between structure and regulation was conceptualized, for the first time, in the report of the Working Party on Public Broadcasting in 1975. This report pointed out that a corollary of shifting the concept of diversity to structure lessened the need for obtaining "adequate and comprehensive" output from individual stations, and therefore lessened the need for detailed regulation.

Over about the last decade, Australia's policy on non-English-speaking migrants has changed from one of integration to multiculturalism. In response to this, and at the particular instigation of a few people associated with the government, the Labor government set up two ethnic radio stations. Ostensibly they were for an experimental period, but it was a fair presumption that they would become permanent. (This has since happened.) They were run by committees appointed by the minister, and financed by the government.

The Labor government also added to the ABC a station intended to broadcast in popular format, in Sydney, and an access station in Melbourne. The former showed for the first time what an ABC station, following the modern mode of strip programming and pitched to a specific audience, could do. It achieved high ratings. For that reason, the commercial sector reacted strongly against it, claiming that popular programming was not the ABC's role. The access station, which also had a high non-English language component, admitted people and organizations to the air who had never previously participated. There was an attempt to "de-professionalize" and broaden the base of broadcasting.

A trenchant and vocal campaign against the Labor government's initiatives was waged by the commercial sector, ostensibly on the grounds that they were ad hoc, and that there was no "orderly plan for broadcasting." This campaign was taken up by the Conservatives in their opposition role, again largely on the grounds of ad hocery. Considerable hysteria developed around Labor's media initiatives (including the Press Council proposal referred to above). They had come in a year of unprecedented turbulence in Australian federal politics, which led up to the dismissal of the Whitlam government in late 1975 and media developments were inextricably bound up with those events.

After the fall of the Labor government, the new Conservative government took office with avowals of reform, partly motivated by a different, more traditional policy, and partly because of a heavy investment in rhetoric while in opposition. The effect on emerging lines of policy was quite marked. The government immediately restricted the funds of the ABC and rescinded plans for relay of the new ABC station to Melbourne. It began inquiries into the access and ethnic radio situation, and into the administrative structure of broadcasting (Department of Postal and Telecommunications 1976. Because the inquiry was headed by F.J. Green, secretary of the department, this report has become known as the "Green Report.") It replaced the Department of the Media with a Department of Postal and Telecommunications. Ironically, although the head of the department was replaced, the new department retained the same functions with respect to media policy as the old department. Concurrently, the commercial federations released policy statements calling for restriction of both the ABC and public radio to a complementary, minority role. There was considerable feeling against the ABC in some influential government quarters and a firm intention to bring it and commercial broadcasting under one overall authority. Most public broadcasters feared that the sector would be abolished or at least frozen. In the event, the Green Report did not recommend a single authority, nor did it explicitly recommend a complementary role for the ABC. But it did for the public sector. It recommended the abolition of the ABCB, which then had a majority of Labor government appointees.

These recommendations were accepted, with the ABCB being replaced by an Australian Broadcasting Tribunal (ABT), comprised of three former commercial-industry people out of four members. Under the amendments of the 1977 Broadcasting and Television Act, the tribunal was to conduct public hearings for all license renewals, and much emphasis was given to public participation. The tribunal itself, at the government's direction, conducted an inquiry into self-regulation for broadcasters, and recommended a substantial degree of self-regulation, except in certain areas such as children's television, local content, and advertising rules (ABT 1979). The government accepted this recommendation in principle.

Contrary to many expectations and after a long delay, the new Conservative government proceeded with the expansion of the public broadcasting sector. At ministerial invitation, hearings were held, and new licenses granted. There are now some 25 licenses. The expansion of the service has not been as rapid as it probably would have been under a Labor government, and it has been under more restrictive rules than were envisaged in the report of the Working Party on Public Broadcasting (1975). The ethnic stations were retained. Initially there appeared to be a strong desire in the new government to convert them to a commercial system. When this was frustrated by opposition from the ethnic communities, negotiations were opened for ABC control. These failed, and the outcome was the setting up of a completely new body, the Special Broadcasting Service (SBS) to run them, and to fund other ethnic broadcasters using public stations. The legislation for and operation of the new body ensured tight government control. There appeared to be a certain amount of opposition to the method of control from the ethnic communities.

In 1979, however, as a result of a semi-public inquiry into ethnic television, the government has put forward a bill to abolish the SBS and replace it with a new statutory body for both television and radio. Other changes in the bill are designed to avoid criticisms that were made of the SBS. However, when the bill reached the Federal Upper House (the Senate), it was referred to a parliamentary committee for reconsideration because four government senators defected and voted with the Opposition (a fairly rare occurrence in Australia).

The bill is now effectively dead. Part of the opposition to it, especially in the government parties, is that the concept of multiculturalism is equated with "ethnic" broadcasting, and is therefore seen as divisive.

The Labor Party adopted a policy of abolition of the SBS, preferring to see ethnic broadcasting, which it supports, set up under public broadcasting provisions.

In regulatory policy, significant changes have occurred. The ABT, in its 1977 report, recommended a large measure of self-regulation, but placed great stress on the need for public participation in renewal hearings. This concept, of public renewal hearings as opposed to closed ABCB consideration, has been aired frequently over recent years. It had been favorably commented on or recommended in various connections in several reports, including the Green Report of 1976. After accepting the ABT report, the government had legislation passed in late 1977, requiring public hearings. These are now routine practice.

Further evolution of regulatory arrangements is now stalled on two fronts. Firstly, the government brought in legislation to establish a large measure of self-regulation on programming standards for the industry, but it has not been formalized.

Much of the delay in settling the standards question probably lies in a reluctance of government to expose itself to the quite vocal criticism by various community standards organizations that will certainly occur. It also results from a heightened public consciousness over sensitive areas such as children's television. Any appearance of lessening standards could cause unfavorable reaction from vocal sectors of the community.

Secondly, the renewal hearings procedure has proved inadequate. The ABT attempted to establish informal procedures by which the public could give evidence. However, the strong existing legal tradition—primarily designed for adversary situations and property interest cases and not for "public interest" procedures—together with the greater resources of the licensees have foiled the ABT's efforts. It has now been shown that insufficient thought has been given to the 1977 Broadcasting and Television Act, both in intention and procedure. It is also clear that the type of appointments usually made to the ABT, and its predecessor, the ABCB, has been inappropriate in the past for its new function. An administrative law review body has now looked at ABT procedures and reported, but no action has been taken.

Resolution of this situation will be difficult. On the one hand, the government and the ABT have made a heavy investment in the rhetoric of public participation; but on the other, they are up against the power of the commercial lobby. The development of judicial character has reached an impasse in the public renewal hearings area, and further resolution in that area is needed.

There is also something of a trend to separate planning, administrative, and regulatory functions on the one hand, and quasi-judicial functions on the other. The confusion of the two roles was one of the faults of the ABCB. Regulation requires continuous contact with the stations, and because of the almost day-to-day involvement of the regulatory body, it gradually acquires a vested interest in, and responsibility for, the performance of the licensee. It is then virtually impossible for that body to be an impartial judge of performance at license renewal time. After the Green Report (1976), planning was removed to the department but, unfortunately, regulatory control remains with the ABT. The Green Report appears to have accepted the point about separating functions, and recommended a broadcasting council, separate from the ABT, to "oversee" (whatever that precisely meant) the administration of standards. Belatedly, the government has now set up a Broadcasting Council, but it is not clear what role it will have in the administration of standards.

Under the 1977 Broadcasting and Television Act, the new ABT was given power to allot licenses itself, rather than make recommendations to the minister. Through the period 1978–80, the ABT began to develop the "public interest" power given to it in the Act, on a case by case development basis.

There were two important cases. In the first, the ABT refused to sanction the sale of a radio station on the grounds that the buyer would have been given an undue concentration of media ownership in one city (ABT 1979). An appeal to the High Court challenged the ABT's power in this matter, but the court's ruling left the decision intact (High Court 1979). This was an extremely important milestone in the development of public interest law in broadcasting. In the second, the ABT blocked the transfer of a television station on the grounds that this would have resulted in a concentration of power within a loose network that was contrary to the public interest. On appeal, the Australian Administrative Appeals Tribunal overturned the decision (1981).

In 1981, however, an effective stop was put to the development of the ABT's power to flesh out the public interest provisions. Under a new minister, Parliament passed extensive amendments to the Broadcasting and Television Act that have the effect of removing the ABT's discretionary power. The amended Act states specific powers that would probably not have enabled the ABT to make those earlier decisions. The amendments also facilitate takeovers and liberalized foreign ownership.

The motivation for these changes is not altogether clear, but they are alleged to be in the interest of certain companies that successfully influenced the government. They have been greatly deplored by those who were delighted with the development of public interest law.

The policy of local ownership and control is also under attack arising from the planning of the domestic satellite. This is probably the strongest attack ever made on the policy.

Much time, effort, and rhetoric has been invested in the policy of local ownership and control. The intention to limit ownership, first expressed in the fairly simple regulation made in 1935, and incorporated in the Broadcasting Act in 1942, and later enacted for television, has been maintained. But over the years, there has been a succession of successful attempts to find loopholes in the Act, mainly relating to "control," followed by post facto amendment. (In 1956 the ownership and control sections of the Act comprised 14 lines, by 1960 they occupied 300 lines, and by 1965, 600 lines.)

Prevention of programming control, by provisions formally forbidding licensees to be in a position to determine the program of another, has also been maintained. However, if one accepts the dictum that programming is what matters and all else is housekeeping, the attempts to maintain independence, presumably based on the assumption that this would follow through in some meaningful way to programming, have failed. Commercial considerations have dictated what has actually happened in programming. In radio, entertainment programs are certainly localized and independently originated by each station, because radio is now that sort of service in the post-television era. But national and overseas news is largely centrally originated, and local news is often shared with the press. There are some significant network news and current affairs operations. In television, there are three networks, each with a station in each of the four eastern state capitals, Brisbane, Sydney, Melbourne, and Adelaide. They operate as networks on a voluntary basis, despite varied ownership and formal control arrangements. And regional television, as of 1978, averaged only 7 percent of locally originated material. The rest is either produced by one of the major networks or imported.

248

Nevertheless, the issue of actually changing any of the rules is very sensitive, and has been focused by the domestic satellite proposal and attendant networking proposals. Unfortunately, the task force appointed by the government did not deal with the economic and social issues involved. Furthermore, the restrictions have been holy writ for so long, and have been so widely and uncritically accepted by interest groups on the simple ground of being antimonopoly, that any analytical debate about networking has been slow to build up.

The satellite will make provision for a limited direct broadcasting service to remote communities by the ABC. However, because the design is not yet finalized, there is a strong possibility that a similar commercial service will be allowed. Furthermore, the city networks are still interested in more general networking. All of this poses a threat to regional broadcasting interests, which have countered by asking for a second license each in their respective regions as a balance to the networking. This issue is unresolved.

In 1979, a similar issue had been faced in the extension of FM radio broadcasting to the commercial sector.

Australia had begun an FM radio service experimentally in 1948. But the 1948 Broadcasting Act of the then Labor government restricted its use to the ABC. The commercial stations were faced with a difficulty over FM. They did not wish to see an increase in the number of radio stations of any kind, but if FM were to come, they wished to participate—by joint ownership with AM stations. No development in FM took place on the ABC, and the restriction stayed until repealed by the 1956 Broadcasting and Television Act. On several occasions between then and 1970, attempts were made to set planning for FM in motion, but each time the commercial lobby successfully countered them. The experimental service ceased in 1961. By 1970, however, it was obvious that Australia was so far behind other countries with which it compares itself that FM radio could be stalled no longer.

Eventually, the board recommended an FM service, but in the UHF part of the spectrum, out of step with every other country. After an adverse Senate committee report on this, it was shown by an independent inquiry to be better to have a VHF service. A VHF service actually began in a very limited way in 1974, but the independent inquiry also produced another important result. Under pressure from the inquiry and other sources, the board suddenly announced that a great increase in the number of AM or medium frequency channels was possible, with changed planning. By 1976 only the ABC and public radio had gained any FM stations. (In a repeat of the 1948 decision, the Labor Party had adopted a policy of no FM for the commercial sector in 1975.)

The commercial sector faced the same dilemma as in earlier years. Under the rules, no metropolitan station could get a license for FM in its own city (although it could in another city if not otherwise in conflict with the rules). The only ways around this were to relax the rules, or to class

FM as a new service as was done with television, where there are no cross-rules with radio. There was considerable pressure from commercial operators to change the rules, but, nevertheless, the minister for postal and telecommunications eventually announced that commercial FM would go ahead under the existing rules. It was a victory for the time-honored policy of restrictions in ownership. License allocation has now taken place under the existing rules.

In early 1982, the ABT, at government request, was conducting a public inquiry into cable television. Existing licenses are opposed to cable, but other powerful business groups are working for its introduction. It is impossible to predict the outcome, particularly as the issue is linked with wider problems in nonbroadcasting telecommunications.

Conclusion

Future trends in all communication policy areas are difficult to predict. They depend on the interplay of the elements described against the overall political climate.

In the telecommunications area, progress toward automation and greater capacity is likely to continue unabated despite some qualms about the social effects of rapid technological change. The present government has begun an inquiry into the effects of technological change, and the Labor Party has addressed itself to the issue in recent policies. It is likely that the policy results will be slow and erratic in coming, but when they do, they are more likely to be in the context of overall industry policy than unique to communications. In the press, publishing, and cinema areas, economic factors will be the most important determinants, with the government assistance structures described for the last being likely to persist. There may be a greater input of television industry money into filmmaking. In the absence of pressure, it is not likely that government policies will change much, whichever party is in power.

In broadcasting, the issues of public participation and renewal procedures, program regulation, ethnic and multicultural broadcasting, and basic structure are all very active. An official inquiry into the ABC, with very wide-ranging terms of reference, has been concluded (Committee of Review of the Australian Broadcasting Commission 1981). Developments are proceeding on a number of fronts, with very little cross-referencing between them, in the usual ad hoc fashion.

Each political party has come a long way since 1970. The conservative parties have been forced to come to grips with the issues. Within the government, there are some very conservative elements, some quite subservient to the most powerful lobbies, that is, the industry, and some who accept the inevitability of change and evolution, and promote it, provided it is under what they see as responsible control. The Labor Party has an official policy that is more reformist than the Conservative's, but it is still very much inclined to fall back on old articles of faith, without much analysis. Much of the running is being made by pressure groups. Press interest and coverage of the issues is still considerable.

Further sophistication of the debate can be expected, and there will be changes in the relative strengths and importance of the participants, but there will be no change in the methods of policy formation.

References

Australia Council
1978   *The Reading and Buying of Books in Australia*. North Sydney.

Australian Administrative Appeals Tribunal
1981   Re Control Investments Pty Ltd and Australian Broadcasting Tribunal, No. 80/109, December 1981.

Australian Broadcasting Control Board
1958   *Report and Recommendations to the Postmaster-General on Applications for Commercial Television Licences for the Brisbane and Adelaide Areas*.

Australian Broadcasting Tribunal
1977   *Self Regulation for Broadcasters*. Canberra: Australian Government Publishing Service.

1979   *Annual Report, 1978-79*. Canberra: Australian Government Publishing Service.

Australian Labor Party
1979   *Australian Labor Party Platform, Constitutional and Rules, as Approved by the 33rd National Conference, Adelaide, 1979*. Canberra.

Australian Telecommunications Commission
1975   *Telecom 2000: An Exploration of the Long-term Development of Telecommunications in Australia*. Melbourne.

Commission of Inquiry into the Australian Post Office
1975   *Report*. Canberra: Government Printer.

Committee of Review of the Australian Broadcasting Commission.
1981   *The ABC in Review: National Broadcasting in the 1980's.* Canberra: Australian Government Publishing Service.

Commonwealth Government Task Force
1978   *National Communications Satellite System.* Canberra: Australian Government Publishing Service.

Department of Postal and Telecommunications
1976   *Report on Australian Broadcasting: A Report on the Structure of the Australian Broadcasting System and Associated Matters* (Green Report). September. Canberra: Australian Government Publishing Service.

Green, F.J.
1976   *Australian Broadcasting: A Report on the Structure of the Australian Broadcasting System and Associated Matters.* Australian Government Publishing Service.

High Court
1979   Re Australian Broadcasting Tribunal and Others; ex parte 2HD Pty Ltd, 27 ALR 321 (1979).

House of Representatives
1956   *Hansard.* 19 April, p. 1538.

Parkhill, Archdale
1935   *Hansard.* House of Representatives, 3 December, p. 2368.

Parliamentary Joint Committee on Wireless Broadcasting
1942   *Report.* Canberra.

Royal Commission on Taxation
1934   *Report.* Canberra: Government Printer.

Royal Commission on Television
1954   *Report.* Canberra: Government Printer.

Royal Commission on Wireless
1927   *Report.* Canberra: Government Printer.

Senate Select Committee on the Encouragement of Australian Production for Television
1963   *Report.* Canberra.

UNESCO
1978   "General Declaration on Mass Media." *United Nations Monthly Chronicle* 15 (11).

Working Party on Public Broadcasting
1975   *Report to the Minister for the Media.* Canberra: Australian Government Publishing Service.

8

Communication Policy in New Zealand: Overseas Influence and Local Neglect

Donald E. Stewart
Logan Moss

Stewart and Moss describe a communication policy that has been influenced and shaped primarily by the demands of a capitalist economy. New Zealand is a small country that developed pursuing egalitarian ideals and forward-thinking social policies. However, the rhetoric describing how things ought to be is often in conflict with the way things are. Media models and their associated technologies have been imported into New Zealand from both the United Kingdom and the United States. This has often meant that not just structures, hardware, and software, but also people and ideas, have been imported. Several inquiries have drawn on experts from the United Kingdom. Thus the initial concerns with the unique characteristics of New Zealand and the social dimension of communication policy have been subordinated to the dictates of sophisticated and expensive technology.

Like Australia, New Zealand has not yet succeeded in establishing a clear direction in communication policy and has fallen into the same patterns of party political decision making and pragmatic, shortsighted solutions to problems and issues.

New Zealand is situated in the South Pacific, slightly west of the International Date Line, 1,600 kilometers east of Australia and 11,000 kilometers southwest of San Francisco. In area the country is about 269,000 square kilometers, consisting mainly of the North and South Islands, separated by the narrow Cook Strait. Large areas of the South Island and the central North Island are mountainous, with 19 peaks over 3,000 meters. While much of the country has been cleared of natural forest for farming purposes, distance, rough terrain, and a scattered population have made communication difficult. About 73 percent of the population of 3,168,000 live on the North Island and about 83 percent live in urban areas. Most of the population (86%) is European in origin, with significant minorities of those of Maori descent (12%) and the other mainly Polynesian groups (2%). Since the 1820s, the United Kingdom has provided most of the European settlers, and English is the most commonly used language (Department of Statistics 1980).

The concentration of population in the major cities, especially those of the North Island, accompanied by what many see as an unwarranted centralization of the decision-making process, has been a central issue in New Zealand politics since the late 1960s. Both major political parties have expressed a concern that this trend be halted or reversed, though policies in many areas do not always reflect this.

New Zealand's government is closely modeled on the Westminster system and parliamentary elections are held triennially. During the last fifty years these elections have been contested by two principal political parties, Labour and National, though minor parties have, from time to time, emerged. Each of the major parties pursues policies that from some perspectives might be termed socialist. However, the socialism of the National Party is strongly tempered by a private enterprise ethic, an influence that has become more marked in recent years. The Labour Party has been concerned to disavow any association with radical socialism, attempting instead to take as its model the social democratic parties of Europe.

About the end of the nineteenth century, a number of innovative and forward-thinking social policies were enacted, in pursuit of an egalitarian ideal, earning for New Zealand a label as the "social laboratory of the world" (Sinclair 1961). Underlying social policy formulation is an often unspoken and implicit doctrine rooted in the ideology and theory of a small island state founded upon principles of Christian social democracy. Doctrine in this case is considered to be a set of normative and prescriptive ideas which, inchoate and unformulated, and commonly enunciated only in the context of discussions about how things *ought* to be in the country, provides the infrastructure upon which social policy is articulated (see Smith 1980).

In terms of communication policy, the doctrinal basis of the early progressive years of social democracy is exemplified by the concern for information equality, with the telephone being introduced only a matter of months after it was invented. An attempt at increased participatory democracy was evident in the broadcasting of parliamentary debates several decades before it was done in Britain. Likewise, regionalism, with local radio, was an important feature of the New Zealand broadcasting system long before this was the case in Britain. In recent years economic and technical factors appear to have dominated policy planning, and it is difficult to discern any overall, coherent communication policy. Each of the parties has formulated a policy relating to each of the media. While some official reports have recognized that there is a social component in mass communications, this has generally been accorded only a secondary consideration.

Mass communications in New Zealand have been influenced and shaped by the demands of a capitalist economy. Media models and their associated technologies have been incorporated into the country from the major nations of the Western world. Since the assumptions upon which the development of these models were based proved amenable to the demands of New Zealand's economy, there has been little impetus to develop alternatives. Certainly local adaptations have been made, but even these changes are frequently the result of consultation with overseas "experts." Not only hardware and software have been imported, but also people and ideas—with their capacity to reproduce unreflectingly products founded upon alien social doctrines.

Our contention is that even though there has been some token acceptance of the importance of the social dimension in communication policymaking, there has been a decreasing concern with the multidimensional nature of communication. With the introduction of more advanced, sophisticated, and expensive technology, the fundamental social philosophy, commonly accepted by many New Zealanders as being unique, has been neglected.

The Press

About three-quarters of the average newspaper's income comes from advertising. While the press operates within the context of a capitalist framework and is subject to the same sorts of commercial and economic pressures as any other business in New Zealand, it has specific guidelines, conventions, and regulations which are of more significance to it than other nonmedia business organizations. Press organizations, as business organizations, strive to maintain profitability in the face of the rapidly rising costs of newsprint, machinery, and labor. These costs are closely monitored, if not controlled, by government; for example orders for general wage increases have to be paid by management to their staff. In addition, the amount of government subsidy for newsprint is a powerful weapon in the arsenal of any government, and licenses for the importation of new plant are subject to political control. These types of control are common throughout industry in New Zealand.

The press not only reflects the social and economic reality within which it operates, but also helps to shape and define that reality through objectification of ideas and arguments, facts and opinions, into the symbolic orders of language and picture. This concept is paralleled by policy decisions with regard to the press. In their role as business enterprises embedded in the capitalist framework, newspapers are subject to common laws and regulations. In their role as "shapers of reality" they are subject to stringent codes of conduct and legal restraints. Control occurs not only through general economic directives applicable to all industries, but also in specific response to their culture-creative qualities.

An understanding of the present-day structure of the press in New Zealand is possible only in the light of the peculiar historical and geographical context of the country. Communications between the early European settlements were so irregular and slow that the establishment of local newspapers became common practice. About five hundred newspapers have been founded since the first, the *NZ Gazette*, was established in 1840. The oldest survivor, the *Taranaki Herald* (established 1842) and the oldest daily, the *Otago Daily Times* (established 1861) were involved, with others, in the fierce rivalry and keen competition of the early years. Journalism in the early days has been described as "powerful, dogmatic, sometimes virulent and irresponsible" (Department of Statistics 1980:353).

Since the 1860s, however, that process of amalgamation and conglomeration—a feature of press ownership throughout most of the Western world—has occurred, beginning in 1865 when several Christchurch newspapers joined as subscribers to the first telegraphic news service. The central government set up a line from Bluff, in the south of the South Island, so that overseas news arriving by ship from Melbourne, Australia, could be flashed northward. As the telegraph lines lengthened, provincial items went on the wire and the demand for news services increased. In 1879, newspapers formally joined a cooperative service, the New Zealand Press Association (NZPA), which has played a dominant role up to the present day.

Through the last half of the nineteenth century, associated with the problems of distribution, the weeklies developed—a special service of importance to farmers, prospectors, and outback settlers. Often these made cooperative use, with the dailies, of machinery, facilities, and talent. Once better communication by road was available, the weeklies were superseded by dailies, with the NZPA providing comparable world news to the country.

The newspapers were predominantly family owned, and while concerned with profit, found it hard to escape from intimate local involvement. The newspaper had to be acceptable to the community, and readers easily enforced their standards of acceptability. Since the 1900s, the importance of capital investment in competitive plant has become increasingly clear, and attempts to start new dailies, with the exception of the Wellington *Dominion* (established 1907) have generally failed. Since 1910 there has been a gradual decline in numbers of newspapers printed, from 193 (of which 67 were dailies) in 1910, to 76 (40 dailies) in 1967, and by 1979 there were 34 dailies. Of these, 7 of the daily newspapers serve the four metropolitan areas, with a total circulation of about 700,000, and the remaining 27 serve the smaller cities and provincial towns, with a total circulation of over 250,000.

Newspaper publishing is now dominated by a few large corporations, and the process of amalgamation and concentration has been clear. In 1969, about 75 of the 100 major publications registered in New

Zealand were owned and operated by nine major firms. Three major firms dominate the ownership structure in 1982—New Zealand News Ltd.; Wilson and Horton Ltd.; and Independent Newspapers Ltd. (INL).

While the press supports the virtues of free enterprise and competition, proprietors protest stridently under the threat of external attempts to invade their strongholds and alter the cozy balance of their cartel. In 1964 the Thomson organization made highly publicized and controversial attempts to take over the *Dominion* of Wellington. This attempt by an overseas newspaper group to break the internal press monopoly was fought off by the newspaper proprietors, and their strong lobbying of the government resulted in the News Media Ownership Act (1965) restricting overseas ownership of newspapers or private radio stations to 15 percent or less. Direct foreign competition was avoided and a situation of artificial equilibrium maintained. Competition remains sluggish, both for circulation and for news. Although this legislation was rescinded, other antimonopoly provisions were made in 1975 so that similar moves could be prevented if necessary.

The NZPA in its structure and functioning represents some of the dominant values underlying the press structure of the country as a whole. It is a collective organization, set up by the newspaper proprietors to cover both overseas and domestic news. As a cooperative, nonprofit-making agency, it is financed by striking an annual budget from its members, scaled according to circulation. However, the Chairman's Report for 1980 (NZPA 1980) indicated that costs are rising and would increase by at least 16 percent that year. Membership involves an obligation for any member to file a local story promptly with the association, to be made available throughout the country.

For its overseas news, the NZPA relies mainly on Reuters and the Australian Associated Press (AAP). It has been a partner with Reuters since 1947, but also uses other sources. (See Figure 8-1.)

Control of the NZPA is in the hands of directors elected from among the newspaper proprietors, and the staff of about twenty-five is based in Wellington, with staff correspondents in London, Washington, Sydney, and Hong Kong. World news reports are compared, and a selection used for the NZPA report. However, this subediting is mainly carried out in the Sydney newsroom of the AAP. No single newspaper or group of papers could afford a comparable system, and small-town local papers are provided with a complete up-to-date news service that would otherwise be unavailable.

During 1979, a multiplex system between Sydney and Wellington was introduced, improving the capacity for bringing international news into New Zealand, and enabling the NZPA in conjunction with Reuters to launch the Reuters Monitor Service in New Zealand. All NZPA members may draw on the major news agency material for overseas news, and indeed a nationwide internal service—beyond the resources of most individual newspapers—provides news from other regions of the country.

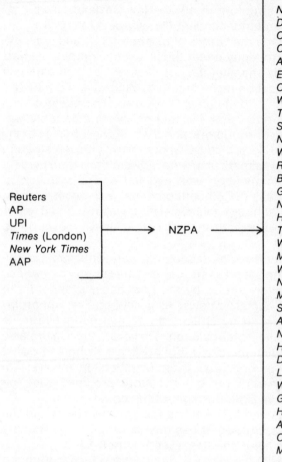

Reuters
AP
UPI
Times (London)
New York Times
AAP

→ NZPA →

New Zealand Herald
Dominion
Christchurch Press
Otago Daily Times
Auckland Star
Evening Post
Christchurch Star
Wanganui Chronicle
Timaru Herald
Southland Times
Northern Advocate
Waikato Times
Rotorua Daily Post
Bay of Plenty Times
Gisborne Herald
Napier Daily Telegraph
Hawkes Bay Herald Tribune
Taranaki Herald
Wanganui Herald
Manawatu Standard
Wairarapa Times-Age
Nelson Mail
Marlborough Express
Southland News
Argus Leader
Northland Times
Hawera Star
Dannevirke News
Levin Chronicle
Westport News
Greymouth Star
Hokitika Guardian
Ashburton Guardian
Oamaru Mail
Mataura Ensign

Figure 8-1
The New Zealand Press Association

Until recently, under NZPA terms, member newspapers were severely restricted in their freedom to gather news independently, and were not allowed to compete "unfairly" with others—there were bitter protests when the *Levin Chronicle* (circulation 3,154 in 1964) telephoned Mr. Khrushchev to question him over the Cuban crisis. However, after almost a century of association monopoly of cables, member newspapers are now allowed to obtain their own cabled reports from other parts of the world, though collecting, editing, and distributing world news remains solidly in NZPA hands.

The cooperative reliance on the monopolistic association has been blamed for the lack of variety, absence of the outstanding, uniformity, and structural similarity of an industry that produces "rivals in conformity" (Cleveland 1970c). Taking crude UNESCO figures, New Zealanders rank near the top of the scale in daily newspaper readership, with circulation per thousand inhabitants listed as Australia 394 (1975); New Zealand 365 (1972); United States 287 (1975); Canada 235 (1973) (Department of Statistics 1980:353). However, these figures take no account of the quality of the individual papers. Throughout New Zealand the high degree of uniformity, with similar views and news selections made in all newspapers, leads to a conscientious, inoffensive mediocrity. The NZPA, as a response to size and isolation as well as the need for an adequate service from limited resources, has been the subject of some praise and considerable criticism—not least because of the unintended bias involved in some four or five major gate-keeping decisions that occur before NZPA material is printed.

The problem of news selection is a real one. The diverse audience and the relatively large-scale nature of the operation produce an emphasis on quantity rather than quality, and there is information overload. Studies of the use made by 16 New Zealand dailies of a sample of NZPA wire-service copy received by all of them reveals that only 27 percent of the total number of items, which were theoretically available to all these newspapers to publish, were in fact used (Cleveland 1970c, 1971). However, a further major constraint producing the prevailing caution and inoffensiveness, are the restraints imposed by the legal system. While overt censorship or nationalization seems unlikely, the main state restraints on the New Zealand press come from the actual or threatened use of the libel and indecency laws, together with the Official Secrets Act (1951), and executive directions to public servants to withhold information from the news media.

It is in the area of legal restraints that communication policy is most clearly revealed. The major legal restraints lie in the law of defamation, law concerning contempt of court, law concerning indecent publications, the Official Secrets Act, and the law regarding ownership of news media services. Although bringing a libel action is a risky business for plaintiffs, the risks attendant upon publishing material which may be defamatory are serious and these risks cause the New Zealand media to engage in a good deal of self-censorship (Palmer 1975). There is no lack of examples of politicians willing to take the risks attendant to libel actions in order to defend their honor and reputation (e.g., *Mills* v. *The Otago Daily Times Co*, 1898; *Massey* v. *The New Zealand Times Co.*, 1900; *Peerless Bakers Ltd.* v. *Watts*, 1955; *Truth (NZ) Ltd.* v. *Holloway*, 1960; *Eyre* v. *NZPA*, 1968; *News Media Ownership* v. *Finlay*, 1970). The law of defamation has a delicate relationship with the principle of freedom of expression. In this, New Zealand follows the British tradition of the common law of libel, rather than the American tradition with its First Amendment of the Bill of Rights.

The law regarding defamation is highly complex, and protection by privilege or qualified privilege not immediately apparent. Comment and explanation, investigation and probing are inhibited because of the ease with which defamation actions may be brought, and the possible heavy damages. In a recent case, for example, the *NZ Listener* (1979*b*) claimed that Prime Minister Muldoon's actions in handling the collapse of the civil servants' investment society were motivated by malice, and were directly related to an industrial dispute in which some society members were involved. The prime minister claimed defamation, and within five days received a check for NZ$12,000 from public money in settlement, without a writ even being issued. The *Listener* subsequently expressed its deep regret for the distress and embarrassment caused him.

The extremely sensitive relationship between the press and the courts has been one of the primary causes of press material being criticized as overwhelmingly consensual, timid, and bland. Any litigation may gag the press, as a matter becomes sub judice, and newspapers criticizing legal officers may be found in contempt. One means of preventing further press publicity is by the issue of a writ for defamation —with no intention of proceeding. To discuss in detail matters that are in any way undergoing the judicial process is to risk punishment for contempt of court. Thus the law of defamation serves to dampen down public debate.

With regard to the law of contempt, the very wide powers of the courts to maintain their autonomy and to protect the rights of citizens to a fair trial, and to protect themselves and court officers from undue pressure or influence, has been held to intimidate the news media in New Zealand. On the one hand, trial by newspaper or pretrial publicity has to be guarded against, and thus the press cannot speculate on legal proceedings once they have started; on the other hand, there is the practical question of whether or not publication is in the public as opposed to the private interest.

During recent years the question of access to government information has arisen in a number of cases, such as the Import Licensing System administered by the Department of Trade and Industry, and a wide range of environmental issues such as the decisions regarding the building of a hydroelectric facility on the Clutha River in Otago. This issue has been the subject of a report from a group of lawyers (Randerson et al. 1978).

During 1980–81, the general and supplementary parts of the report of the Committee on Official Information, "Towards Open Government" (the "Danks Report"), were released, and a draft Official Information Bill came before a select committee in Parliament. This bill is predictably conservative, and while it may increase public access to innocuous official information, information relating to politically and economically contentious issues will still be hard to come by.

The Official Secrets Act (1951), under review in 1980-81, makes it an offense for any public servant to disclose any document or information that has been obtained through his or her position. The breadth of this section is immense—every kind of public servant and all kinds of information may, if wanted, be included. The government has an absolute right to withhold any information unless at its own discretion it decides to disclose it.

While there is no Freedom of the Press Act as in Sweden (1969), which provides for considerable freedom of access to official documents, and there is no equivalent of the U.S. Freedom of Information Act (1966) with its later related measures, or the proposed Australian Federal Freedom of Information Bill (1981), there are growing demands, even from the government benches, for a more open approach to government. It has been suggested that a commission of inquiry or a nonpartisan parliamentary task force could be established to examine the question of a Freedom of Information Act in New Zealand. Meanwhile, in dealing with contentious matters in many areas, be it defamation, obscenity, contempt, or the Official Secrets Act, the golden rule of journalism has been "when in doubt leave it out."

Newspaper owners have traditionally been characterized as pro the conservative National Party and this has long been a Labour Party criticism. It was the Labour Party's belief that it was being given unfavorable publicity by a hostile and biased press that stimulated the introduction of broadcasting of parliamentary debates in 1935.

In 1946 the Labour Party established in Wellington a second morning newspaper, which lasted only five years. The only Labour-supporting daily in the country, the small-scale *Grey River Argus* ceased publishing in 1966. *The Week*, an analytical, investigative weekly of considerable merit, lasted for only a matter of months in 1976; priced at 40 cents per copy and lacking advertising, it simply failed to survive.

The business connection is most clearly seen in the pattern of ownership and direction exhibited by the various press organizations. To take the *Otago Daily Times* as an example, in 1979 the chairman was also a director of a woolen mill and a construction company. His fellow directors between them managed a local radio and television company, a rope and twine company, chaired a city motor company, directed other provincial newspapers, sat on the Otago Development Council, and generally played active roles in such bodies as the local Chamber of Commerce. As a further illustration, in 1981 the *Otago Daily Times* was the subject of a fierce takeover battle between a produce marketing company and an airline/tour operator. The former was ultimately successful, and changed the company's name to Otago Press and Produce Ltd.

Newspaper editors have strenuously maintained that "they receive no directives or suggestions from either managements or boards on editorial or news content" (Nevill 1975:13), but this may well be unnecessary since the self-censorship and informal norms covering collection and distribution of news and comment make management directives superfluous. Editorial appointments are made by boards and management and the tendency is to appoint persons in their own image (*New Zealand Tablet* 1978).

Anonymity, both in letters to editors and in staff reports, is common. Very few journalists command their own by-lines, and it may be the exigencies of a small, homogeneous society that cause letter-writers to use pen names.

In many ways, however, the potentialities of the local newspaper as a means of participatory democratic activities are realized. The papers remain firmly local in orientation and have a clear role in airing local issues and publishing readers' letters. While journalists as a group in no way reflect the population structure, the cities and towns in which they operate are generally small enough to provide face-to-face daily contact with a fair cross section of their audience. In smaller communities, local newspapers, though affectionately characterized as "the one-minute silence," do allow for a multidirectional flow of messages and for considerable public participation. However, they are scarcely likely to engage in investigative reporting or to disturb the status quo.

As in many nations where the press is free to print what it likes and freedom of expression and freedom of the press are basic rights, these freedoms are curtailed by legal constraints, a structure of formal guidelines and policies, and informal norms and values accepted among press personnel and management. These have become so widely held and institutionalized that the New Zealand press has been described as timid, consensual, and dull, and that "the journalist's relationship to the state resembles that of a well-behaved draft horse rather than a vigilant watchdog" (Cleveland 1969:39). Unlike the Swedish experience, no radical attempt to foster an alternative press outside the established commercial structures has achieved long-term success. Despite the many noncommercial public-service roles claimed by the press, the marketplace is the final arbiter of existence.

Publishing

Publishing provides an unusual mixture of commercial free enterprise and close moral supervision. In business it has remained relatively independent of policy strictures, whereas in content it has been strictly regulated. This normative element in communication policy indicates a long-standing puritanical concern to shield members of society from perceived moral dangers, and is perhaps a reflection of the moralistic element in New Zealand's social doctrine.

264

When compared with larger markets overseas, the whole of the New Zealand publishing scene can be described as a regional market. However, with a historical preference for centralization, even such a small-scale society as New Zealand has been able to support comparatively strong bookselling and publishing industries. Unlike many industries in the country, a recent in-house magazine, *Forum* (Whitcoulls' Group), claimed that it was hard to believe that book printing in New Zealand not only received no assistance or encouragement from the government—it was actively discouraged and hindered. Unlike the Australian bounty scheme or publishing assistance in Canada and the United States for example, there is no assistance for locally produced books in New Zealand. Debate as to the merits of government assistance is fierce.

On the other hand, government policy in the publishing world is felt more keenly in the area of "nudery-prudery," and pressure groups concerned with community standards. It is a deeply held political belief, ostensibly supported by election and by-election results, that a hard line on moral questions, such as abortion, sex education, and contraception issues, secured for the National government some very important block voting. The book industry has been involved in such politicized questions through a continuing battle over definitions and age qualifications.

The industry as a whole is served by a number of associations and organizations, such as the Booksellers' Association, the Book Publishers' Association, the Book Trade Organisation, and the Book Council. The Booksellers' Association, formed to protect a fledgling industry in 1921, is a strong and confident association, with about three hundred full members (about one bookshop to every 10,000 people). Of these, about two-thirds employ two or fewer staff, with most selling other goods besides books. The major company, Whitcoulls (which also prints and publishes—a complete vertical coverage), accounts for about one-third of the country's retail trade. The subscription for the association also finances the Book Trade Organization (BTO), a body that represents booksellers and British and New Zealand publishers. The BTO, founded in 1968, has nine members, three each from the Booksellers' Association, the New Zealand Book Publishers' Association, and the British Publishers' Representatives' Association in New Zealand. It has sponsored some research, and has established the New Zealand Book Council with a small annual grant.

While New Zealanders appear to be avid readers (*New Zealand Census of Libraries* 1974:3), the manufacturing sector of the industry is in considerable turmoil. A Commission of Inquiry (1976-78) into the book production industry provided no solutions and merely recommended increased cooperation between publishers and printers (Industries Development Commission 1978). Arguments have been voiced against government subsidy, claiming that it might inhibit literature discussing adversarial politics and lay the industry open to pressure from powerful minorities. A protective tariff on imported books is not feasible, not only because the government has about 40 percent of the book market through its public and departmental libraries, but also because of the various international conventions guarding freedom of information, to which New Zealand is signatory.

As far as book manufacturing and selling are concerned, therefore, the main feature of the present situation is the lack of policy. The industry appears to be relatively uninfluenced by the governmental communication policy. However, political opportunism in response to moral panics related to indecency is more clearly visible. The Indecent Publications Tribunal was set up in 1964 as a final arbiter of what is indecent or pornographic in books and magazines. Control of pornography in New Zealand is relatively simple since almost all of it is imported. Publishers, the Customs Department, or moral crusaders can submit a publication to the tribunal for a ruling on whether or not it is indecent.

To many, it has appeared that the tribunal has acted as a buffer of reason between the paternalism of those who demand conformity to their concepts of family, and the importers of exploitative pornography. However, members of the tribunal are selected by political appointment, and, although so far they have seemed relatively immune to political pressure, in the scramble for votes with both parties flirting with the reactionary element of the law and order groups, increasingly repressive legislation has restricted the scope of the tribunal. Recent decisions indicate that the tribunal has extended its concept of "indecent" to include publications that, in the view of the Tribunal, encourage or assist in breaking the law. To date such decisions have been largely tied to drug-related publications.

The Abortion, Contraception and Sterilisation Act (1977) overrides the Indecent Publications Act of 1963, so that books which outline contraceptive methods cannot be exhibited before anyone who might be 16 or under. In this, the regressive example of Australia is followed, in the introduction of "the back room." It also has a further effect on the employment of young bookshop staff, who might catch a glimpse of forbidden back-room material in the unpacking and warehousing stages. A recent article in *Printers News* (1979:5) termed New Zealand publishing "another endangered species." Industry leaders, together with unions, expressed their disquiet in the face of government inaction. The lack of financial assistance representing a policy of nonintervention is viewed by many publishers as arrant folly. On the other hand, the industry is equally disquieted by the triennial rectitude of governments courting votes from the moral guardians of the nation.

Film and Cinema

In New Zealand, no less than in the United States or Europe, filmmaking is a business, and the primary orientation is toward profits.

266

Businesses rely on investors to provide the necessary funds to meet the cost of production, and in return investors expect to share in the profits. No matter what form that share takes, be it interest or dividends, investors are unlikely to provide funds unless they can foresee their eventual return being greater than their initial investment. They are even more reluctant if there is even a possibility that their initial investment will not be returned.

The New Zealand film industry faces just this situation—many people wishing to make films, but very few willing or able to finance them. The result has been the virtual absence of film production other than as an adjunct to other business enterprises, in the form of commercials or public relations material. To date only about sixty feature films have been made in New Zealand. The activities of the handful of companies working in this area are supplemented by the National Film Unit, a division of the government Tourist and Publicity Department, which is engaged primarily in the production of promotional, documentary, and information films covering all aspects of New Zealand life.

Prior to 1940, New Zealand showed all the signs of developing a thriving feature-film industry, and about twenty feature films and a great many short films were created in this period. But with the advent of sound and the resultant rise in costs, the number of feature films dropped dramatically. The mid-1960s saw a slight revival, though the most ambitious project, *Runaway* (1964) was a financial disaster and its successor *Don't Let It Get You* (1966) fared no better. Eleven years elapsed before the release of the next locally produced feature film.

Television, once established, provided some opportunity for New Zealand filmmakers, particularly in the period 1971–74, with the NZBC providing NZ$350,000 in commissions to independent filmmakers in 1974. However, with the advent of the independent corporations, the commissions ceased—both channels concentrated on producing their own material.

Throughout its history the major obstacle to the industry has been the lack of money. Despite this, the mid-1970s saw a comparative revival in film production, with several New Zealand-made feature films released, and several more in production, and since released. As David Gascoigne (ex-president of the New Zealand Federation of Film Societies) has commented, to finance such films demanded a degree of commitment "bordering on the fanatical." For example, one recent production, *Sleeping Dogs* (Aardvark Films 1977), initially budgeted for NZ$300,000, finally cost nearer NZ$450,000, of which the producer and crew members contributed nearly NZ$100,000, while NZ$150,000 was invested by a merchant bank, and Television One secured television rights and a portion of the profits for NZ$50,000. The bank saw its investment, in part at least, as a public relations exercise, clearly an unstable basis for an ongoing industry. The possibility of making a profit is very unlikely. A local filmmaker could expect to receive from box office sales as cash in hand between a quarter and—at most—half of the receipts. Since the average box office return for an overseas film is between NZ$35,000 and NZ$40,000, to recover costs, this local film would need to become the second biggest grossing film ever, slightly behind *The Sound of Music* (NZ$1,000,000) and significantly ahead of *Jaws* (NZ$750,000), indeed a remote prospect (1977 figures).

It is only in the last few years, indeed, since the revival of New Zealand filmmaking with three feature films on the screen in 1977, that there has been interest expressed at the policy level. In November 1977, the Interim Film Commission was set up, and in October the following year the New Zealand Film Commission—a statutory body—was established. These bodies were to assist in the production of New Zealand films, and were modestly financed with NZ$100,000 for the interim commission, and NZ$500,000 for the statutory commission. Up to July 1981, ten feature films had received commission support. The commission has created momentum in film production, which has encouraged talent and employment in the industry, and through its marketing activities overseas, has considerably boosted sales of New Zealand films.

Such policy decisions, do not, however, indicate a fundamental reappraisal by policymakers of the role of film in New Zealand society. Despite the growing realization of the problems facing filmmakers, the policy still seeks solutions in terms of those imposed by the business framework. The commission's NZ$500,000 budget is not to be used to finance filmmaking directly, but to aid potentially profitable ventures. The framework appears to be a business orientation toward film, with the commission acting as a broker investigating the various possible cash sources. It encourages, assists, and facilitates, including encouraging private investors to invest—but it does not perceive film in terms of its communications potential. It is possible due to the commercial success of several films throughout 1981 that there will be much more assistance forthcoming for New Zealand filmmakers (Sheat 1981:3).

If filmmaking has been considered primarily a competitive business enterprise, and film as a medium of communication has received only secondary consideration, this order of priority is reversed in policy relating to the exhibition of films. The nature of the medium makes the position problematic within the framework of the kind of communications system envisaged in the UNESCO Medium-Term Plan (Najar 1977). Film is essentially a medium of dissemination, and its incorporation within the framework of a multidirectional communication process can be achieved only if policymakers accept that providing for greater access to the medium must be their primary concern. Filmmaking as a business enterprise means that access to this medium other than as recipients is effectively denied to all but the few with the necessary financial capital.

New Zealand cinema is totally dependent on imported films, the vast majority of which are produced in the West, with about 50 percent coming from just two countries, the United States and Britain. Table 8-1

Table 8-1
Films Screened in New Zealand,
by Country of Origin, 1976–78

| | Films Screened | | |
| | On Television* | Feature Films‡ | |
Country of Origin	No.	No.	%
United States	770	114	37
United Kingdom	127	34	13
Italy	11	7	2
France	2	15	5
West Germany	1	15	5
Co-production‡	—	29	9
Australia	—	12	4
Greece	—	12	4
India	—	10	3
Other§	4	63	20
Total	**915**	**311**	**102‖**

Notes: *Figures are for the period 22 May 1976 to 25 May 1978.
  †Feature film has been defined as any film of over 60 minutes'
  duration. Data are for films certificated by the censor between
  1 April and 30 September 1977.
  ‡Involving only United States, United Kingdom, West Germany,
  France, or Italy.
  §Includes 13 co-productions (4%) involving at least one of United
  States, United Kingdom, West Germany, France, or Italy.
  ‖Discrepancy because of rounding.

shows the country of origin of films screened on television and feature
films certificated by the censor for selected periods in 1976 to 1978. The
cinema in New Zealand may be seen as a reflection of assumptions about
films made outside the country and imposed as a consequence of the
virtual absence—until recently—of domestic film production. In a basically capitalist economy like New Zealand's, such assumptions found
ready acceptance, with the result that the showing of films is regarded as
primarily a commercial enterprise. However, while commercial considerations have been important, they have not been alone in shaping the
cinema. The potential of film as a medium of communication has not
been completely ignored by policymakers, although they have tended to
dwell on the negative aspects.

Policy expresses a concern to restrict films that may prove "injurious
to the public good." New Zealand has had film censorship since 1916,
when the Cinematograph Film Censorship Act requiring all films to be
submitted to a government-appointed censor for approval was passed.

From 1916 until the 1976 Cinematograph Films Act, the censor's terms of reference remained unaltered. No film could depict any matter that was "against public order or decency" or "undesirable in the public interest." Many films were banned or cuts made because of the portrayal of explicit sexual practices, but more recently the censor's attention has turned to the depiction of violence. Language, too, seems to have been the bane of film censors. The award-winning film *One Flew over the Cuckoo's Nest* suffered between forty and fifty cuts because of the language used, while *Last Tango in Paris* so shocked the censor that it was banned until 1978. Twenty-three percent of the films exhibited in 1979 suffered cuts. In the late 1960s the censor passed the film *Ulysses* uncut, but restricted it to sexually segregated audiences. Besides banning or cutting films the censor's primary function is to classify those films that are approved. Films are approved for "General Exhibition" or "Restricted," usually to those above a particular age, though the 1976 legislation allows films to be restricted to particular audiences, based on considerations other than age, such as particular ethnic interests.

During the early 1970s censorship came under increasing attack, both from those who wished to see censorship abolished completely, and those who wished to see a more moderate approach. The censor was included among the critics (*NZ Listener* 1977:14). However, the existence of a vocal, well-organized procensorship lobby, the Society for the Promotion of Community Standards, seems to have made politicians reluctant to advocate any drastic change. The political significance of the moral lobby has already been noted in our discussion of publishing.

Many significant films, particularly those from non-English-speaking countries, are never screened in New Zealand cinemas. To fill this gap, film societies, at present numbering 45, have been formed, but their activities have in the past been severely hampered by censorship. Being nonprofit-making organizations, they cannot afford the cost incurred in bringing films to New Zealand, only to have them rejected by the censor. As a result, such film societies are active in campaigning against censorship. However, the public, long since accustomed to accepting what the commercial cinema offers and consequently unaware of the alternatives, have acquiesced and shown remarkably little interest in the issue. The assumption that a fundamental agreement on ethical concerns may be found, and that a middle view will prosper over extremism is one that is rarely fractured.

The major cinema chains, Amalgamated and Kerridge-Odeon, are subsidiaries of multinational film corporations. Amalgamated is wholly owned by Twentieth Century-Fox, while Britain's Rank organization, itself associated with Universal of Hollywood, has a 50 percent (and recently increased) stake in Kerridge. Both chains are primarily interested in the highly standardized products of the multinational film corporations. The Cinematograph Films Amendment Act (1980) was intended to reduce the power of these large chains and to give small independent operators an increased share of box-office revenue. However, it is possible that the Act may have the opposite effect—with more free enterprise meaning no enterprise at all. Removing licensing controls on cinemas is unlikely to affect the well-entrenched chains.

The recent increase in local film production will undoubtedly have some cultural benefit. While acknowledging the necessity of guarding against xenophobia, our films may at last allow the depiction of situations, people, and places that are uniquely our own. However, it is not enough simply to follow the suggestion of the minister of the arts and "create and define our own heroes" (*NZ Listener* 1977:14). For even the place of heroes may not be immutable, and their cultural origin, if not their ideological implications, should at least be recognized. Ultimately, it is to be hoped, we may see the development of a means of communication which, in both structure and content, evinces a reality that is truly New Zealand's. If this possibility is to be realized, the strictures of the moralist pressure groups and the restrictions imposed by purely economic considerations must be overcome.

Broadcasting

There have been four major broadcasting Acts (see Figure 8-2). Prior to the 1937 Broadcasting Act the government had contractual arrangements with the Radio Broadcasting Company (1925–31) and later a public Broadcasting Board (1931–36). From 1937 to the Broadcasting Corporation Act of 1961, broadcasting came under the aegis of the New Zealand Broadcasting Service. In 1962, associated with the introduction of television, control was placed in the hands of a public body, the New Zealand Broadcasting Corporation (1962–75). The 1973 Broadcasting Act set up three separate and independent public corporations designed to be competitive and yet complementary. The 1976 Broadcasting Act abolished these corporations and transferred control to one central corporation. In February 1980 further reorganization of the television services occurred, with the stated intention that wasteful duplication should be avoided, and Television New Zealand is now a unified two-channel operation.

Radio

The 1903 Wireless Telegraphy Act required the licensing of "stations for the purpose of receiving and transmitting telegraph messages . . . by what is commonly known as 'wireless telegraphy'." However it was not until 1922 that the first regular broadcasting station was established in Wellington. Since 1931, broadcasting has been under public control, though until 1937 and again in the 1960s, a handful of privately owned stations operated in the main cities and several provincial centers. It was in the period of early development that the framework within which all

271

Year	Governments	Acts	Broadcasting Organizations	Major Reports and Events
1980	National	Broadcasting Act	Broadcasting Corporation of New Zealand	
1975	Labour		Broadcasting Council of New Zealand	June 1975, Second Television Channel
				July 1973, "Broadcasting Future for N.Z."
1970	National		New Zealand Broadcasting Corporation	July 1971, Broadcasting Authority Report on Second Television Channel
				1968, Broadcasting Authority Established
1965				
1960	Labour	Broadcasting Corporation Act		June 1960, Television Commences
1955	National		New Zealand Broadcasting Service	
1950				

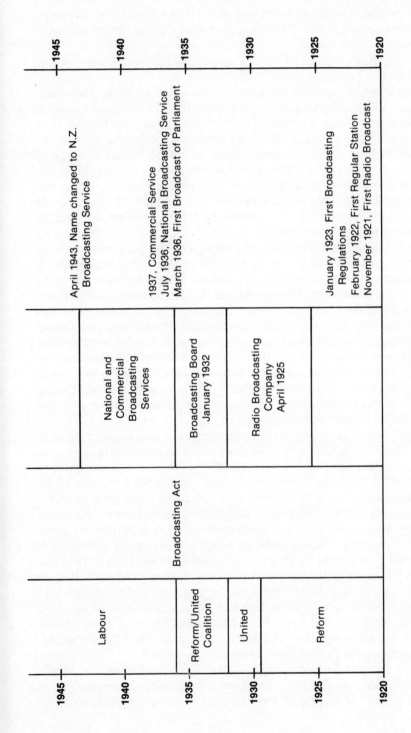

Figure 8-2

The Political and Organizational Structure of Broadcasting

future policy would be formulated was established. Radio was developing as an instrument of distribution, a means of disseminating information to a mass audience.

By taking this concept of radio's role as given, policymakers have been concerned primarily with organizational and audience problems rather than with the communications system itself. Just why radio has been viewed as a household utility may be explained by Boyd-Barrett's (1977) suggestion that the shape of each medium has been the result of certain commercial choices made in the light of perceived market conditions. In New Zealand's case many of these choices have been made in other countries and imported along with the technology, for which New Zealand remains dependent on overseas nations. Given the concept of radio providing a one-way flow of information, the question of who will disseminate what information becomes problematic and of central concern to policymakers.

The 1903 Wireless Telegraphy Act had given the government some degree of control over the activities of radio broadcasters. However, as the full impact of the medium was appreciated, the government moved to establish limits over what was broadcast. Early regulations, issued in 1923, prohibited "the dissemination of propaganda of a controversial nature." However it was permissible to broadcast "matter of an educative or entertaining character such as news, lectures, useful information, religious services, music or elocutionary entertainment and such other items of general interest as may be approved by the Minister from time to time" (Regulation for Broadcasting 1923). The regulations established a principle that the broadcaster was answerable to government and this remained so for more than fifty years.

In 1925, the regulations were extended to forbid broadcasts of a seditious, obscene, libellous or offensive nature. Broadcasters were also required to transmit any communication the government, or any department, desired to send out. These regulations were applied zealously and several instances of both ministerial and self-censorship were evident.

In cultural terms the nature of broadcasting content was quite clear. It was to be useful and self-improving material from a narrow range of culture and ideology. For example, in 1932 the Wellington station 2YA withheld the news of riots by groups of unemployed workers. In 1934 the script of a talk to be given by the Indian philosopher Krishnamurti was rejected as, according to the minister, it was "too controversial and perhaps objectionable from some points of view" (Downes and Harcourt 1976:23). In 1935, on the eve of a general election, the government authorized the jamming of an Auckland station which it feared would strongly endorse the then oppositional Labour party.

In 1925 the government entered into a contract with the Radio Broadcasting Company of New Zealand to provide radio service in the four urban centers of Auckland, Wellington, Christchurch, and Dunedin.

This service was still quite limited, since by the end of the 1920s only one home in seven had a radio receiver. The activities of the company were to be financed from the radio license fee. During this period, the question of advertising assumed central importance. It had been allowed subject to the permission of the minister concerned, but in effect this meant a complete ban, since advertising was considered a newspaper preserve. It was only with the nationalization of radio in 1937 that advertising commenced.

The example of broadcasting in Britain was emulated in 1932, with the activities of the company being taken over by the Broadcasting Board. The latter was charged with the responsibility for extending and improving the broadcasting service, which at the time of its inception comprised 18 stations and 71,500 license holders. The terrain of New Zealand provides major obstacles to the provision of extensive, efficient broadcasting services, and with this difficulty the board faced several tasks. Upgrading of existing equipment was a major priority, as was establishing alternate program stations in the four main centers. In order to provide service to more remote areas, some financial assistance was offered to provincial "B" stations (those private stations that survived from before the time of the broadcasting company). However, the effective ban on advertising remained in force.

The biggest controversy during the period 1923–35 was over the right to advertise and ultimately the problem of finance. The issue is an early example of a continuing feature of New Zealand's communication policy: typically, issues relating to communication policy become party oriented, and decisions are made on the basis of short-term political gain. Thus, immediately prior to the 1935 general election the leader of the theoretically leftist Labour Opposition, M.J. Savage, arguing that "economic interests are stifling broadcasting" strongly advocated the right of the B stations to advertise. (Here we see another paradox, frequently mirrored in later years, of a Labour leader arguing for an increase in competitive capitalism.)

The Labour Party had traditionally perceived the press as hostile and intent on frustrating its objectives. The Broadcasting Board, composed as it was of business interests, seemed little different. It was also perceived as a threat by the members of the new Labour government, who saw difficulties ahead if they were unable to explain to the public their new, and in some cases radical, policies unhindered. Savage explained it well:

> The government has a duty to the people not to keep them in the dark. What the newspapers neglect to do the Broadcasting Service will do. We have a far-reaching programme and we want the people with us everywhere. The government is going to be the master of publicity. (Savage 1936)

Consequently, the government abolished the Broadcasting Board in 1936, and control of broadcasting was placed in the hands of a department of state, the National Broadcasting Service. The B stations had been promised advertising and this they were given. The government had conceived of a plan for establishing its own commercial service. B station owners could join this network by selling to the government, or they could remain independent, without advertising, but with a subsidy. The National Commercial Broadcasting Service was established in July 1936 with the purchase of the Auckland station. The service was to derive its revenue primarily from advertising while the "National Service" in contrast, was to draw its finance from license fees. The two departments were amalgamated in 1943 amidst increasing acrimony between the then Labour Prime Minister Peter Fraser, and the Controller of the "Commercial Service," Rev. C. G. Scrimgeour. Radio broadcasting underwent no further reorganization until 1962, when control was once again placed in the hands of a public body, the New Zealand Broadcasting Corporation (NZBC), but this time the changes were brought by the introduction of television.

Throughout the 1960s, radio, under the control of the NZBC, was allowed to become television's poor relation. In short, radio was stagnating. Private enterprise was not long in perceiving this state of affairs, and by the mid-1960s approaches were being made by several groups with a view to obtaining broadcasting warrants (licenses). But as the power to grant these warrants had been vested in the NZBC, approval was not forthcoming. However, one group, spurred by the exploits of the "radio pirates" off the English coast, overcame the difficulties by transmitting programs from beyond the three-mile territorial limit. Public support for the activities of Radio Hauraki and the crew of their "pirate" ship, *Tiri* (and later *Tiri II*) was so widespread that the government was forced to intervene and remove some of the restrictions facing private radio. This they did in 1968 by establishing the Broadcasting Authority, a three-member board empowered to grant broadcasting warrants as well as act as watchdog over broadcasting standards. Over the next few years seven warrants were granted.

Radio was restructured in 1975, following the Adam Committee Report (1973), as part of a large-scale reorganization of broadcasting services. The committee emphasized the differences between the two media—radio and television—and proposed separate structures to allow for the independent development of each. It saw radio as a medium that permitted a much greater flexibility in providing for community participation. The possibility of using radio to "forward the understanding and enjoyment of community life" was raised by the committee, particularly in relation to the provision of a Polynesian station in Auckland (Adam 1973). The committee felt that the aim of such a station could be furthered by the establishment of a "system of committees representative of Auckland's Polynesian communities . . . to furnish informed guidance on programme policies" (Adam 1973). Yet underlying such comments was an implicit acceptance of the hegemony of a dominant culture; it was argued that the Polynesian station would need to carry advertising to assist the Maoris and Pacific Islanders in adjusting to and learning about city life.

An assimilationist approach to multiculturalism has long been characteristic of New Zealand; concepts of society and community deriving from beyond a Western cultural tradition have, in general, been ignored. During the 1970s this situation was increasingly challenged as Maori and Polynesian groups endeavored to establish their cultural identity, though as yet there has been little recognition of this challenge in policy. The potential role of the media in the development of a multicultural society remains largely unexamined by policymakers. Despite such limitations, the Adam Committee Report (1973) acknowledged the importance of social research (albeit of a restricted nature) in ensuring that the broadcast media more accurately reflected the concerns of the community. However, it still appears that economic considerations and political expediency continue to be the dominant forces shaping radio.

Increasing competition, from both commercial radio stations and television, continued through the 1970s. Public commercial radio has had to adapt to the competitive pressures for audience and revenue brought about by the advent of private commercial radio. This adaptation appears to have been quite successful, but to some has produced a tension between the conceivably incompatible goals of commercialism with its emphasis on profitability and mass entertainment, and public service with its educational and minority information roles. Future developments might include the withdrawal of "state radio" from commercial activities if current pressure from private commercial stations is successful. A report giving the green light for the establishment of FM broadcasting in New Zealand has recently been published (Slane 1981:11). However, very definite guidelines have been laid down, both in terms of where stations should be established and who should establish them. For instance, it has been suggested that initially stations should be allowed only in the major centers of population, especially the Auckland area. It was also recommended that stations should not be permitted to broadcast programs in both AM and FM.

In brief, while broadcasting was confined to radio it retained some degree of flexibility in responding to the needs of the community it served, despite the limitations imposed by the concept of one-way dissemination of information. Radio did develop in and respond to conditions peculiar to New Zealand. Real efforts were made to use radio as a means of increasing the receivers' involvement in the community. The Labour Party, upon gaining office in 1935, moved immediately to introduce the broadcasting of Parliament, and even before this, the broadcasting of sports events was widespread. In 1946 the National Orchestra of the Broadcasting Service was founded.

277

The advent of the commercial service resulted in a greatly increased public involvement in the activities of radio (Downes and Harcourt 1976). Once a station had been established it was a relatively simple matter to record and transmit programs of local interest, thus responding to and expressing the concerns of at least some sections of the community. Certainly this development took place within the restricted bounds imposed by the 1923 regulations, but it was an aspect of broadcasting that was to disappear almost completely in the case of television.

During the period when radio was the dominant form of broadcasting, certain well-defined social ends were in concurrence with the medium, to the point where there was a relatively good fit between social doctrine, communication policy related to radio, and the medium itself. In comparison, radio today has been eclipsed by television and has suffered relative neglect at the policy level. New Zealand was close on the heels of other nations in establishing radio broadcasting—indeed a program was broadcast in Dunedin within two years of the establishment of the first British station. Television, however, was much longer arriving.

Television

The late 1950s would seem to have provided an ideal opportunity for a complete evaluation of the role of the electronic media in New Zealand society. The Broadcasting Service had established an extensive radio network and the introduction of television was imminent. But with an election scheduled for 1960, television, which was first introduced in that year in Auckland under the direction of the Broadcasting Service, became just another carrot for the politicians to hold before a public eager to experience the new medium, and both parties formulated their planks in unseemly haste. Labour championed the application of the existing system to television—a government department originally set up by that party in 1936. National espoused the vague ideal of control by a corporation "like the BBC" (Jackson 1962:109).

In retrospect, what gives the greatest cause for regret was that the opportunity to shape the medium in accordance with a specifically New Zealand culture was lost, possibly forever, at that time. Through the changes in policy and media structure in the ensuing twenty years, issues of doctrine concerning the values and norms of New Zealand society and the significance and relevance of media products to the enrichment, enhancement, and invigoration of a specifically New Zealand culture have received scant attention. A technology-driven future appears to be the assumed model of development, and the normative concerns that fired the policymakers of the early "social laboratory" have had little impact on more recent communication policy.

The shape of the new medium, taken for granted by the politicians, was to follow that developed in the major capitalist nations of the West. To have done other than accept overseas models would have taken time, a commodity in short supply for political parties anxious not be outdone by their opponents. A directly imported system that would allow for a rapid extension of services once established clearly had obvious appeal to politicians sensitive to electoral pressures. There was little experimentation to adapt an imported technology to an indigenous culture. In any case the possibility of an original and unique New Zealand culture was only dimly perceived. In a country that still looked toward Britain as "home," there existed an uncertainty as to what was or is the indigenous culture. Elihu Katz (1977) has recorded the debate about the introduction of television to developing countries and how, after much controversy over its potential impact on indigenous cultures, television is introduced often with the highest of motives to serve these cultures and nations. Despite this clear awareness of doctrinal issues, factors as much related to demand as to supply ensure the rapid broadcast of *Kojak* and other U.S.-packaged series in such countries. How much greater such pressures must be in a society unsure of its own identity and lacking the strong voice of cultural concern in communication policymaking.

In terms of finance, to adopt a concept of the medium already extensively developed elsewhere was far less expensive than developing one's own. However, in establishing any television system, some consideration must be given to what is to be transmitted—and it is here that the strongest argument emerges for the adoption of imported concepts. In 1959 the secretary of industries and commerce, W. B. Sutch, delivered a highly controversial address in which he dealt with the problem. He argued that "it would be impossible to provide sufficient programmes of standard approaching the best that is available and that the cost of New Zealand programmes would be too great for a young and expanding service to bear" (Sutch 1959). On the other hand he did argue that "a decision to make local programmes should be a deliberate act of policy to ensure that the service provided was one especially suited to New Zealand's needs." Though not an official government view, the opinions expressed were undoubtedly influential, coming as they did from such a high-ranking civil servant whose department would be closely concerned with many aspects of television. More importantly, they served to illustrate some of the factors that appeared to make the adoption of existing models so attractive.

Sutch displayed the optimism typical of administrators in newly established television services regarding the possibility that television would allow an unhindered exchange of the best programs throughout the world. Such a view failed to recognize that many nations were in exactly the same position as New Zealand—in an effort to develop a service they had opted to be receivers, not originators. By the end of

1961, 88 percent of New Zealand's television programs were imported. Though this had decreased to 73 percent by November 1980 (based on the program times published in the *NZ Listener*), it reflects a worldwide pattern as studies by Schiller (1969), and Nordenstreng and Varis (1973) have shown.

Though Sutch's (1959) paper provoked controversy, it was not because of the arguments he put forward in support of a particular concept of the medium and policy orientation toward that medium, but rather because he advocated state control of the television system. Parliament was divided over the issue of who should control the service. The ruling Labour Party seemed to favor the existing Broadcasting Service, while some in the Opposition favored private enterprise. Control was a political issue, and there seems to have been relatively little debate other than over who should be in charge.

In the 1960 election, National ousted the incumbent Labour Party, and once in power the government set about enacting legislation that placed both radio and television under the control of a public corporation "like the BBC," the NZBC. This body was to be responsible to a minister of broadcasting, and was expected to comply with the general policy of the government of New Zealand with respect to broadcasting, as well as complying with any general directions given in writing by the minister.

In practice, ministerial directives were infrequent (McKinnon 1973:10). However, there seems little doubt that the government of the day was able to exert considerable influence over the activities of the corporation (Cleveland 1970*b*:52). The necessity for major capital expenditure to be approved by the government provided one avenue of control, but perhaps of more importance were the range of informal pressures acting on NZBC staff. A former producer of current affairs programs on the NZBC, Bick observed:

> In a small intimate society where relationships are very informal, pressures can easily be applied on a friendly basis by a mere telephone call. Ministers, the Director-General and departmental heads are all on first-name terms. They have to live with each other and depend on each other's cooperation. (Bick 1968:104)

The government also appointed the members of the Broadcasting Corporation, and its appointees were criticized for being business and establishment oriented (Gregory 1978; Cleveland 1969; Holcroft, 1969). As the Australian chapter demonstrates, an analysis of policy formulation cannot ignore the influence and interaction of personalities.

The issue of "political interference" in the activities of the NZBC dominated public debate over the media, and throughout the 1960s and early 1970s fears for the independence of broadcasting were expressed frequently. This issue concerned policymakers as well, with both parties expressing their belief in the importance of an independent broadcasting system. By the late 1960s an extensive television coverage of the country had been achieved—over 80 percent of the households were operating a set—and the introduction of a second television service became an issue. But once again debate and policy focused on the problem of control rather than social issues. The major issue was whether the second service should be developed by the government or by private enterprise.

During the 1960s, under the control of the NZBC, radio had been eclipsed by television. However, public support for the English-style radio pirates in the mid-1960s led to the establishment in 1968 of the Broadcasting Authority discussed above. The authority's major activity was its inquiry into the establishment of a second television system.

The National Party government tended to favor some form of private enterprise involvement in the development of any second television service, but requested the authority to conduct an inquiry into television services. In its report (Peacock 1971), the authority declined to make any firm recommendations on whether the NZBC or private enterprise should be granted the warrant to establish a second service, suggesting instead that no final decision be made on the matter until color transmission had been established and in operation for some time. Guidelines were drawn up to cover both eventualities. In the event, the only recommendation to be implemented was that concerning color, for the government was to change the following year.

However, the report provided a clear indication of what had become the dominant concept of television in New Zealand—that of a unidirectional medium. The possibility of community involvement, except as a passive receiver of a transmitted signal, was largely ignored. The tribunal appears to have been more concerned with financial and technical considerations than in seeking new ways to use the medium. The minimal consideration given to social factors is perhaps best shown by the fact that the shortest chapters in the report were the two that dealt with the social implications of any change (Peacock 1971).

With the Labour Party coming to power in late 1972, political reality and the principles voiced as the Opposition Party had to coalesce. The party had maintained a strong belief in public control of broadcasting, and indicated a growing realization that community involvement in broadcasting was important. However, it also accepted that a competitive element could provide a stimulus to service and programs.

A Labour cabinet study of broadcasting in January 1973 resulted in the establishment of a committee to inquire into broadcasting in New Zealand. Its scope was limited—the government already possessed a policy. What it now wanted to know was how to implement it. The committee's chairman was Kenneth Adam, a former director of BBC television. The government had sought the advice of an overseas "expert"—a long-standing tradition in a country evolving from a colonial heritage.

The committee spent more than three months preparing its report, receiving more than 1,500 submissions and traveling widely. Informally the committee "took every opportunity to talk to drivers, chambermaids, sportsmen, receptionists, people in bars," which, according to Adam (1974), "may have been less than scientific, but was certainly illuminating." The Labour government seemed more concerned to prevent any repetition of the charge of political interference than to explore new concepts of the media. Its professed social democratic base was not revealed in any concern for a distinctive New Zealand interpretation of the television-audience relationship.

The central concern of the Labour government was with the impartiality, independence, and integrity of broadcasting as three of the major aims of the Broadcasting Corporation. Following the committee's recommendations (Adam 1973) three corporations were set up in 1975. One, Radio New Zealand, controlled radio; the others, Television Service One and Television Service Two, were designed to be competitive yet complementary. This concept has remained central to discussions of broadcasting since that date.

Existing concepts of both radio and television as instruments for the dissemination of information and entertainment were taken for granted. The committee's role was principally administrative—its terms of reference were to improve the dissemination process. It was not particularly concerned to develop new models for pluri-dimensional or multiple feedback media in the communications process. Though the committee touched on the problem of providing access to the media for all, this remained only a peripheral concern.

The government's other concern—to provide choice through competition—was also founded in a unidirectional model of the media. Competition was seen as a means of making the receiver an active participant through exercising choice over programs. Such a view is deceptive, and the degree of participation possible only minimal, since although he or she may exercise control over which signal is received or whether any signal is received, the receiver is unable to influence what the signal itself will be.

The committee pointed out the importance of audience research. But in practice, such research as was carried out tended to be of the head-counting type, which, in a situation of competition for income derived from advertising, became a service primarily for the benefit of advertisers.

The Labour government, in effect, was trying to combine a market-oriented, commercial, profit-oriented system with a public-service system sensitive to the needs of minorities, the maintenance of program standards, and, as Adam (1973) put it, "without the full penalties which would be involved in an all-out race for audiences." The notion that evolved was one of "guided" competition, and one of the major problems in adopting such an approach was that of cost. The corporations would be working within the budgets made available by the sale of advertising and their share of revenue from licenses, which was limited. For the year ending 31 March 1976, the television stations derived about two-thirds of their revenue from advertising, and Radio New Zealand about half.

Given such restrictions, the appeal of overseas programs, especially American and British, was obvious. In 1976 the average cost to New Zealand of a U.S.-produced feature film was between NZ$1,300 and NZ$1,700. The cost of producing *The Governor*, a series of six 90-minute programs dealing with the life of a former governor and later prime minister of New Zealand, Sir George Grey, was more than NZ$500,000 in TV-1's above-the-line costs and total costs were probably in the range of NZ$1 million.

Imported programs have continued to dominate New Zealand television screens despite the recommendations of both the committee (Adam 1973) and earlier, the Broadcasting Authority (Peacock 1971), that New Zealand content should not fall below certain minimum levels. In general the aim has been that at least one-third of programs be produced in New Zealand. But according to Nordenstreng and Varis (1973), such a figure, if achieved, would leave unchanged New Zealand's standing in 1970 as the fourth highest consumer of imported programs.

In any event, this innovative, though perhaps hasty, ill-considered, and ultimately contradictory, system had no time to prove itself. In opposition, the National Party was strongly critical of the new broadcasting arrangements. It saw in the three corporations an unnecessarily expensive duplication of services. Further, in view of the amount of public money involved, they felt that the absence of a minister able to accept parliamentary responsibility for the affairs of broadcasting removed a necessary safeguard. On their return to office following the dramatic reversal of the 1975 general election, they wasted little time in setting about a further restructuring of broadcasting. This time the major concerns were financial as well as requiring from the broadcasting service a greater degree of accountability through ministers to Parliament (*NZ Listener* 1976:16). In 1976 the Broadcasting Act was passed by Parliament and from 1 February 1977 the Broadcasting Council and the three corporations ceased to exist as separate entities.

The responsibility for the operation of the three corporations was transferred to a new body, the Broadcasting Corporation of New Zealand, the current organizing body, which retains many of the functions of the Broadcasting Council. However, it differs in composition, in that all of the seven to nine members are appointed by the government. In addition, since 1977 the chairperson of the corporation has served in the capacity of "executive chair"—a new role that has occasioned considerable debate.

There was wide opposition to the 1976 Broadcasting Act, both inside and outside Parliament, but the National government's parliamentary majority was sufficient to ensure its passage. After the 1976 Act was passed by a party supposedly supportive of the principles of competition and decreased central government involvement, the prospect was for a centralized public corporation responsible to Parliament, through the minister of broadcasting. The minister may direct the corporation in writing, but any such direction must subsequently be gazetted and laid before Parliament. The corporation became responsible for three operating services, Radio New Zealand (RNZ), Television Service One (TV-1), and Television Service Two (TV-2). It also publishes the weekly *NZ Listener* and assists in the administration of the New Zealand Symphony Orchestra.

Throughout 1979 further changes occurred (Broadcasting Amendment Act 1979) and radical changes (including the suggestion that TV-2 should be abolished) were mooted. Under the latest system, established in February 1980, competition for ratings and revenue—a fight that has absorbed TV-1 and TV-2 since their inception—were intended to disappear. TV-1 and TV-2 are no longer mirror images of each other in structure and intent, and instead a single television enterprise known as Television New Zealand (having as its stated basis "the highest degree of complementary") serves the two television channels. The stated intention of this unified two-channel operation was to give a wider range of programming to viewers and to rationalize the use of facilities by the channels. Such a cooperative system was to offer the public wider scope for regional television, eliminate annoying competitive practices, cater to minority and cultural audiences at more suitable times than had previously been possible, and fulfill the social, cultural, and educational potential of television. It was hoped that with independent private productions, the percentage of local output across both channels would reach 40 percent in 1981. The chairperson of the corporation (a government appointee) considers that this retreat from competition, instituted paradoxically by a Labour government and eliminated by the more conservative National government, indicates the resurgence of the BBC ideal of public-service broadcasting.

This latest organizational change—the fourth in as many years—has been prompted, according to official reports, principally by questions of economics and finance (*NZ Listener* 1979a:14). Many consider the political decision that New Zealand should have two television channels too ambitious in light of the country's resources and the quality of programs available. License fees provide only about one-third of broadcasting's revenue, and advertising the remainder. Yet in April 1979, an appeal for a raise of NZ$10 in the cost of license fees (currently NZ$27.50 for monochrome, NZ$45.00 for color, per year) was judged politically unacceptable. Instead, new cuts were encouraged. Cost-consciousness, cost-saving, and close scrutiny of expenditure are the key to the future. A further indication of a possible future trend was the formation of several companies to pursue private television broadcasting, with the intention of either leasing one of the existing channels or setting up their own. There was some resistance from the NZBC, and the question of loss of revenue was raised. However, the major political parties have policies that call for some level of private enterprise involvement in television, so this issue will no doubt be resurrected.

The present situation, set against a background in which it is acknowledged that New Zealand overextended itself in providing a second television channel, which both political parties were keen to see established, results from the lack of regard for continuity and long-term planning. Equally, the partisan nature of policy decisions, informed by little more than short-term political gain and "ad hocery," have combined to inhibit the development of a coherent communication policy related to broadcasting.

Telecommunications

The present government has shown an increased awareness of the need for a clearly articulated and widely debated telecommunications policy, as the impact of telecommunications is felt on homes and industries alike. This was evidenced by the establishment of the Communications Commission in June 1976 "to survey the evolution, present use and existing forward planning of telecommunications as affecting New Zealand" (Communications Commission 1977:4). Following the report of the Communications Commission (1977), the government decided to establish a Communications Advisory Council as the advisory body to which it could look to formulate, coordinate, review, and recommend longer term national telecommunications policy. Membership of this council was to be drawn from government and private sectors, the tertiary education sector, and the New Zealand Planning Council. The current considerations of the advisory council relate to data transfer networks, the training, recruiting, and retention of data processing personnel, and measures to assist the New Zealand electronics industries. Studies mooted for the future include information transfer systems, including videotext systems, and the potential for domestic satellites.

Most of the equipment, and particularly major items, used in New Zealand results from developments overseas—frequently supplied direct by overseas manufacturers. Within the critical economic constraints of a country with just over three million people, a balance has had to be struck between economic and social demands for improved telecommunications, and the ability to pay for and profit from them.

By March 1976 about 3 percent of the total work force (30,000 people) were employed in the manufacture or servicing of telecommunications equipment or were involved in the provision of telecommunications services. At the same time, capital assets (including land, buildings, and equipment) or organizations providing telecommunications equipment and services were more than NZ$700 million. Probably less than 30 percent of telecommunications equipment currently in use is locally manufactured.

In terms of the current penetration of the telecommunications services available, New Zealand has been able to keep abreast of developments. But there is an increasing disquiet that new developments in technology represent changes in kind, which cannot be catered to by policies based on historical values. The principal government agency that has been responsible for the provision, operation, and maintenance of public telecommunications services in New Zealand has been the Post Office, responsible to the postmaster-general. The uniformity of the national telecommunications systems is accounted for by this long-standing monopoly system. The early collaboration between government and overseas companies indicated the pattern of future policy collaboration for the mutual benefit of both New Zealand and the overseas company. A recent example is the establishment of the Austral Standard Cable factory, a subsidiary of IT&T, and the supply arrangement entered into whereby the New Zealand Post Office oversees production costs in return for a guarantee that 90 percent of its underground cable orders will be placed with the firm. Typically, New Zealand relies on competitive world tendering for a centrally unified system.

The Post Office Act (1959) gives the Post Office sole responsibility for regulation (except broadcasting) and provision of public telecommunications services, such as the establishment and operation of inland and international telephone and telegraph services, and, through a licensing system, the right to decline to allow private apparatus to be connected to the Post Office-operated telephone network. Such licenses have been strictly regulated. It also has the particularly sensitive responsibility for control of the radio-frequency spectrum. Requests to open up new radio stations are made to the Post Office, which, in its role as guardian of the scarce spectrum-space resource, and with its scale of priorities regarding national and international coordination, has frequently declined requests, and thus earned a reputation for inflexibility.

A postwar trend which has become increasingly apparent is the development of private systems in the radio sphere. Mobile radio services have developed in government organizations such as Police, Forestry, Defence, and Electricity Supply, which has caused the Post Office to complain of increasing fragmentation in the area of coordination. Indeed, the major conclusion of the 1977 Communications Commission report—which took into account the revolutionary potential of the emerging information sector—was that there was "a need in New Zealand for more effective coordination in the overall development of telecommunications."

As a policy issue, public telephony as a whole receives little or no public comment. Decisions are taken, with regard to technological changes, based on advice and information from an indigenous group of experts. Bearing in mind the continuing availability of maintenance spares, this advice is tempered with such independence and innovation as is possible in the international marketplaces. Decisions regarding improvements follow, as may be expected, the demographic and political power contours of the country. Subscriber Toll Dialling (STD), for example, was introduced first in the northern cities and more tardily in the south. On 31 March 1981 it was available to 51.4 percent of subscribers. The majority of two-or-more-party lines (9% of total subscribers in 1976) are in rural areas, as are the majority of the 107 (1976) manual exchanges. However, improvements in the service to rural subscribers have been a recognized long-term policy. Telephone exchanges are grouped into 291 free-calling areas within which there is, following the U.S. pattern, no charge for local calls. The long-term objective is to reduce the number of free-calling areas to about 80 (Department of Statistics 1980).

Since the mid-1960s, New Zealand has been among the top five nations in terms of density of telephone connections. This consistently high demand for residential connections has been attributed to the relatively low cost of the service, wider area free-calling, the isolation of a fair proportion of the community, and increases in the number of dwellings. In addition, it continues a concern of more than a century to allow as many people as possible access to the means of person-to-person communication—with the implications for information egalitarianism that this indicates.

For its first half-century of existence, the telegraph provided the country's basic internal communication service. More recently the decline in usage has been rapid, from 4.9 million telegrams lodged in the year ending 31 March 1974, to 2.5 million in the year to 31 March 1981. The number of teleprinter offices, which form the public telegraph network, has also declined from 120 in 1976 to 111 in 1979. These offices interwork through "Gentex" (automatic circuit switching), augmented by point-to-point circuits between five major cities. On the other hand, the fully automated inland and international telex, introduced in 1964, has shown a substantial immediate and continuing demand for service. From a total of 647 subscribers at the year ending 31 March 1967, there were 3,883 subscribers as of 31 March 1978. The international service is available with 183 countries. Rentals have increased steeply, from NZ$650 per year (standard machine) and NZ$900 per year (teleprinter plus tape reperforator and transmitter) in 1975 and 1976, to NZ$1,350 and NZ$1,800 per year respectively in 1978 and 1979. Public access to telex facilities is available at all chief post offices (Department of Statistics 1980:345).

The 1976 Communications Commission felt itself most hindered by lack of information in the area of data transmission, since it stated that there had been no comprehensive survey of computer usage and applications in New Zealand (Communications Commission 1977). In general, however, the government sector estimates that data transmission accounts for about 75 percent of current usage. Almost all major hardware is imported, and figures for the import costs of data-processing machines and accessories clearly indicate recent trends: in 1971 almost NZ$2.95 million, in 1976 NZ$30.26 million.

The use and requirements of data-transmission telecommunications facilities has also grown rapidly, with the increase in number and use of remote terminals. Because of the wide geographical distribution of government departments and the centralized computing resources of the government, the State Services Commission (Computer Services Division), in its forecast to the Communications Commission (1977), predicted that the provision of computer networks will be one of the main areas of development from 1976 to 1981. This development reflects the worldwide move to dispersed computer-processing facilities. Again, the telecommunications services developed for both inland and international data transmission have been provided by the Post Office. As with telex facilities, charges for data modems have increased sharply by over 100 percent over a two-year period. For the Datel Service, allowing the exchange of data using switched local, toll, and international telephone networks, the rent of Post Office modems is mandatory. In addition, subscribers must rent a business telephone connection. As with standard telephone calls, there is no charge for Datel calls within each free-calling area. In the early days firms found themselves persuaded into buying systems to solve problems they did not have, and there were a number of "burnt fingers." However, it is apparent from submissions to the Communications Commission that both government and industry fully appreciate the impact and special importance of data processing and transmission. The Post Office has noted (Communications Commission 1977) that a probable need would develop in the future for a digital package switching, common user systems, and end-to-end digital links.

New Zealand has international telecommunications links via cable, satellite, and radio to almost all countries of the world, and has been linked by telegraphic cable to Australia for over one hundred years. With increasing demands, further major developments have included COMPAC telephone cable (1962–63), SEACOM (1967), the Post Office Warkworth Satellite earth station (1971), and the Australia–New Zealand TASMAN submarine cable (1975). TASMAN has a total capacity of 640 circuits; COMPAC, nearing the end of its recognized twenty years of economic life, has a capacity of 80 telephone channels. The Warkworth Satellite earth station operates via the Pacific INTELSAT 4A satellite, which has become increasingly important for simultaneous television transmission of overseas events. New Zealand is represented on the Board of Governors of INTELSAT through membership of the Asia Pacific Group. Originally formed in 1967, with eight members, this group has consisted since 1973 of five Commonwealth countries (New Zealand, India, Singapore, Sri Lanka, and Malaysia).

International Subscriber Dialling was introduced on 1 December 1979, and initially the service was available to seventeen countries, which handle most of the international telephone traffic. This facility is available only to subscribers with STD and is conducted through an international gateway telephone exchange in Auckland, which handles all of New Zealand's outgoing and incoming international calls. This new exchange is intended to cater to the growth of international telephone traffic and to meet international standards not possible with the present exchange. A service providing access to data bases and computing facilities connected to the Tyonnet and Telenet networks in the U.S. was opened in September 1979. This service, named OASIS (Overseas Access Service for Information Systems), is intended to be extended to similar facilities in other countries. Such international considerations are of critical importance in policy planning and implementation, and the overall development of telecommunications in New Zealand. The Post Office acts as administrative member, cooperating with other interested organizations, with the ITU, INTELSAT, INMARSAT (Intergovernmental Maritime Consultative Organization), the Commonwealth Telecommunication Organisation, COMPAC, SEACOM, and TASMAN. The degree of independence in planning decisions is circumscribed by the need to conform to internationally agreed arrangements. In addition, standards are set for transmission performance and compatible signaling systems to enable traffic to be satisfactorily interconnected via the international network.

In many vital regards New Zealand's telecommunications policy is circumscribed by developments overseas. For example, once decisions have been made for equipment supply, even though the policy is one of competitive tendering on the world market, the demands of system and equipment compatibility and international agreements limit the choices available. Because of costs and the limited resources available to a small country, a stringent order of priorities is needed, and many features familiar to consumers in other developed countries (such as International Subscriber Dialling, FM broadcasting, CATV, cable television, and educational television) are either lacking or are introduced some years after initial development overseas. This problem of a lengthy lead time inherent in telecommunications planning is well recognized by the Post Office, together with the difficulty of changing direction, reversing a trend, or recovering from an unsatisfactory situation.

It is quite clear that there are insufficient resources to match the growth in demand—both for existing services, and for new developments in telecommunications. Implementation of policies, and the prior planning of such policies, is a profoundly political question. While existing telecommunications systems may have developed through the political pressure of heavy public demand, the rapidity of progress in communications over the last decade has meant that policy decisions regarding technical matters have had to be well in advance of the public at large.

The development and evolution of new concepts of communication have had to be established ahead of, rather than evolving through, public demand based on historical values.

In common with much decision making relating to recent, high-cost, imported communications technology, a relatively small group—principally drawn from the Post Office and broadcasting institutions—has made such decisions. The critical relationship between communication policies and national economic policies has been recognized and institutionalized through the establishment of the Communications Advisory Council. However, it is questionable whether this body will become the forum for public discussion of the relationship between new communications technology and its social impact.

Conclusions

The peculiar constraints of New Zealand, as of course with all nations, have provided the general parameters within which policy has been enunciated. There has not been, and arguably—with the revolutionary potential of successive forms of communication—never can be a blueprint for the future. Policy formulation, adaptation, and change has had to be an iterative process. An ad hoc a day has kept policies in play.

Within these parameters, a narrow general concept of communication has been dominant. The concept of communication in its true sense (from the Latin *communicare*: to make common, to share) has been only glimpsed in certain less visible areas. The *UNESCO Courier* (Najar 1977:23) noted this change in concept as "requiring the active participation of all concerned in the communication process, which thus becomes a pluri-dimensional flow of information with multiple feedback." New Zealand has failed to establish a distinctive and unique approach to communication policy, in part because it has imported, with technology and software, the dominant concepts from overseas.

In the absence of an overall coordinated communication policy, control has principally been achieved through piecemeal legal limitations. Many of these limitations have been imposed as a consequence of expedience, pragmatism, and political opportunism. Some of the acts passed have had purposes, such as public protection from obscenity, which, while appearing tangential to a coherent communication policy, enshrine in legal form the normative framework within which such policy is articulated. Self-control, through the form of a generalized consensus, is apparent in some media. The press, for instance, offers an example of restrained competition among collectively minded operators. With the constantly looming economic constraints in broadcasting, many believe it is becoming increasingly timid and banal. Associated with the financial situation, recent pressure from both parties has attempted to decrease government involvement in industry as a whole, and such pressure could be expected to be reflected in media organizations.

The current economic retrenchment is of great concern to communications organizations. In November 1979 one of the major metropolitan newspapers closed down. In addition, there has been widespread discussion about the financing—and possible dismemberment—of television and radio services. Such factors have placed communications to the fore in public debate. The Communications Commission report (1977) and increasing public disquiet concerning the role of silicone chip technology vis-à-vis threats to employment and the changing job structure in industry have contributed to the debate. It is expected that communication policy will become an increasingly important and central issue.

References

Adam, K.
1973   *The Broadcasting Future for New Zealand: Report of the Committee on Broadcasting*. Wellington: Government Printer.

1974   "The Broadcasting Future for New Zealand." *Gazette* 20: 162–70.

Bick, G.
1968   *The Compass File*. Christchurch: Caxton Press.

Boyd-Barrett, O.
1977   "Media Imperialism: Towards an International Framework for the Analysis of Media Systems." In *Mass Communication and Society*, edited by J. Curran, M. Gurevitch, and J. Woollacott, pp.116–35. London: Edward Arnold.

Chappel, G.
1977   "New Zealand Films: A New Wave?" *NZ Listener*, 5 March.

Cleveland, L.
1969   "The New Zealand Mass Media System: Functions and Responsibilities." *Political Science* 21 (2):36–47.

1970*a*   "The New Zealand Mass Media System: Problems of Broadcasting." *Political Science* 22 (1):38–51.

1970*b*   "The New Zealand Mass Media System and the Broadcasting Authority." *Political Science* 22 (2):50–61.

291

1970c   "The Structure and Function of the Press in New Zealand." Ph.D. dissertation, Victoria University of Wellington.

1971   "The NZPA and the Newspaper System." *Political Science* 23 (2):2–60.

The Commission of Enquiry into the Dismissal of Alexander Macleod
1975   Extracts in *New Zealand Politics: A Reader*, edited by S. Levine, pp. 277–90. Melbourne: Cheshire.

Communications Commission
1977   *Telecommunications in New Zealand: Report of the Communications Commission*. Wellington: Government Printer.

Department of Statistics
1976   *New Zealand Official Yearbook.* Wellington: Government Printer.

1977   *New Zealand Official Yearbook.* Wellington: Government Printer.

1980   *New Zealand Official Yearbook.* Wellington: Government Printer.

Downes, P., and Harcourt, P.
1976   *Voices in the Air: Radio Broadcasting in New Zealand*. Wellington: Methuen NZ Ltd.

Gregory, R.
1978   "Public Broadcasting and Ministerial Responsibility." In *Politics in New Zealand: A Reader*, edited by S. Levine. Sydney: George Allen & Unwin.

Holcroft, M.
1969   *Reluctant Editor: The " 'Listener' " Years 1949–67*. Wellington: Reed.

Industries Development Commission
1978   *Commission of Inquiry into the Book Production Industry*. Wellington: Government Printer.

Jackson, K.
1962   "Broadcasting and the Election." In *New Zealand Politics in Action: The 1960 General Election*, edited by R. Chapman, K. Jackson, and A. Mitchell. London: Oxford University Press.

Katz, E.
1977   "Can Authentic Cultures Survive New Media?" *Journal of Communication* 27 (2):113–21.

McKinnon, J.
1973   "Interview with C. Fry." *NZ Listener*, 5 March, p. 72.

Najar, R.
1977   "A Voice from the Third World, towards a 'New World Order of Information'." *UNESCO Courier*, April.

Nevill, H.
1975   "The Press in New Zealand: Papers and Opinions." *NZ Listener*, 9 August, pp. 12–14.

New Zealand Census of Libraries
1974   Wellington: Government Printer.

New Zealand Press Association
1980   *Chairman's Report*. Wellington.

New Zealand Tablet
1978   26 July.

Nordenstreng, K., and Varis, T.
1973   *Television Traffic: A One-Way Street?* Reports and Papers on Mass Communication no. 70. Paris: UNESCO.

NZ Listener
1977   "Interview with the Minister of the Arts." 19 March, 14–17.

Palmer, G.W.R.
1975   "Politics and Defamation: A Case of Kiwi Hunting?" In *New Zealand Politics: A Reader*, edited by S. Levine. Melbourne: Cheshire.

Peacock, T.
1971   *NZ Broadcasting Authority: Extension of Television Services in New Zealand*. Held in the General Assembly Library, Wellington.

Printers News
1979   "Another Endangered Species." February, pp. 5–7.

Randerson, A.P., convener
1978   *Freedom of Information*. Public Issues Committee of the Auckland District Law Society.

Savage, M.J.
1936   Speech reported in *New Zealand Herald*, 9 June.

Schiller, H.
1969   *Mass Communication and American Empire*. New York: A.M. Kelley.

Sinclair, K.
1961   *A History of New Zealand*. London: Oxford University Press.

Smith, A.
1980   "The Doctrinal Context of Telecommunications Policy in Developed Countries." In *Pacific Telecommunications Conference: Proceedings*, edited by D.J. Wedemeyer. Honolulu: PTC.

Sutch, W.B.
1959   *The Economics of Television*. Wellington: New Zealand Department of Industries and Commerce.

Variety
1977   "Global Prices for Television Film." 5 January, p. 96.

CONTRIBUTORS

Anne W. Branscomb is an attorney specializing in communications law. She has published numerous articles and reports on emerging technologies and the First Amendment, on cable television, public broadcasting, the broadcast reform movement, computerized information systems, and United States communications policies and structures. She has served on the United States Department of Commerce Technical Advisory Board, the Department of State WARC Advisory Committee, as a trustee of Educom, a director of National Public Radio, as communications counsel for the Teleprompter Corporation, and as vice president and chair of the Board of Kalba Bowen Associates, communications consultants.

Patricia Edgar is a sociologist with experience in broadcasting regulation in Australia. She is a senior lecturer at the Centre for the Study of Educational Communication and Media, La Trobe University, Melbourne. She has an M.A. from Stanford University and a Ph.D. from La Trobe University in the sociology of communications. She has produced and directed three documentary films and published many books and articles on the mass media, including *Under Five in Australia* (1973), *Media She* (1974), *Children and Screen Violence* (1977), *The Politics of the Press* (1979), and *The News in Focus* (ed.) (1980). She has served on a number of government committees including the Australian Broadcasting Control Board, the Australian National Commission of UNESCO, the Council of the Australian Film and Television School, and the Australian Broadcasting Tribunal's Children's Program Committee (chair). She is currently director of the Australian Children's Television Foundation.

Geoff Evans is a public servant and policy analyst. He was educated at the University of Sydney and at Cornell University, and originally trained and worked as a research scientist. After seven years he changed fields in early 1972 to work for a committee of the Australian Senate. This led to an involvement in broadcasting policy. He became an adviser to the second minister for the media in the Labor government of 1972–75, and was a member of the Australian Broadcasting Control Board in its final year. Currently he is secretary to the deputy Opposition leader in the Senate and is engaged in a range of policy areas, including communications.

Göran Hedebro is an economist. He is an assistant professor at the School of Journalism at the University of Stockholm, and was a visiting scholar at the Institute for Communication Research at Stanford University 1976–77. He has been involved in communication research for over ten years, with a special focus on communication and development. Recent publications include "Communication and Change in Developing Nations: A Critical View" and "The Challenge of Cooperation: A Study of Alternative Communication and the New International Information Order in Latin America."

Jean McNulty is a political scientist with a special interest in communication policy analysis. She was educated at the University of Dublin, the University of South Wales, and at Carleton University of Ottawa. Since 1971, she has been a research associate with the Telecommunications Research Group in the Department of Communication at Simon Fraser University, Vancouver. In 1979–80, she spent a year with the federal Department of Communications in Ottawa, under the auspices of a government-university exchange program. With Gail Martin and Patricia Hindley, she has written a book on basic issues in Canadian communication policy. Other research projects and publications over the past ten years have been concerned with community media in Canada and the development of cable television systems.

Gail M. Martin is an associate professor of communication at Simon Fraser University, Vancouver, Canada, and is also research director of the University's Telecommunications Research Group. She is a graduate of the College of New Rochelle, New York, and has a master's degree in psychology from New Mexico. She has served as an adviser and consultant to a number of government and community bodies and has published widely on communications issues.

Logan Moss spent six years as a school teacher following graduation from Otago University. He returned to the university in 1977 to undertake further studies in education and social anthropology. He is currently a lecturer in the Education Department, Waikato University, New Zealand.

Syed A. Rahim is a senior researcher and project leader of the communication policy and planning project, Communication Institute, East-West Center, Honolulu, Hawaii. He has a Ph.D. in communication from Michigan State University. His recent publications include *Perspectives in Communication Policy and Planning* (1977), and *Planning Methods, Models, and Organization: A Review Study for Communication Policy*

Making and Planning (1978). Dr. Rahim has many years of research experience on development in less developed countries, and has worked as chief of the rural development sector, Bangladesh Planning Commission. He is a member of the Board of Trustees, Pacific Telecommunications Council.

Anthony Smith is director of the British Film Institute in London. He has been a producer of television current affairs at the BBC and a Fellow of St. Antony's College, Oxford, and has written extensively on broadcasting, newspapers, and telecommunications. His most recent publications are *The Geopolitics of Information: How Western Media Dominate World Culture* (1980), *Goodbye Gutenberg: The Newspaper Revolution of the 1980's* (1980), and *Newspapers and Democracy* (1980).

Donald Stewart is a sociologist who is currently a senior research fellow in the Institute of Family Studies, Melbourne. He is a graduate of Durham, Oxford, Leicester, and Otago Universities. He has lectured for several years in Southeast Asia, at Notre Dame University, Philippines; Chulalongkorn University, Thailand; and Singapore University, as well as at Otago University, New Zealand. During 1978–79 he held a scholarship at the Communication Institute, East-West Center, Honolulu, researching communication and innovation. His master's degree from the Centre for Mass Communication Research, Leicester, and his Ph.D. were both in the sociology of mass communications. He has published articles in this general area in various journals.

Ed Wittich is a sociologist. He has a master's degree in sociology from La Trobe University, Melbourne, and taught sociology there from 1973–76. He has published a number of articles and monographs on a range of sociological topics and issues. He was invited to Germany on an Academic Exchange Programme scholarship to the University of Bielefeld (1977) and the Ludwig Maxmilian University, Munich (1978). Guidance for the current contribution was afforded by Professor D. Baacke (Bielefeld) and Professor H. Holzer (Munich). His current position is lecturer in Sociology, Preston Institute of Technology, Melbourne.